# COUNTERING CULTURE

# COUNTERING CULTURE

*Arming Yourself to Confront Non-Biblical Worldviews*

DAVID NOEBEL
and
CHUCK EDWARDS

BROADMAN
&HOLMAN
PUBLISHERS

Nashville, Tennessee

Copyright © 2004 by David Noebel

Published in 2004 by Broadman & Holman Publishers
Nashville, Tennessee

Unless otherwise noted, Scripture quotations have been taken from the *Holman Christian
Standard Bible®*, copyright © 1999, 2000 by Holman Bible Publishers.
Used by permission.

Cover and interior design by
The Gregory Group and Paul T. Gant, Art & Design—Nashville, TN

ISBN 0-8054-5888-3

1  2  3  4  5    08  07  06  05  04

# TABLE OF CONTENTS

# INTRODUCTION

When it comes to most social, political, and moral issues of our day, the majority of Christian youth, according to a nationwide survey, hold views more like atheists than Christians. Another study finds that up to 51% of "born again" Christians lose their faith during four years in college.

Why is this happening?

A major reason is because Christian young people do not understand how to think like Christians. As a dean of students at a major Christian university puts it, "Students come here with a love for God in their hearts, but their minds think like pagans."

Yet the problem does not rest with the younger generation but with adults—the parents, Sunday school teachers, and youth workers—who, themselves, do not understand how to navigate the world of ideas that confront Christians on every side.

According to the "Cultural Mandate" of Genesis 1:28, God's original intent was for man to shape culture according to His principles. In addition, Jesus calls on His disciples to be the "salt and light" of society, and Paul pleads for Christians to sharpen their minds in order to shape the culture instead of being conformed to it (see Matthew 5:13-16 and Romans 12:2).

In order to fulfill these biblical directives, Christians need to recover the ability to instruct the head as well as inspire the heart. Best-selling author and well-known speaker Josh McDowell captures the issue when he says, "The heart cannot rejoice in what the mind rejects." To retain warm hearts for Christ, we must know why we believe what we believe. And we must engage the minds of our youth if they are to withstand the assaults on their faith from every side and lead the church and society in the 21st century.

For more than 40 years, Summit Ministries has been a leading force to train Christians in worldview analysis, equipping them to champion the Christian faith and inspiring them to love God with their hearts and minds (for more information, see www.summit.org). *Countering Culture: Arming Yourself to Confront Non-Biblical Worldviews*, Summit's latest worldview study, is the second of the Worldviews in Focus series. The text, video, and lesson plans introduce learners to the ideas that are shaping our culture and provide an understanding of why our society is moving in the direction it is headed. More to the point, it demonstrates why a biblical Christian worldview is the only viable solution to the rapidly deteriorating moral conditions we find in our culture.

As you participate in this study—whether on your own or in a group—you will gain insight into the major worldviews that oppose much of what Christians affirm. You also will be presented with practical steps to take to mount a counter-offensive, helping those who have been captured by deceitful philosophies to see the light of God's truth. In comparison to Secular Humanism, Postmodern Marxism, and the New Age, biblical Christianity shines noon-bright.

This study equips Christians to take a reasoned stand for biblical principles in the classroom as well as the boardroom. By understanding non-biblical worldviews, Christians gain a deeper appreciation of how to draw non-believers to want to know more about what Christ offers. And to prevent our own capture by the culture, we must understand it:

Therefore as you have received Christ Jesus the Lord, walk in Him, rooted and built up in Him and established in the faith, just as you were taught, and overflowing with thankfulness. Be careful that no one takes you captive through philosophy and empty deceit based on human tradition, based on the elemental forces of the world, and not based on Christ.
—Colossians 2:6-8

(Unless otherwise noted, all scriptures cited in *Countering Culture* are taken from the *Holman Christian Standard Bible*®.)

To challenge the culture effectively, we must offer better arguments:

For although we are walking in the flesh, we do not wage war in a fleshly way, since the weapons of our warfare are not fleshly, but are powerful through God for the demolition of strongholds. We demolish arguments and every high-minded thing that is raised up against the knowledge of God, taking every thought captive to the obedience of Christ.
—2 Corinthians 10:3-5

To change the culture, we must set captives free:

The Lord's slave must not quarrel, but must be gentle to everyone, able to teach, and patient, instructing his opponents with gentleness. Perhaps God will grant them repentance to know the truth. Then they may come to their senses and escape the Devil's trap, having been captured by him to do his will.
—2 Timothy 2:24-26

We trust that this text will encourage your thirst to know and love God and will equip you to be the much-needed "salt and light" in our increasingly tasteless and dark society. May God bless your time spent in this study and in teaching others who, in turn, will be equipped to train still others (2 Timothy 2:2).

David A. Noebel, President
Chuck Edwards, Director of Bible Study Curriculum
Summit Ministries
Manitou Springs, CO
March, 2004

# SECTION I
# WORLDVIEWS IN CONFLICT

Ever since the first century, Christians have influenced society wherever they have gone. Christians founded hospitals, orphanages, soup kitchens, schools, and universities. They advocated the abolition of slavery, the rights of women and children, and promoted racial equality. It was a biblical view of the universe that propelled scientists to explore God's creation, leading to technologies that make our lives healthier and more carefree. And while critics point out the church's at times checkered past, almost every major social improvement has been initiated because of a biblical worldview. Yet in recent years, the church's influence has been waning.

The first chapter of *Countering Culture* presents an overview of why this study is important. We suggest the blame for the current state of affairs in the United States does not rest so much with those who tear down the moral fabric of our nation but rather with Christians for abandoning the institutions that build our moral framework—education and government. While the home and church create a foundation for moral citizens, schools and the state must work in concert with church and home to maintain a civil society.

In chapter two, we define a worldview as reflected in ten subject categories: theology, philosophy, biology, psychology, ethics, sociology, law, politics, economics, and history. A fruit free illustrates the concept of "worldview thinking" and shows how each worldview category interacts with the others. To understand the significance of a worldview, one must understand the connections between these categories. We also demonstrate how three worldviews—Secular Humanism, Postmodern Marxism and Cosmic Humanism—currently dominate our culture, especially in our education, politics and media, and we show how they are replacing our Christian heritage with atheistic and pantheistic views.

# CHAPTER 1

# Engaging Our
# Post-Christian Culture

"…as a society we are in the midst of
secularization, and therefore we are an utterly
irreconcilable mix of rival views of the universe,
of human nature and the human good….
The culture wars are cosmological wars."[1]
—BENJAMIN WIKER

"When we American college teachers encounter
religious fundamentalists, we do not consider
the possibility of reformulating our own
practices of justification so as to give more
weight to the authority of the Christian
scriptures. Instead, we do our best to convince
these students of the benefits of secularization.
Rather, I think these students are lucky to find
themselves under the benevolent Herrschaft of
people like me, and to have escaped the grip of
their frightening, vicious, dangerous parents."[2]
—RICHARD RORTY

A mother's tear-stained letter describes what happened when her daughter went off to college: "Our daughter was raised in Christian schools and in a Christian home where we taught her Christian values and morals. . . . Two years out of high school —at 20 years old, she enrolled at the University. . . . Unfortunately she was overwhelmed by the professors and began to believe their philosophies. . . . and has turned her back on all that she believed in."

How tragic! Yet this one example represents a growing trend: Kids raised in Christian homes lose their faith while attending college. What causes a bright young woman to turn her back on all she has been taught to believe for 20 years? James Dobson and Gary Bauer have an answer to why a once faithful college student would turn her back on Christ. In their book, *Children at Risk*, Dobson and Bauer write, "Nothing short of a great Civil War of Values rages today throughout North America. Two sides with vastly differing and incompatible worldviews are locked in a bitter conflict that permeates every level of society."[3] They go on to describe the present civil war as a struggle "for the hearts and minds of people. It is a war over ideas."

> ### I CHRONICLES 12:32
>
> *From the Issacharites, who understood the times and knew what Israel should do: 200 chiefs with all their kinsmen under command.*

The centerpiece of the conflict is the battle between competing worldviews. The Christian worldview stands on one side while on the other are the humanistic worldviews which can be divided into three branches: Secular Humanism, Postmodern Marxism, and Cosmic Humanism (including New Age pantheism and Neo-paganism). Although these three worldviews do not agree in every detail, there is one point on which they unanimously concur—they oppose biblical Christianity.

"Someday soon," Dobson and Bauer note, "a winner [in the battle for hearts and minds] will emerge and the loser will fade from memory. For now, the outcome is very much in doubt."[4] In order to survive on the front lines, much less emerge victorious, Christians must mimic the ancient tribe of Issachar which led the nation of Israel because they had an understanding of the times and knew what they ought to do (see 1 Chronicles 12:32).

## SALTY CHRISTIANS

As with the Israelites centuries ago, there is a need for faithful people today to understand the times in which they live. The late theologian and philosopher Francis Schaeffer observed, "The basic problem of the Christians in this country [referring to the United States of America in the mid-1980's] in the last eighty years or so... is that they have seen things in bits and pieces instead of totals."[5] Schaeffer suggests that most Christians view their lives as a set of isolated, independent areas which do not necessarily interact with each another. They fail to see how their belief in God and the Bible interrelates with their personal, social, and community lives, and they do not understand or act as if Christianity is a total world and life view.

There are at least two consequences of this "bit and piece" focus. First, we have not understood the scriptural admonition to develop a total Christian mind. Recall that Jesus' Great Commandment in Matthew 22:37-38 includes loving God with our minds as well as our hearts. The failure to heed both aspects of this command has led to an intellectually anemic Christianity. George Barna explains the result of this anti-intellectual approach, "Without a biblical

> **MATTHEW 22:37-38**
>
> *He [Jesus] said to him, "You shall love the Lord your God with all your heart, with all your soul, and with all your mind. This is the greatest and most important commandment."*

worldview, all the great teaching goes in one ear and out the other. There are no intellectual pegs . . . in the mind of the individual to hang these truths on. So they just pass through. They don't stick. They don't make a difference."[6] No wonder most Christians can't remember on Monday what the sermon was about the day before!

Second, a "bit and piece" focus causes many Christians to make a distinction between what is "sacred" (e.g., Bible study, prayer, church attendance, witnessing) and other areas of life that are "secular"(vocation, political involvement, education, psychology, etc.). Thinking about life in this sacred/secular dichotomy has resulted in the church generally withdrawing from those areas considered to be secular. This withdrawal by Christians actually began in the mid-1800's and accelerated in the early twentieth century as the church abandoned first one area of public life and then another. Those with a humanistic worldview, far removed from the biblical Christian perspective, filled the void in the public arena left by Christians.[7]

The results of this shift in worldview have been the demise of both public and private morals, a debasement of law and politics, an undermining of

> Author Heather MacDonald notes simply that we are now living under a heavy "burden of bad ideas."

educational values, and the corruption of media and popular culture. Over the past two decades, several authors have noted the rapid decline of our society's soul. Chuck Colson, President of Prison Fellowship, describes our social decline as an approaching storm ready plunge our culture into a new Dark Age.[8] Judge Robert Bork suggests that our nation has become like a beast heading toward a modern-day Gomorrah.[9] And author Heather MacDonald notes simply that we are now living under a heavy "burden of bad ideas."[10]

In contrast to the way many Christians approach life today , Jesus taught that the church ought to have an upbuilding and enlightening influence on society (see Matthew 5:13). With the removal of a distinctly Christian influence in areas of public concern, the outcome has been an increasingly tasteless and dark society—as evidenced every day on the news. The antidote is that Christians need to replace our narrow "bit and piece" focus with a broader understanding and application of the total picture of biblical truth.

> **MATTHEW 5:13**
>
> *You are the salt of the earth. But if the salt should lose its taste, how can it be made salty? It's no longer good for anything but to be thrown out and trampled on by men.*

It was God's intent all along that man should apply righteous principles to every area of life. After creating Adam and Eve, God instructs them to have dominion over all living creatures (see Genesis 1:26-28)— historically referred to as the Cultural Commission. Chuck Colson and Nancy Pearcey comment, "Until the sixth day, God has done the work of creation directly. But now he creates the first human beings and orders them to carry on where he leaves off: They are to reflect his image and to have dominion (Gen. 1:26). From then on, the development of the creation will be

**CHUCK COLSON**

**Chuck Colson's** first major entry into public life came as the 29 year-old manager of the 1950 California senate campaign for Congressman Richard Nixon. More than two decades of unflinching loyalty to the man who became the 36th president of the United States brought him to the forefront of the Watergate crisis—and to the frontlines of America's spiritual battle. In 1974, his newfound faith led him first to prison and then to begin one of the most powerful prison ministries in U.S. history. During the past 30 years, he also has become a leading spokesperson for biblical worldview thinking, through both his writing (such as *How Now Shall We Live?*) and his "Breakpoint" daily radio program. Taken from the 2003 biography *Charles Colson: A Story of Power, Corruption, and Redemption* by John Perry (Broadman & Holman Publishers), the following excerpt reflects Colson's courageous defense of the faith from his earliest days as a Christian.

Just before lunch the switchboard at Dickstein, Shapiro & Morin sprang to life. Every reporter in Washington, it seemed, wanted a statement from Chuck Colson. This was what happened every time some big announcement was made. *At last*, Colson thought, *the indictments have come through.*

The first call he took was from Aldo Beckman, Washington bureau chief of the *Chicago Tribune*. There were reports on the news wires about Colson attending a prayer meeting at the White House, and Colson and Hughes becoming friends. "And then there's something else here about your having found religion."

Colson's face flushed with anger. "My religion is my own business and I'm not about to talk about it in the public press."

"Jerry Warren announced it. It's already public."

As calls poured in, Colson asked his secretary to make a list of them. Then he thought about what had

happened that morning. He had been to the White House many times since resigning from the presidential staff. Why had [Dan] Rather decided to ask about this particular visit? Why hadn't Warren brushed the question aside?

Colson briefly supposed it could be a one-in-a thousand coincidence, but then had another thought: this was all God's doing. He was recognizing Chuck's commitment and at the same time making sure he couldn't backtrack on it. Chuck Colson was now locked into living his life for Jesus. He couldn't deny it, couldn't soft-pedal it, so he did his best to explain it, calling back all the reporters and telling them he had accepted Christ.

***Colson offers these reflections
in the biography's epilogue:***

I can see the pattern that God has used in my life and the things he's led me into. And the one thing I can tell you . . . is that I never planned any of this out. I didn't plan to start a resurgence of the born again movement. I didn't plan to try and be the driving force in getting people to take up the gospel, salt and light, in the form of prison ministry.

I wasn't the guy who sat down and thought, "You know maybe some time we should start talking about Christian worldview because we live in an era of radical individualism and people need to be thinking about these things." I didn't strategize that, I just felt a real hunger for it, and studied, it, greatly influenced by Francis Schaeffer. And I started to pick that up after Schaeffer died; it was just a natural thing.

It was a kind of outgrowth of what I was doing, and an outlet for my own intellectual pursuits. And yet it's turned out to be extremely timely, certainly after the terrorist attacks of September 11 [2001]: this is a worldview clash that we're in the middle of, the battle of worldviews between Islam and Christianity.

primarily social and cultural: It will be the work of humans as they obey God's command to fill and subdue the earth (Gen. 1:28)."[11]

In the life of Daniel in the Old Testament, we find an example of a man living out the Cultural Commission in the midst of a pagan culture. Daniel was trained in the "language and literature of the Babylonians" (Daniel 1:4), excelled in a high government position, and yet maintained a strict devotion to God.

## STAYING OUT OF CAPTIVITY

The Scriptures warn us not to be taken captive by the deceptive philosophies pervading our culture (Colossians 2:8). What makes non-Christian worldviews deceptive? A deception is anything that pretends to be the real thing but is not. A deceptive worldview looks good on the surface, but in fact does not conform to the way things actually are. It is a counterfeit of the real thing.

Some Christians insist that believers should stick only to studying the Bible and not waist time becoming familiar with deceptive philosophies. Some even use the example that U.S. Treasury agents supposedly are trained to spot counterfeit currency by analyzing only real bills. But this is actually an urban legend. In reality, agents have a thorough knowledge of faked bills as well. By knowing how to spot both the real and the counterfeit, they are not fooled when presented with a cleverly designed fraud. Similarly, Christians must be aware not only of why a biblical Christian worldview represents the real thing, but also of the earmarks of a false worldview.

Besides being a need for every Christian person-

**COLOSSIANS 2:8**

*Be careful that no one takes you captive through philosophy and empty deceit based on human tradition, based on the elemental forces of the world, and not based on Christ.*

ally, it is critical for Christian parents and teachers to endow younger people with protection against deceptive philosophies. In fact, not to prepare the next generation to understand other worldviews sets them up for nearly certain failure. Professor William McGuire conducted experiments to study how students respond when a persuasive speaker tries to change their minds about a commonly held belief. The study used as an example the idea that brushing teeth is good for oral health.[12] McGuire found that students who were given only a general verbal reinforcement of what they already believed (called a "concept boost")—in this experiment, that brushing one's teeth is good—were found to change their minds in greater numbers than those who were given clearly delineated reasons for refuting arguments presented by the speaker.

The findings of this study parallel what happens to many Christian young people today. If Christian teens are given only a "concept boost" by their parents, pastors, and youth leaders—that they should "believe in God and the Bible"—then when they are confronted in college with persuasive arguments against believing in God and the Bible by articulate non-Christian faculty, these students are defenseless. In contrast, students who understand why non-Christian worldviews are false are able not only to withstand attacks on their faith, but also are equipped to go on the offensive by using winning arguments of their own. Adult Christians experience the same thing. They become intimidated and afraid to speak out for what is moral and true because they are not sure what to say, how to say it, or why their view makes sense.

# HOW ARE WE DOING?

Christian students are especially vulnerable to being captured by alien worldviews while attending college. UCLA has surveyed students attending universities and colleges across America and has found that between 34 and 51 percent of the students who claim to be "born again" as freshmen no longer place themselves in that category by their senior year.[13] This is a tremendous dropout rate!

Evidently, we are not preparing Christian young people to face the worldview challenges of a college education. But what can account for a shift of this magnitude away from Christianity? Which worldviews have the greatest influence during the teen years? To explore this issue, the Nehemiah Institute developed a survey to determine the worldviews of high school students in five key areas: politics, education, economics, religion, and social issues (P.E.E.R.S.). This survey evaluates the degree to which the student's worldview aligns with biblical Christianity. The instrument yields a score from negative one hundred to positive one hundred. A score in

the 70 to 100 range means a student is answering the questions in line with an essentially biblical Christian viewpoint. Students who score between 30 and 69 are embracing a more moderate Christian worldview and could well move away from a biblical viewpoint on a number of key issues if presented with persuasive arguments. From 0 to 29, the student is thinking like a Secular Humanist in the majority of key areas. Even though students in this range may say they have a love for Jesus in their hearts, they are approaching life's major issues as practicing atheists. A student with a score of less than zero is responding to the questions as a Marxist-Leninist.[14]

Christian students in over 45 states have taken the P.E.E.R.S. survey since 1988, and their average scores show a steady decline. For Christians from evangelical churches who also attended public schools, the score in 1991 was 33, barely in the moderate Christian category. By 2001, the average for the same group had dropped to 8.2—a strong Secular Humanist position.

Stop and let that sink in a minute. Our best and brightest Christian youth actually are thinking like atheists when it comes to the major moral, social,

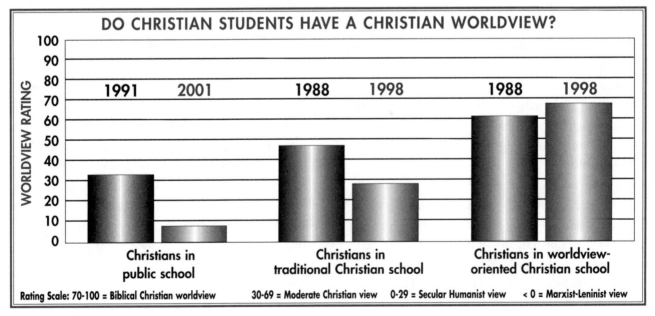

political and educational issues of our day! If this trend continues, it is estimated that the church will have lost an entire generation of Christian youth by the year 2015.

Unfortunately, students attending "traditional" Christian schools do not fair much better. A traditional Christian school is defined as one which may have chapel services, Bible classes, and begin classes with prayer but does not provide an inter-disciplinary worldview approach in every subject. From an average high of 47.2 in 1988, student scores fell to 29.7 by 1998. Only in Christian schools that emphasize a worldview approach in every class was there a gain over this same ten-year period, from 61.2 to 67.7.

The results of the P.E.E.R.S. survey tell us two things. First, Christian students in typical educational settings (whether government schools or "traditional" Christian schools) are being influenced more by secular culture than by a biblical worldview. Second, when presented with a well-planned approach to worldview issues, teens can embrace and defend the biblical perspective on those issues.

## SPIRITUAL FOUNDATIONS

George Barna, in his book *Generation Next*, helps us understand the youth to whom we will soon entrust the future of Western civilization. Barna reports:

> Because the Bible and most religious activities are foreign to them and seem irrelevant to what "real life" is all about, they perceive two parallel worlds coexisting: the spiritual, impractical world that contains many pure and absolute (and impracti-cal) dictums (such as truth, morality, love, faith), and the real world, the one they inhabit, which deals with

the hard stuff of daily living. Truth may be a wonderful concept, but many teens don't have sufficient interest in such an "impractical" or unrealistic concept to explore it further. *Millions of those who do have the interest do not have the philosophical, intellectual and spiritual foundations to take such an exploration to the next level.* [emphasis added][15]

Barna concludes that even among those who have a desire to follow the truth (which presumably would include many of the youth in our Christian homes and churches) they do not have the "spiritual foundations" on which to build! One Christian college administrator put it this way: "Students come here with a love for God in their hearts, but their minds think like pagans." To reverse this disturbing trend, parents, pastors, and youth leaders must teach the next generation how to think biblically and how to take the lead in making positive changes in our culture. That may mean parents, pastors, and youth leaders must themselves learn to counter our culture with godly insight!

## SETTING CAPTIVES FREE

Not only are we warned about falling victim to deceitful philosophies, we also are instructed to set free those who have been captured by these same philosophies (2 Timothy 2:24-26). In 2 Corinthians 10:5, Paul explains how to do this. He tells Christ's followers to "...demolish arguments and every high-minded thing that is raised up against the knowledge of God, taking every thought captive to the obedience of Christ."

The best way to demolish an argument is to point out its inconsistencies and offer a better argument in its place. All non-biblical worldviews have distinct weaknesses because they are out of sync with the real world. Once these weaknesses are brought to light, they can be contrasted with the strength of the biblical position. In the New Testament, the Apostle Paul provides an excellent example of putting into practice what he preached.

In Acts 17 we read that upon entering Athens, the intellectual and cultural center of the Roman Empire, Paul observed the pagan altars and idols that abounded in the city. As a result, "his spirit was greatly troubled" (v. 16). But instead of being depressed and discouraged, Paul took action. He "reasoned in the synagogue… and in the market-

> **2 CORINTHIANS 10:4-5**
>
> *We demolish arguments and every high-minded thing that is raised up against the knowledge of God, taking every thought captive to the obedience of Christ.*

> **2 TIMOTHY 2:24-26**
>
> *[24] The Lord's slave must not quarrel, but must be gentle to everyone, able to teach, and patient, [25] instructing his opponents with gentleness. Perhaps God will grant them repentance to know the truth. [26] Then they may come to their senses and escape the Devil's trap, having been captured by him to do his will.*

place every day …" with those who happened to be present (v.17). The same should be true for Christians today. When we observe our culture and see how it is dominated by secular and pagan worldviews, we should feel compelled to rescue those captured by alien worldviews and take appropriate action.

Paul's action was a "reasoned" dialogue—a public debate. This caught the attention of the city leaders, who invited him to address their council. Never underestimate God's ability to use our efforts to spread His truth. For instance, a graduate from one of Summit Ministries' summer leadership camps was motivated to take an active role in shaping society.

When she noticed an article in the local newspaper highlighting a proposed sex-education curriculum for the local schools, she wrote a letter to the editor expressing her opposition to it, providing a well-reasoned argument why teaching "safe-sex" techniques in school was not in the best interest of the students nor the community. This caught the attention of a businessman who invited this young lady to present her views to those in his civic club. This, in turn, led to other invitations to speak to other civic groups. On one occasion, a state senator attending the meeting was so impressed that he asked her to testify in the state capitol before a subcommittee on education. All of this from writing one letter!

It is worth noting that as Paul stood before the leaders of Athens the first words out of his mouth was a compliment. He said, "I see that you are religious in every respect" (v. 22). Instead of haranguing his audience for their false beliefs, Paul attempts to gain their ear. He was addressing the Epicurean and Stoic philosophers, whose philosophies are comparable to the atheists (Secular Humanists and Postmodernists) and pantheists (Cosmic Humanists) of our day. During Paul's speech, he demonstrates his knowledge of their beliefs by quoting from their own authorities. In finding common ground between his worldview and theirs, Paul acknowledges God's general revelation to all men (Romans 1:19-20). Every worldview has some points of contact with the way God has made the world; otherwise no one would believe it. Paul used this to his advantage, and similarly, we need to discern where a person's beliefs intersect the truth and use that knowledge to lead him or her out of deception and into the light of God's truth.

Paul begins his apologetic by addressing the question

## PAUL'S SERMON TO THE ATHENIAN LEADERS

While Paul was waiting for them [Silas and Timothy] in Athens, his spirit was troubled within him when he saw that the city was full of idols. So he reasoned in the synagogue with the Jews and with those who worshiped God, and in the marketplace every day with those who happened to be there. Then also, some of the Epicurean and Stoic philosophers argued with him. Some said, "What is this pseudo-intellectual trying to say?"

Others replied, "He seems to be a preacher of foreign deities"—because he was telling the good news about Jesus and the resurrection.

They took him and brought him to the Areopagus, and said, "May we learn about this new teaching you're speaking of? For what you say sounds strange to us, and we want to know what these ideas mean." Now all the Athenians and the foreigners residing there spent their time on nothing else but telling or hearing something new.

Then Paul stood in the middle of the Areopagus and said: "Men of Athens! I see that you are extremely religious in every respect. For as I was passing through and observing the objects of your worship, I even found an altar on which was inscribed: TO AN UNKNOWN GOD. Therefore, what you worship in ignorance, this I proclaim to you. The God who made the world and everything in it—He is Lord of heaven and earth and does not live in shrines made by hands. Neither is He served by human hands, as though He needed anything, since He Himself gives everyone life and breath and all things. From one man He has made every nation of men to live all over the earth and has determined their appointed times and the boundaries of where they live, so that they might seek God, and perhaps they might reach out and find Him, though He is not far from each one of us. For in Him we live and move and exist, as even some of your own poets have said, 'For we are also His offspring.' Being God's offspring, then, we shouldn't think that the divine nature is like gold or silver or stone, an image fashioned by human art and imagination.

"Therefore, having overlooked the times of ignorance, God now commands all people everywhere to repent, because He has set a day on which He is going to judge the world in righteousness by the Man He has appointed. He has provided proof of this to everyone by raising Him from the dead."

When they heard about resurrection of the dead, some began to ridicule him. But others said, "We will hear you about this again." So Paul went out from their presence. [34]However, some men joined him and believed, among whom were Dionysius the Areopagite, a woman named Damaris, and others with them.

of theology, "What about God?" Because Paul had "looked carefully" at their religious expressions and understood their worldview, he found an opening for the truth. He pointed to one of their altars erected "TO AN UNKNOWN GOD," and realized that built into their belief system was an unanswered question, "What if there is a God whom we don't know?" The Greeks had filled a pantheon with gods to oversee every conceivable situation in life. Yet, even with thousands of gods, they feared that some god might be left out. So in order to cover their bases, they built this altar. Paul used their lack of knowledge to explain that this "unknown God" is the Creator of "the world [cosmos] and everything in it," and that He is "Lord of heaven and earth and does not live in shrines made by hands" (v. 24). This declaration counters the Epicureans' practical atheism that placed the "gods" in another realm, inaccessible to the material universe. It also corrected the Stoics' pantheistic belief that the various Greek gods reflected different representations of the "world soul."

Paul then turns from theology to psychology

*The Acropolis in Athens, Greece remains today near the site where Paul of Tarsus argued the truth of Christianity with Stoic and Epicurean philosophers.*

("What about man?"). He declares that man receives "life and breath and all things" from the one Creator and that "from one man He [God] has made every nation of men..." (v. 25-26). The purpose of each individual, Paul continues, is to "seek God and perhaps they might reach out and find Him, though He is not far from each one of us" (v. 27). Then Paul quotes two Greek poets who had written similar ideas. Epimenides, the 6th century BC philosopher, has said, "For in him we live and move and exist" and the Stoic, Aratus, a poet who had lived 300 years earlier, wrote, "We are also His offspring" (v. 28). While these comments were originally directed toward Zeus, not Yahweh of the Hebrew Scriptures, Paul recognized the ideas expressed were essentially correct.

By way of application, Paul then says, "Being God's offspring, then, we shouldn't think that the divine nature is... an image fashioned by human art and imagination" (v. 29). Paul had just made it clear that the Athenians' "unknown God" was the exact opposite of an idol—it was His skill that designed us, not the other way around. That being the case, God calls all men to repent because "he has set a day on which He is going to judge the world in righteousness" (v. 30). Paul makes the connection between theology, psychology and ethics by presenting the notion

that God is holy and just and man is sinful and separated from God's righteousness and needs to repent of his moral failings (for an explanation of these ideas, see Paul's letter to the Romans, chapter 3, verses 21-26).

Why should those listening to Paul believe this picture of reality? ("How do I know?" is a key question of philosophy.) Paul affirms that God "has provided proof of this to everyone by raising Him [Jesus] from the dead" (v. 31). As the capstone of Paul's argument, he appeals to the resurrection of Jesus (the central issue in the worldview category of history). His argument rests on a historical event validated by numerous eyewitnesses (this is detailed in Paul's account found in 1 Corinthians 15:3-8).

Those who heard Paul that day responded in one of three ways: with contempt (probably the Epicureans because their worldview precluded a bodily resurrection), contemplation ("We will hear you about this again," most likely echoed by some of the Stoics), or commitment ("some... believed.") (v.32-34). We can expect the same range of responses as we share with others that Jesus is the Way, the Truth, and the Life.

## WHAT IS THE FAMILY?

When it comes to demolishing deceptive philosophies, consider a contentious question of our day: What is a family? A national debate currently rages

over this issue. On one side are the humanists who define family in a way that is fluid and changes with the times. They claim the biblically prescribed family (one man and one woman married for life in order to establish a home and raise children) is not necessarily the only way or even the best way to define marriage and the family. In fact, both Secular and Cosmic Humanists insist that people should have the freedom to establish any kind of marriage they desire—two men living together, two women together, or any other combination of their choice.

Does the biblical view offer individuals and society a better answer to the "What is a family" question? Does it have a better "fit" with the real world? Numerous social, psychological, and demographic studies reveal that husbands, wives, and children are all better off emotionally, physically, spiritually, economically, and academically when the traditional family unit is maintained. The following are just two examples from the many that could be cited:

> • Married mothers are hallikely to experience domestic violence as are never-married mothers.
> • Teenagers from intact, two-parent families have a 20 percent lower rate of sexual activity than their counterparts living with a single, divorced, remarried, or cohabitating parent.[16]

The answer to the family question clearly is: "Yes, the traditional family is best for individuals and for society."[17]

As these statistics suggest, general revelation (also described as "natural law," i.e., what we can discern from studying the world around us) works in concert with God's special revelation (the Bible) to present a consistent picture of reality. Thus, a biblical worldview

appeals to natural law as well as divine law in demonstrating how a biblical perspective offers the best course for life. As Christians, we should be actively persuading our friends and fellow citizens of the truth of God's design for life. As we do this, we are fulfilling Jesus' call to be "salt and light" in our world.

## FACING THE CHALLENGE

As the Apostle Paul faced the religious worldviews of his day, so faithful and aware Christians must face the false philosophies of our day. In the West, this means facing humanism and postmodernism in all forms. Since there are biblical and practical reasons to study other worldviews, where should we begin? This text provides an introduction to Secular Humanist, Postmodern Marxist, and Cosmic Humanist worldviews while presenting an intelligent defense of biblical Christianity. We intend to present these views as accurately as possible. No humanist, upon reading this text, should find that we misrepresent the humanist position. When we say Secular Humanism is atheistic, we show you why by presenting what Secular Humanists say about the issue. When we note that Cosmic Humanist ethics are morally relative, you will read supporting statements from their own books and articles. When we contend that Marxist sociology relies on class warfare, you will hear that from Marxist sociologists. No quote has been taken out of context purposely. We have, in the best tradition of Christian scholarship, allowed proponents of alternative worldviews to have their say as they wish to say it.

> The heart of Christian theology is theism, just as the heart of Secular Humanist biology is evolution or the heart of Cosmic Humanist ethics is relativism.

| FOUR WESTERN WORLDVIEW MODELS | | | | |
|---|---|---|---|---|
| | **BIBLICAL CHRISTIANITY** | **SECULAR HUMANISM** | **POSTMODERN MARXISM** | **COSMIC HUMANISM** |
| **SOURCES** | THE BIBLE | HUMANIST MANIFESTOS I, II, III | MARX, NIETSCHE, FOUCAULT, PRORTY | WRITINGS OF SPANGLER, FERGUSON, ETC. |
| **THEOLOGY** | Theism | Atheism/Skepticism | Militant Atheism | Pantheism/Paganism |
| **PHILOSOPHY** | Supernaturalism | Naturalism | Anti-Foundationalism | Non-Naturalism |
| **BIOLOGY** | Creation | Darwinian Evolution | Chaos Theory | Cosmic Evolution |
| **PSYCHOLOGY** | Dualism:Mind/Body | Monism:Self-Actualization | Nihilism: Will to power | Monism:Higher Consciousness |
| **ETHICS** | Moral Absolutes | Ethical Relativism | | Individual Autonomy |
| **SOCIOLOGY** | Traditional Home, Church and State | Non-Traditional Family | Culturally Constructed Values | Non-Traditional Home, Church and State |
| **LAW** | Biblical and Natural Law | Positive Law | Muliculturalism | Self-Law |
| **POLITICS** | Justice/Freedom/Order | World Government | Victim Group Empowerment | New Age Order |
| **ECONOMICS** | Stewardship of Property | Interventionism | Power Politics | Enlightened Production |
| **HISTORY** | Historical Resurrection | Historical Evolution | Socialism | Evolutionary Godhood |

We paint the picture of these three worldviews with broad strokes. Since each subject could fill countless pages by itself, we do not address every subtlety but rather attempt to capture the kernel of each worldview's perspective on the key disciplines most influential in shaping our culture. Following C. S. Lewis' formula in striving to capture "mere Christianity," we attempt to present mere Secular Humanism, mere Postmodernism, and mere Cosmic Humanism. The heart of Christian theology, for example, is theism, just as the heart of Secular Humanist biology is evolution or the heart of Cosmic Humanist ethics is relativism. Thus, we examine the core, the central foundation, of each worldview. For a summary of how each worldview approaches each of ten major subject categories, see the chart above.

This course of study is based on the belief that by learning to contrast worldviews, a Christian improves his overall conceptual skills. We contend that by seeing worldviews compared, readers will better understand their own worldview and be positioned to offer a persuasive and intelligent defense. Many people today do not have the foggiest notion what they believe; it is the duty of Christians to share God's truth with this spiritually rootless generation. The Apostle Peter says as much when he exhorts believers in Jesus Christ to "always be ready to give a defense to anyone who asks you a reason for the hope that is in you" (1 Peter 3:15).

As you proceed through the text, our prayer is our that you will see the full value, truthfulness, and superiority of the Christian worldview and grow in the grace and knowledge of our Lord and Savior, Jesus Christ.

## RECOMMENDED READING

Colson, Charles and Nancy Pearcey. *How Now Shall We Live?* Wheaton, IL: Tyndale House, 1999.

Dobson, James C. and Gary L. Bauer. *Children at Risk: The Battle For the Hearts and Minds of Our Kids*, Dallas, TX: Word, 1990.

Schaffer, Francis A. *How Should We Then Live?* Wheaton, IL: Crossway Books, 1983.

## ENDNOTES

1. Benjamin Wiker, *Moral Darwinism: How We Became Hedonists* (Downers Grove, IL: InterVarsity Press, 2002) p. 301, 314.

2. Robert B. Brandon, Editor, *Rorty and His Critics* (Malden, MA: Blackwell Publishers, 2000) p. 21-2.

3. James C. Dobson and Gary L. Bauer, *Children at Risk: The Battle For the Hearts and Minds of Our Kids* (Dallas, TX: Word, 1990), p.19.

4. Ibid., p.19.

5. Francis A. Schaeffer, *A Christian Manifesto* (Westchester, IL: Crossway, 1981), p. 17.

6. Quoted in *How Now Shall We Live?*, Charles Colson and Nancy Pearcy. (Wheaton, IL: Tyndale House, 1999) p. ix.

7. For more on the historical development of the "pietistic movement" among Christians in America from the mid-1800's and into the twentieth century, see *Love Your God with All Your Mind*, by J. P. Moreland. Moreland traces the steps taken by the church in the United States to arrive at the point where one's emotions are the primary vehicle for relating to God. He then builds a case from Scripture that God has designed people with rational minds as well as emotional hearts, and to neglect the mind is to miss the mark of a true Christian.

8. See Charles Colson, *Against the Night: Living in the New Dark Ages* (Ann Arbor, MI: Servant Publications, 1989).

9. See Robert H. Bork, *Slouching Towards Gomorrah: Modern Liberalism and American Decline* (New York: HarperCollins Publishers, 1996).

10. See Heather MacDonald, *The Burden of **Bad** Ideas: How Modern Intellectuals Misshape Our Society* (Chicago, IL: Ivan R. Dee, Publisher, 2000).

11. Charles Colson and Nancy Pearcey, *How Now Shall We Live?* (Wheaton, IL: Tyndale House, 1999), p. 295.

12. See William McGuire's article, "Inducing Resistance to Persuasion" in *Advances in Experimental Psychology, Vol. 1*, Leonard Berkowitz, ed. (Academic Press, NY, 1964) p. 192-231.

13. Gary Lyle Railsback, "An Exploratory Study of the Religiosity and Related Outcomes Among College Students," Doctoral dissertation, University of California at Los Angeles, 1994.

14. If you would like to use the P.E.E.R.S. survey to test students or adults in your church or Bible study, contact Nehemiah Institute, Inc., 3735 Harrodsburg Rd., Suite 150, Lexington, KY 40513, (800) 948-3101, nehemiah@midco.net, www.nehemiahinstitute.com. There is a charge for the full 70–question survey and evaluation.

15. George Barna, *Generation Next* (Ventura, CA.: Regal Books, 1995), p. 33.

16. Patrick F. Fagan, et. al. *The Positive Effects of Marriage: A Book of Charts*, "The Effects of Marriage on Children," http://www.heritage.org/Research/Features/Marriage/index.cfm

17. The issues raised in this example will be covered in more detail in chapter eight. It is included here to illustrate how a consistent biblical Christian worldview provides a framework to understand the connections between the various disciplines and the real world. We also suggest a careful reading of George Gilder's *Men and Marriage*.

(1) Chuck Colson: From Charles Colson: A Story of Power, Corruption, and Redemption by John Perry (2003 Broadman & Holman Publishers: Nashville, TN)
(2) Acropolis: From Countering Culture video (2004 Summit Ministries: Manitou Springs, CO)

# CHAPTER 2

# Worldviews Seeking
# To Capture You

"Who are you?… Then, who am I?…
Was nothing real?"
—Truman (from the final scene of *The Truman Show*)

"In the United States of America, our
traditional, Western, Judeo-Christian culture is
collapsing. It is not collapsing because it failed.
On the contrary it has given us the freest and
most prosperous society in human history.
Rather, it is collapsing because we are
abandoning it."[1]
—William S. Lind

"… the clash that is coming—and that has,
indeed, already begun—is… between those who
claim the Judeo-Christian worldview and those
who have abandoned that worldview in favor of
the 'isms' of contemporary American life—
feminism, multiculturalism, gay liberationism,
lifestyle liberalism—what I here lump together
as a family called 'the secularist orthodoxy.'"[2]
—Robert P. George

In *The Truman Show*, the hit comedy film starring Jim Carey, Truman is a man who has lived his entire life confined in an enormous Hollywood studio, never realizing his every move was seen live by millions of television viewers around the world. Everyone in his life was an actor, playing the part of wife, neighbors, and friends, yet Truman was playing only himself. Talk about a strange twist on reality TV! But Truman begins to suspect all is not as it appears in his sound-stage world, and he finally determines to face reality by walking off the set.

In the final scene, Truman makes his way in a boat to the edge of the "ocean" and locates a set of stairs leading to an exit. As Truman opens the door, the voice of Christof, the show's director, booms through the loudspeaker, apparently coming down from the sky. Truman asks Christof a series of three sweeping questions. The first, foundational to the others, is "Who are you?" (with the clear implication, "Who are you, God?"). This ultimate question is the central question of theology.

After considering Christof's answer, Truman asks a second question: "Then who am I?" This time, Truman seeks knowledge about his own being, which is the focal issue of psychology. Finally, after pondering Christof's response, Truman asks, "Was nothing real?" Here is the great philosophical question, as bright as day. To this Christof answers, "*You* were real. That's what made you so good."

Truman's three questions are the ones every person on earth must answer in some way. The answers form the bedrock for how we understand our world and our relationships to God, ourselves and our fellow human beings. Together, they are the cornerstone of a total worldview.

## WORLDVIEW THNKING

If Truman's questions are the starting point, how should a total worldview be defined? There are various ways of slicing the "worldview pie," depending on whom you read, but we find a great advantage in segmenting the framework for a worldview into the following ten disciplines:

1. **Theology.** At some point, everyone asks the question, "What about God?"
2. **Philosophy.** We are curious about the nature of reality and how we know what is true.
3. **Biology.** We have questions about the origin of life.
4. **Psychology.** We wonder about ourselves.
5. **Ethics.** How do we go about making moral choices?
6. **Sociology.** We question how society ought to be structured.
7. **Law.** How should legal issues be solved?
8. **Politics.** We're concerned about how government should be structured.
9. **Economics.** We ponder what is the best system by which to make and spend money.
10. **History.** What can we learn from the past?

*Thinking Like A Christian,* the first study in the Worldviews in Focus series, explores these disciplines in detail. It examines how a biblical Christian approach addresses each issue and demonstrates how these ten disciplines provide a comprehensive framework of life—a total worldview. The Western educational enterprise is structured around these disciplines. Universities, in particular, offer courses in each area, corresponding to how Western civilization approaches life's crucial questions.

## THE WORLDVIEW TREE

Defining a worldview through these ten areas also helps one understand the inter-relationships between the various disciplines. To visualize these interrelationships, think of a fruit tree supported by a root system. The tree draws nourishment from the roots, transfers it through the trunk, and produces fruit at the end of the branches. Although the fruit is separated from the underpinnings of the tree, it is nevertheless organically connected to the roots.

Jesus said of his disciples, "You'll recognize them by their fruit" (Matthew 7:16). Similarly, a worldview operates as an organic whole. Fruit (outward behavior) flows naturally from the root (inner beliefs). The root system of every worldview is composed of the twin disciplines of theology and philosophy. Together, these form assumptions about God, reality, and knowledge. From these *religious* roots flow implications for each of the other eight disciplines, the branches of the tree. And at the end of these branches is the fruit—the outworking of these assembled beliefs in a person's life.

## CULTURAL RADICALS

For nearly 2,000 years, Western culture has grown and blossomed as it drew nourishment from biblical answers to the questions raised by the ten disciplines outlined above. Yet in recent years, voices calling for radically different answers have gained a hearing. William S. Lind describes the serious implications of these new and different answers: "In the United States of America, our traditional, Western, Judeo-Christian culture is collapsing. It is not collapsing because it failed. On the contrary it has given us the freest and most prosperous society in human history. Rather, it is collapsing because we are abandoning it."[3] To use our tree analogy, Western society is abandoning the Judeo-Christian roots that have been its very source of nurture.

What could cause such a dramatic and widespread shift in perspective? Lind also comments on some of the people and strategies that have been used to initiate this mutation of culture which in the past has served us so well:

Starting in the mid-1960s, we have thrown away the values, morals, and standards that define traditional Western culture. In part, this has been driven by cultural radicals, people who hate our Judeo-Christian culture. Dominant in the elite, especially in the universities, the media, and the entertainment industry, the cultural radicals have successfully pushed an agenda of moral relativism, militant secularism, and sexual and social "liberation."[4]

*The diagram shows a tree with branches labeled:* Government, Psychology, Ethics, Law, History, Sociology, Science, Economics, with "Outward" and "Behavior" on the trunk. The roots are labeled Theology, Inner Beliefs, Philosophy.

When we consider the significant moral and social issues of today, we see disturbing fruit emerging. "Cultural radicals" seek to cut off a biblically-based root system and graft in another that is composed of drastically different answers to the foundational religious questions. The radical ideas now taught in the classroom, promoted through the media, and encouraged by entertainment industry are simply the result (fruit) of a revised view of life and reality. These ideas fall into one of the three specific worldviews outlined in chapter one—Secular Humanism, Postmodern Marxism, and Cosmic Humanism.

To fully understand the current culture war, we need to recognize each of these divergent worldviews and apprehend their influence throughout our society —even in many of our seminaries and churches.

# SECULAR HUMANISM

Perhaps the single most important reason Secular Humanism exerts such a dramatic influence on our society is that it is the dominant worldview in our secular educational system. Proponents of this atheistic view have long recognized the classroom as a powerful place to indoctrinate young minds. Writing in the 1930's, humanist Charles Potter penned these words:

> Education is the most powerful ally of humanism, and every American public school is a school of humanism. What can the theistic Sunday schools, meeting for an hour once a week, and teaching only a fraction of the children, do to stem the tide of a five-day program of humanistic teaching?[5]

And how are humanists doing in their goal of changing the educational landscape? They are doing quite well.

In recent years, Christianity has been deliberately—some would say brilliantly—erased from America's educational system. In the subject of biology, for example, the only view allowed in the classroom is naturalistic evolution, one that excludes the possibility of God's involvement in creation. When Christians have attempted to introduce a balanced treatment of the origin of life by including the concept of an Intelligent Designer, there has been an uproar that favors banning any mention of a Creator in science classes.[6]

In the area of social studies, humanists also are taking the upper hand by eradicating the study of Christianity from textbooks, or if Christians are mentioned, it is usually in a negative light. Professor Paul Vitz systematically reviewed textbooks used in schools across the United States[7] and summarizes his findings from books used in first through forth grades:

> …this sample of forty social studies texts, which were ostensibly meant to introduce students to American society as it exists today (and, to a lesser extent, how it existed in the past), did not contain a single reference in word or image to today's powerful Protestant religious world of the Bible belt…. Nothing about the world of mainline Protestantism was acknowledged even once. The books placed a heavy emphasis instead on such things as today's job market and the world of recreation.[8]

Regarding U.S. history textbooks used in an estimated 60 percent of the country's eleventh and twelfth grades, Vitz noted that "Not one of these texts recognized, much less emphasized, the great religious energy and creativity of the U.S. . . . although a few of them mentioned the Scopes trial."[9] So the only image of religion most students receive is cast in the negative light of the

*Early 20th century humanist Charles Francis Potter envisioned public school education as a way for humanism to replace Judeo-Christian beliefs as our culture's dominant philosophy.*

Scopes "monkey trial" in Tennessee! Five other independent studies confirm the same religious bias revealed by Vitz.[10]

Furthermore, if you step into any psychology class on the average university campus, you will study the major contributors of "modern psychology"—B.F. Skinner, Sigmund Freud, Abraham Maslow, Carl Rogers, and Erich Fromm. What you probably will not hear is that each one of these men was an atheist, and every single one except Freud was selected as "Humanist of the Year" by the humanist movement.

## INDOCTRINATION 101

From grade school to graduate school, the results of this shift away from a biblical understanding of course

material is evident. Many professors are unapologetically indoctrinating their students into their humanist worldview. Professor Richard Rorty boldly states his purpose: "We are not going to tolerate you bigoted Christians. We liberal Profs try to change the fundamentalist students... away from their bigoted parents."[11] To grasp how far Rorty is willing to take our Christian students, one need only read *Achieving Our Country: Leftist Thought in Twentieth Century America*. While he insists, for example, that he is a militant anti-communist and believes the war against Stalin was legitimate,[12] he also finds the Communist Party USA useful in recruiting "a few good agents for Soviet intelligence" and praises those who apologized for Stalin since they "helped change our country for the better."[13]

Attorney and author David French recalls the indoctrination into liberal thinking he received in law school when he comments:

> I was surprised by both the unrelenting liberalism of my professors and by their daily zeal in advancing their various worldviews.... [M]y criminal law class was an exercise in coercing a reexamination of our attitudes towards race and poverty.... My family law professors tried to persuade their students to abandon traditional conceptions of childhood, gender, and parental roles. My human rights teachers spent much of the class attacking religious fundamentalism of all stripes.... [14]

French goes on to relate that the most discouraging part of his law school experience was how the other students accepted uncritically their professors' teaching. Often, he was the only one willing to challenge the blatantly outrageous ideas expressed from the front of the classroom.

Recent surveys support this anecdotal evidence of

anti-Christian and liberal bias in much of education. The fall 2001 survey conducted by the Higher Education Research Institute at UCLA's Graduate School of Education and Information Studies finds that 29.9 percent of students entering four-year colleges and universities characterize their political views as "liberal" or "far left," the highest percentage in two decades... [while] just 20.7 percent consider themselves "conservative" or "far right."[15] This demonstrates that liberal indoctrination is not confined to the university campus. Evidently, many students are introduced to liberalism through their high school experience! Charles Potter's words in 1930 clearly were prophetic.

## HUMANIST INFLUENCE IN POPULAR CULTURE

This brings us to another reason for examining the Secular Humanist worldview: many humanists have gained positions of considerable influence in our society. Most mainline media—including nightly news broadcasts, television shows, movies, and even much of popular music—present opinions, story lines and lyrics consistent with the humanist vision. For instance, in the film, *The Cider House Rules*, the viewer is presented with six convincing arguments for abortion on demand as the main character, played by Toby McGuire, moves from pro-life to pro-choice by the end of the story. And in *John Q*, starring Denzel Washington, the story from beginning to end is an impassioned case for universal health care, yet another cause championed by liberals.

For a closer look at how the mainstream media exhibit a consistent bias toward liberal causes in reporting the news, one need look no further than Bernard Goldberg's book, *Bias*. An award-winning broadcast journalist who worked for more than three decades at CBS News, Goldberg offers an insider's take on major news organizations. He describes how "during the Clinton impeachment trial in 1999, as the senators signed their names in the oath book swearing they would be fair and impartial, Peter Jennings, who was anchoring ABC News's live coverage, made sure his audience knew which senators were *conservative*—but uttered not a word about which ones were *liberal*."[16] Goldberg explains why this incident is revealing: "On that particular day, Peter identified the conservatives because he thought it mattered. He thought his viewers needed to know.... In the world of the Jenningses and Brokaws and Rathers, conservatives are out of the mainstream and need to be identified. Liberals, on the other hand, *are* the mainstream and don't need to be identified."[17]

Goldberg also highlights numerous other examples of liberal bias. He spends a chapter discussing how the media *created* the AIDS "scare" by misinforming the public about the nature and transmission of HIV. This was due to the media elite's reluctance to expose AIDS as a disease transmitted primarily through homosexual acts.

The press reveals their bias not only by over-reporting certain items, but also by under-reporting others. Goldberg points out the almost non-existent reporting of the declining health and well being of "latch-key kids." About the lack of reporting on a major study on children, he makes clear that journalists do not want to take on the feminists' love affair with daycare. If it were widely reported that children in daycare centers generally do not fare well, then many working moms might feel guilty, thus subverting the feminist goal of liberating all women from the constraints of husband and children. Goldberg does not suggest media elites are engaged in a "vast left-wing

## EXCERPT FROM *BIAS* BY BERNARD GOLDBERG

*(Regnery Publishing, Inc.: Washington, DC, 2002), pages 57-59*

This blindness, this failure to see liberals as anything but middle-of-the-road moderates, happens all the time on network television. The Christian Coalition is identified as a conservative organization—so far, so good—but we don't identify the National Organization for Women (NOW) as a liberal organization, which it surely is.

Robert Bork is the "conservative" judge. But Laurence Tribe, who must have been on the CBS Evening News ten million times in the 1980s (and who during the contested presidential election in 2000 was a leading member of Team Gore, arguing the vice president's case before the U.S. Supreme Court), is identified simply as a "Harvard law professor." But Tribe is not simply a Harvard law professor. He's easily as liberal as Bork is conservative.

If we do a Hollywood story, it's not unusual to identify certain actors, like Tom Selleck or Bruce Willis, as conservatives. But Barbara Streisand or Rob Reiner, no matter how active they are in liberal Democratic politics, are just Barbara Streisand and Rob Reiner.

Rush Limbaugh is the conservative radio talk show host. But Rosie O'Donnell, who while hosting a fund-raiser for Hillary Clinton said Mayor Rudy Giuliani was New York's "village idiot," is not the liberal TV talk show host.

During the Clinton impeachment trial in 1999, as the senators signed their names in the oath book swearing they would be fair and impartial, Peter Jennings, who was anchoring ABC News's live coverage, made sure his audience knew which senators were conservative—but uttered not a word about which ones were liberal.

As the senators each signed the oath book, Jennings identified several Democrats, including Barbara Boxer and Ted Kennedy, two of the most liberal members of the Senate, without ever mentioning that they are indeed liberal. That would have been just fine, except for what happened later. When Senator John McCain signed the book, Jennings said, "Senator John McCain here of Arizona, left-hander. More right than left in his politics and intending to run for president of the United States." Jennings, spotted another conservative. "Senator McConnell of Kentucky, very determined conservative member of the Republican Party."

When Jennings identified the next senator to sign the book it was, "Senator Mikulski of Maryland."

Plain and simple. Unadorned. Senator Mikulski of Maryland. Not a word that Senator Mikulski is a liberal Democrat from Maryland.

Then, a few second later, Jennings, with pinpoint precision, continued identifying the conservatives. "Senator Rick Santorum, one of the younger members of the Senate, Republican, very determined conservative member of the Senate. That's Senator Daschle there in the left-hand side of your picture."

Santorum was a conservative Republican but Tom Daschle, a liberal from South Dakota, was simply...Senator Daschle.... On that particular day, Peter identified the conservatives because he thought it mattered. He thought his viewers needed to know. And he was right. He didn't identify the liberals, obviously because he thought it didn't matter. And he was wrong. In the world of the Jenningses and Brokaws and Rathers, conservatives are out of the mainstream and need to be identified. Liberals, on the other hand, are the mainstream and don't need to be identified.

conspiracy," but rather, that they are merely living out their worldview, assuming theirs is the correct way to look at the world and oblivious to their own biased inclinations. These observations highlight our contention all along: worldviews matter!

# POSTMODERN MARXISM

Like Secular Humanism, Marxism-Leninism is a well-developed atheistic worldview. Over the past century, followers of Marx and Lenin have crafted a perspective on each of the ten disciplines—generally in great detail. Marxists often produce a "champion" of their perspective in various fields (e.g., I.P. Pavlov in psychology, T.D. Lysenko in biology, Stephen J. Gould in paleontology, Michael Hardt and Antonio Negri in politics, or Stanley Fish in humanities).

Yet, over the past 20 years, traditional Marxism-Leninism has morphed into the currently fashionable "postmodernism"—a view animating the "politically correct" ideology prevalent in the majority of our universities today. And while Postmodern Marxism does not offer a perspective as comprehensive in all ten worldview disciplines as traditional Marxism-Leninism, studying this version of Marxism is crucial for Christians in order to understand why so many bizarre-sounding ideas are emanating from college campuses across our land—speech codes, biased admissions practices, celebration of "Gay Pride," mandatory diversity training, radical professors in almost every department, plus many other elements of the radical cultural agenda. Of perhaps even greater significance, Marxism needs to be analyzed because it is currently one of Christianity's most rabid detractors.

# MARXIST INFLUENCE IN EDUCATION

As their atheistic comrades the Secular Humanists have targeted education, so Marxists have recognized the classroom as the key to influencing our nation. As early as the 1950's, U.C.L.A. was referred to as the "Little Red School House" because of the Marxist influence on campus. Not only there, but on campuses across the U.S., "radical" students of the '60's protested the Vietnam War and embraced the Marxist worldview. To secure their stronghold, many of them never left the campus but stayed on to earn their Ph.D.'s and now are tenured professors teaching our current generation of students.

Even as early as 1982, a *U.S. News and World Report* article entitled "Marxism in U.S. Classrooms," revealed that 10,000 Marxist professors were teaching on America's campuses.[18] And by 1987, New York University's Herbert London remarked, "The strides made by Marxism at American universities in the last two decades are breathtaking. Every discipline has been affected by its preachment, and almost every faculty now counts among its members a resident Marxist scholar."[19] Alvin Schmidt describes "a 1992 conference, 'Marxism in the New World Order: Crisis and Possibilities,' held at the University of Massachusetts at Amherst. Only 300 were expected to attend, but 1,500 registered. Nearly all were professors. The conference attendees were diehard believers in Marxism, not realists who recognized that the most inefficient, cruel, and inhumane socioeconomic system had come to an end."[20] Georgie Anne Geyer further states "the percentage of Marxist faculty numbers can range from an estimated 90 percent in some midwestern universities."[21]

> "Marxist academics," writes Arnold Beichman, "are today's power elite in the universities."

"Marxist academics," writes Arnold Beichman, "are today's power elite in the universities."[22] And those in power are not shy about expressing their intentions. Duke University Professor

Frederic Jameson told *Commentary* magazine that "to create a Marxist Culture in this country, to make Marxism an unavoidable presence in American social, cultural, and intellectual life, in short to form a Marxist intelligentsia for the struggles of the future...seems to me the supreme mission of a Marxist pedagogy."[23] It is certainly no accident that the new "Communist Manifesto" for the twenty-first century was published by Harvard University Press and is owned by the fellows of Harvard University.[24]

The Postmodern Marxist influence has reached its most alarming heights in the humanities departments of America's universities. "With a few notable exceptions," says former Yale professor Roger Kimball, "our most prestigious liberal arts colleges and universities have installed the entire radical menu at the center of their humanities curriculum at both the undergraduate and the graduate level."[25] Kimball provides examples of how Duke University has been and continues to be in the forefront of academia's move toward Postmodernism, noting that it has "conducted a tireless—and successful—campaign to arm its humanities department with the likes of the Marxist literary critic Frederic Jameson, Barbara Herrnstein Smith, Frank Lentricchia, Stanley Fish (and his like-minded wife, Jane Tompkins), and other less well known souls of kindred intellectual orientation."[26]

The result of this Postmodern Marxist influence is that the culture wars are fiercest on our campuses, with battles being waged over political correctness, feminism, multiculturalism, and deconstructionism. Yet

> "The shadow university, with its shadow curriculum, dominates freshman orientation, residential programming, extracurricular student life, the promulgations of codes and regulations, and the administration of what passes, on our campuses, for justice."
> —*The Shadow University* (Kors and Silverglate)

many of the most critical battles are shielded from the public eye. According to Professor Alan Charles Kors and lawyer Harvey A. Silverglate, authors of *The Shadow University*, much is going on behind the scenes to further radicalize higher education:

> To know the betrayal of liberty on our campuses, one must understand what has become of their divisions of university life and student life, residential advisors, judicial systems, deans of students and their officers, and of their new and profoundly disturbing student rules and regulations. This threat has developed not in the glare of publicity, debate and criticism, as has been the case with new academic disciplines, courses, and pedagogies, but in the shadows.... The shadow university, with its shadow curriculum, dominates freshman orientation, residential programming, extracurricular student life, the promulgations of codes and regulations, and the administration of what passes, on our campuses, for justice.[27]

As this overview demonstrates, Postmodern Marxism is thriving on the American campus and in the classroom. If Christian students are to survive their college experience with their faith intact, they must understand the weaknesses of a Marxist worldview and be able to articulate a positive biblical response.

# MARXIST INFLUENCE IN POPULAR CULTURE

Once embraced by students, a worldview does not remain confined on campus but gradually influences all arenas of society, such as popular media, film and television. A recent article in *National Review* explains, "In Hollywood, it was—and is—more chic to be a Commie than a conservative."[28] A case in point is TV producer Norman Lear, who has produced and/or significantly influenced numerous popular shows in the early 1970's such as *All in the Family, Maude,* and *The Jeffersons.* According to media observer and Lear fan Robert S. Alley, "no single individual has had more influence through the medium of television in its 50-year history than Norman Lear."[29]

In addition, according to Alley, by 1980 Lear became "alarmed by the radical religious fanaticism of Christian fundamentalists. At first he thought he would use a television series to respond.... He became convinced that another approach would be more effective for him, and in 1982 he founded People For The American Way (PAW) to speak out for Bill of Rights guarantees and monitor violations of constitutional freedoms. By 1996 the organization had become one of the most influential and effective voices for freedom."[30]

What Alley's article fails to mention is that many of the issues taken up by PAW seek to replace traditional morality with a radical liberal agenda. Another article, by former radical David Horowitz, uncovers the worldview that sets the tone for his "voice for freedom" and reveals the source of that voice to be Marxism. Horowitz recounts that a meeting was held in the PAW offices in 2003 to create a new organization called "United for Peace and Justice" to oppose the U.S.-lead coalition against Iraq. The "organizer and head of the new organization," writes Horowitz,

---

*Excerpt from* World *magazine, July 19, 2003, feature article by Marvin Olasky, page 16.*

## MARX LIVES

Socialism in America still attracts some among the counterculturally audacious or embittered.

One morning 34 years ago, my college roommate and I saw a notice in the **Yale Daily News** about a meeting on socialism to be held that evening in one of the university classrooms. We showed up on time and found ourselves the only ones in the room except for a solemn man precisely arranging on a front table piles of publications from the Socialist Workers Party. Saying not a word to us, he focused on squaring each stack and having the distance between each stack exactly the same. My roommate and I took one look at each other and bolted the room, heading down the stairs as the comrade, jolted from his reverie, hurried after us yelling, "Wait, wait."

We didn't wait, that evening. We never went back to that particular clique. But both of us were alienated: I had grown up within Judaism and my roommate within Christianity, but neither of us had absorbed reasons beyond social custom for maintaining our allegiance. I continued drifting left, participating in "peace" marches and joining the Communist Party, before resigning from it late in 1973. My roommate drifted in another way, announcing several years after graduation that he was gay. (In college he had talked about heterosexual pursuits like the rest of us.) I don't know what has happened to him.

Three weeks ago I attended "Socialism 2003," a three-day gathering of 900 leftists, most of them under 30. The International Socialist Organization, publisher of **Socialist Worker**, the same periodical I had seen neatly stacked in 1969, sponsored the meeting. Three decades had gone by since the last Marxist function I attended, and many have proclaimed that Marxism is dead, but judging by the enthusiasm and intensity of the folks I mingled with, Marxism is alive among some deeply alienated individuals, some red-diaper babies who respect their radical parents and hope to replicate the 1965-1974 golden age of unrest, and some graduate students in fields such as sociology and women's studies.

"was Leslie Cagan, a pro-Castro Sixties radical who was still a member of the Communist Party USA after the fall of the Berlin Wall."[31] Unless Cagan has experienced a dramatic change of heart, her radical background continues to animate her current activities in guiding this organization in "peace and justice." And in fact, she called for "protesters to 'disrupt normal life' once the war started."[32]

Along with groups like PAW, the American Civil Liberties Union (ACLU) tends to champion left-leaning causes and bring these issues before the courts. After the 2003 Supreme Course decision striking down the Texas Sodomy law, the ACLU announced its intention to "launch a national campaign and companion Web site—"Get Busy. Get Equal."—to empower lesbian, gay, bisexual and transgender communities to push for equality."[33] Of course this makes sense when one realizes that socialist-communist Roger Baldwin founded the ACLU in 1920.[34]

Because Marxists of every stripe are convinced their worldview is true, they also are committed to seeing their perspective win the hearts and minds of all Americans. And if educational and popular-level indoctrination do not work well enough, they will use any means to have their way, including finding like-minded judges who will overrule through the courts the will of the people as expressed by laws created by duly elected representatives. In this way, Postmodern Marxists force their agenda onto the American public in moral and ethical issues such as abortion, sodomy, gay marriage, and cloning, and in social causes such as affirmative action quotas and universal healthcare.

## COSMIC HUMANISM

Cosmic Humanism consists of a broad mixture of neo-paganism and neo-pantheism, best known as the New Age movement (NAM). Because it disdains any unified dogma, this worldview is less well defined than Secular Humanism or Postmodern Marxism. Indeed, some Cosmic Humanists go so far as to claim that their worldview "has no religious doctrine or teachings of its own."[35]

This attitude, according to most Cosmic Humanists, results from the belief that truth resides within each individual and, therefore, no one can claim a corner on the truth or dictate truth to any one else. "The New Age," explains Christian writer Johanna Michaelsen, "is the ultimate eclectic religion of self: Whatever you decide is right for you is what's right, as long as you don't get narrow-minded and exclusive about it."[36]

The very assumption that truth resides within each individual rather than being externally defined, however, sets the cornerstone for a worldview. Granting to oneself the power to discern all truth is a facet of theology, and this theology has undeniable ramifications. Some Cosmic Humanists actually have begun to articulate their movement as a worldview.

Marilyn Ferguson, author of *The Aquarian Conspiracy* (a book referred to as "The New Age watershed classic"), says the movement ushers in a "new mind—the ascendance of a startling worldview."[37] The skeletal outline of this worldview is summed up by Jonathan Adolph: "In its broadest sense, New Age thinking can be characterized as a form of utopianism, the desire to create a better society, a 'New Age' in which humanity lives in harmony with itself, nature, and the cosmos."[38]

While the New Age movement is still fragmented and lacking focused leadership, it is growing at a remarkable rate. The Stanford Research Institute estimates that "the number of New Agers in America could be as high as 5 to 10 percent of the population—12 million or more people."[39] Others have put the figure as high as 60 million although this includes people who simply believe in the reincarnation and astrological elements of New Age thought. John Randolph Price, a leading spokesperson for the New Age, says, "there are more than half a billion New Age advocates on the planet at this time, working among various religious groups."[40] Further, Malachi Martin lists dozens of organizations that are either New Age or New Age sympathetic. Barbara Marx Hubbard, another outspoken proponent of the New Age, made a bid for the 1984 Democratic vice presidential nomination.

# PAGANISM IN POPULAR CULTURE

A resurgence of paganism is one earmark of Cosmic Humanism, and one of the fastest growing elements of this renewed interest is Wicca, a contemporary rendition of witchcraft. As Craig S. Hawkins writes:

> A threatening storm is brewing on the religious horizon: the winds of occultism are blowing ever more strongly across the land. In

the past two to three decades, America and much of Western Europe have seen a resurgence of paganism and witchcraft. Paganism is attempting a resurrection from the dead, a revival of the old gods and goddesses of pre-Christian polytheistic nature religions and mystery cults (e.g., Celtic, Norse, Greek, Egyptian, Roman, and other traditions of the Western world).[41]

Many teens and adults come to Wicca after reading *The Spiral Dance: A Rebirth of the Ancient Religion of the Great Goddess* (1979), a best-selling introduction to Wiccan teachings and rituals written by Starhawk (née Miriam Simos), a witch from California. Young people also are drawn to this worldview through books and films like *Harry Potter*[42] or by the influence of popular neo-pagan oriented television shows such as *Charmed* and *Buffy, the Vampire Slayer*. A recent Mori poll of 2,600 children aged 11-16 found that over 50 per cent were interested in the occult and that one in six said they were worried about what they had discovered about the supernatural. Some pollsters estimate there may be more than 750,000 adherents of Wicca and related neo-pagan faiths in the United States.[43]

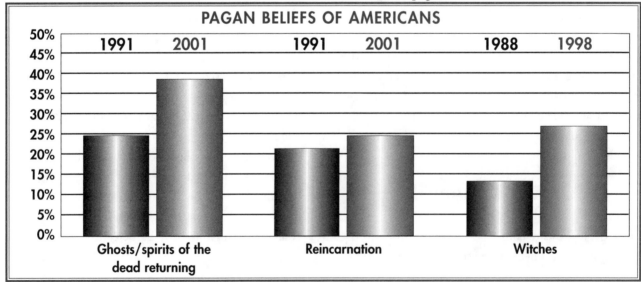

**PAGAN BELIEFS OF AMERICANS**

| | | | | | |
|---|---|---|---|---|---|
| 1991 | 2001 | 1991 | 2001 | 1988 | 1998 |
| Ghosts/spirits of the dead returning | | Reincarnation | | Witches | |

Hollywood, too, is a haven for Cosmic Humanist activity. Irvin Kershner, the director of George Lucas' blockbuster Star Wars episode, *The Empire Strikes Back*, was not shy about expressing his New Age worldview throughout his film. He told *Rolling Stone* Magazine that he wanted to "introduce some Zen here because I don't want the kids to walk away just feeling that everything is shoot-em-up, but that there's also a little something to think about here in terms of yourself and your surroundings."[44]   Other movies carry Cosmic Humanist themes, such as communicating with the dead (*Sixth Sense*) and reincarnation (Robin William's *What Dreams May Come*). These popular films, along with numerous others, reveal the general public's increasing acceptance of paranormal phenomena. According to a 2001 Gallup Survey, the number of Americans who believe that ghosts or spirits of dead people can come back increased over the previous ten years from 25 to 38 percent, and those subscribing to reincarnation went up from 21 to 25 percent. Adults who believe in witches rose from 14 to 26 percent.[45]

But the interest in the occult does not stop with ghosts and reincarnation. Astrology is also on the rise. The July 1997 cover of *Life* blared, "Why So Many of Us Now Believe the Stars Reflect the Soul." The lead article highlighted recent polls showing the trend in which "48 percent [of Americans] say astrology is probably or definitely valid."[46] The article goes on to recount that "the first newspaper horoscopes appeared in the '30's; now they run in the vast majority of dailies. Twenty years ago there were an estimated 1,000 professional astrologers in the United States; today there are something like 5,000. In 1968... the annual market for astrology books was around five million. Today, it is closer to 20 million." Clearly, the "age of Aquarius" is gaining steam.

## CONCLUSION

Marxism and Secular Humanism share a number of similarities. The two are family—Secular Humanism the mother (humanists trace their heritage to the Greeks 400 years before Christ) and Marxism the daughter. At the heart of both worldviews lies atheism, materialism, spontaneous generation, evolution, and moral relativism. Both Karl Marx and humanist advocate and author Paul Kurtz share a similar view of the truth. Marx said it this way: "Communism, as fully developed naturalism, equals humanism."[47]  And Paul Kurtz says Marx "is a humanist because he rejects theistic religion and defends atheism."[48]

If Marxism and Secular Humanism are in the same family, Cosmic Humanism and Secular Humanism are at least very close kin. The New Age movement is essentially a spiritualized Secular Humanism. Take the Secular Humanist's

> Cosmic Humanism claims to meet man's spiritual needs— something Marxism and Secular Humanism cannot claim—but it is stuck with an impersonal, unjust god.

exaltation of self, sprinkle in some meditation, reincarnation, and anti-rationalism, and you've created the Cosmic Humanist worldview. Cosmic Humanism claims to meet man's spiritual needs—something Marxism and Secular Humanism cannot claim—but it is stuck with an impersonal, unjust god. There is little difference between claiming no god exists and claiming everything is god.

The following chapters explore key aspects of these three worldviews as well as how a Christian can respond to each. Our purpose is to equip the church to set free those who have been captured by deceptive worldviews and to actively participate in the community, state, and nation to maintain a safe, sane, and free society.

## RECOMMENDED READING

Ankerberg, John, Craig Branch and John Weldon. *Thieves of Innocence: Protecting Our Children from New Age Teachings and Occult Practices.* Eugene, OR: Harvest House Publishers, 1993.

Clark, David K. and Norman L. Geisler. *Apologetics in the New Age: A Christian Critique of Pantheism.* Grand Rapids, MI: Baker Book House, 1990.

Kurtz, Paul, ed., *Humanist Manifestos I and II.* Buffalo, NY: Prometheus Books, 1973.

_____ , *Humanist Manifesto 2000: A Call for a New Planetary Humanism.* Amherst, NY: Prometheus Books, 2000.

Marx, Karl and Friedrich Engels. *The Communist Manifesto.* New York: Simon & Schuster, Inc., 1964.

LaHaye, Tim and David Noebel. *Mind Siege: The Battle for Truth in the New Millennium.* Nashville, TN: Word Publishing, 2000.

Noebel, David A. *Understanding the Times: The Religious Worldviews of Our Day and the Search for Truth.* Eugene, OR: Harvest House, 1994.

## ENDNOTES

1. William S. Lind, et. al., *Marine Corps Gazette,* December 1994, p. 37.

2. Robert P. George, *The Clash of Orthodoxies,* (Wilmington, DE: ISI Books, 2001) p. 3.

3. William S. Lind, et. al., p. 37.

4. Ibid.

5. Charles Francis Potter, *Humanism: A New Religion* (New York: Simon and Schuster, 1930) p. 128.

6. Recent attempts in Alabama, Ohio and Kansas to critique the standard Neo-Darwinian view of evolution was met with howls of dissent and ridicule from academics and scientists across the U.S. and around the world. We will look in depth at the issue of God and science in chapter 5, where a worldview analysis uncovers the real debate when it comes to teaching students about the

origin of life.

7. Vitz conducted a major study funded by the National Institute of Education. His findings are detailed in *Censorship: Evidence of Bias in Our Children's Textbooks* (Ann Arbor, MI: Servant, 1986).

8. Richard John Neuhaus, General Editor, *Democracy and the Renewal of Public Education,* (Grand Rapids, MI: Eerdmans, 1987), p. 120.

9. Ibid., p. 133.

10. In 1988 the Assistant State Superintendent for Instructional Services of the State Board of Education for North Carolina appointed a committee to address the issue. They surveyed the results of six different studies and found "social studies textbooks to be seriously deficient in their treatment of religion." ("Committee on Placement of Religion in the Social Studies Curriculum," June 7, 1988 Report).

11. Robert B. Brandon, Editor, *Rorty and His Critics,* (Malden, MA: Blackwell Publishers, 2000) p. 20.

12. Richard Rorty, *Achieving Our Country: Leftist Thought in Twentieth Century America.* (Cambridge, MA: Harvard University Press, 1998), p. 57.

13. Ibid., p. 44.

14. David French, *A Season For Justice: Defending the Right of the Christian Home, Church, and School* (Nashville, TN: Broadman & Holman, 2002), p. 190.

15. Shaena Engle, *2001 CIRP Press Release: CIRP Freshman Survey,* January 28, 2002, www.gseis.ucla.edu/heri/heri.html.

16. Bernard Goldberg, *Bias: A CBS Insider Exposes How the Media Distort the News* (Washington, DC: Regnery Publishing, 2001), p. 57.

17. Bernard Goldberg, *Bias.* p. 58-9.

18. David B. Richardson, "Marxism in U.S. Classrooms," *U.S. News and World Report,* January 25, 1982, pp. 42-5.

19. Herbert London, "Marxism Thriving on American Campuses," *The World and I,* January 1987, p. 189.

20. Alvin J. Schmidt, *The Menace of Multiculturalism,* (Westport, CT: Praeger Publishers, 1997), p. 25.

21. Georgie Anne Geyer, "Marxism Thrives on Campus," *The Denver Post,* August 29, 1989, p. B7.

22. Ibid.

23. Quoted in Tony Mecia, "Feminist College President Assumes Control of Duke," *Campus,* Spring, 1994, p. 6.

24. A new work by Duke University Professor Michael Hardt and Italian Professor of Political Science Antonio Negri titled *Empire* has been called "A sweeping neo-Marxist

vision of the coming world order" and the authors referred to as the "Marx and Engels of the internet age" according to comments from the back cover of the book. Harvard University Press published the book in 2000.

25. Roger Kimball, *Tenured Radicals* (New York: Harper and Row, 1990), p. xiii. To grasp what Christian students face in America's colleges and universities, you should read Kimball's book, then Allan Bloom's *The Closing of the American Mind: How Higher Education has Failed Democracy and Impoverished the Souls of Today's Students* (New York: Simon and Schuster, 1987), Ronald Nash's *The Closing of the American Heart* (Brentwood, TN: Wolgemuth & Hyatt, 1990) and finally *Cloning of the American Mind: Eradicating Morality Through Education*, by B. K. Eakman (Lafayette, LA: Huntington House Publishers, 1998).

26. Kimball, *Tenured Radicals*, p. xiv.

27. Alan Charles Kors and Harvey A. Silverglate. *The Shadow University: The Betrayal Of Liberty On America's Campuses.* (The Free Press, 1998), www.shadowuniv.com/introduction.

28. Terry Teachout, "They Admit It!" *National Review*, July 29, 2002, p. 46.

29. Robert S. Alley, in an online article on Norman Lear, www.museum.tv/archives/etv/L/htmlL/learnorman/learnorman.htm.

30. Ibid.

31. David Horowitz, *People Against The American Way (The Nation's Largest Hate Group)*, http://www.gopusa.com/david-horowitz/dh_0519.shtml, May 19, 2003. Horowitz, a former sixties Marxist radical, has written an excellent article exposing the worldview of People for the American Way.

32. Ibid.

33. See the ACLU's news release at www.aclu.org/LesbianGayRights/LesbianGayRights.cfm?ID=13011&c=41.

34. B. K. Eakman, *Cloning of the American Mind* (Lafayette, LA: Huntington House Publishers, 1998), p. 136.

35. Jonathan Adolph, "What is New Age?" *New Age Journal*. Winter 1988, p. 11.

36. Johanna Michaelsen, *Like Lambs to the Slaughter* (Eugene, OR: Harvest House, 1989), p. 11.

37. Marilyn Ferguson, *The Aquarian Conspiracy* (Los Angeles: J.P. Tarcher, Inc., 1980), p. 23.

38. Adolph, "What is New Age?" p. 6.

39. Ray A. Yungen, *For Many Shall Come in My Name,* (Salem, OR: Ray Yungen, 1989), p. 34.

40. John Randolph Price, *The Superbeings* (Austin, TX: Quartus Books, 1981), pp. 51.

41. Craig S. Hawkins, "The Modern World of Witchcraft," *The Christian Research Journal*, Winter/Spring 1990, page 8.

42. See "Harry Potter: Witchcraft Repacked," Jeremiah Films, P.O. Box 1710, Hemet, CA, 92546. 1-800-828-2290.

43. It is difficult to estimate the number of Wiccans and neo-pagans because by the nature of their religious belief and practice, they are not prone to organizing beyond small groups of local adherents who usually do not advertise their existence. Estimates of their numbers in the U.S. range from 5,000 to 5 million according to the Religious Tolerance website (www.religioustolerance.org/wic_nbr.htm).

44. *Rolling Stone*, July 24, 1980, p. 37.

45. Gallup Report, "Americans' Belief in Psychic and Paranormal Phenomena Is up Over Last Decade," June 8, 2001, http://www.gallup.com/poll/releases/pr010608.asp.

46. Kenneth Miller, "Star Struck: A Journey To the New Frontiers of the Zodiac," *Life*, July, 1997, p. 40.

47. Marx and Engels, *Karl Marx-Friedrich Engels: Collected Works*, 40 volumes (New York: International Publishers, 1976), vol. 3, p. 296.

48. Paul Kurtz, *The Fullness of Life* (New York: Horizon Press, 1974), p. 36.


(1) Charles Francis Potter: From Countering Culture video (2004 Summit Ministries: Manitou Springs, CO)

# SECTION II
# SECULAR HUMANISM

Although Secular Humanism has extensive historical roots, its contemporary form was systematized in the 1933 *Humanist Manifesto.* Signed by numerous intellectuals, professors, and scientists, the 1933 document led to other manifestos, the most recent of which was published in the year 2000. From these documents as well as books and articles consistent with the perspective presented in the manifestos, it is clear that Secular Humanists have a well-developed worldview and are convinced theirs should shape future generations.

In chapter three, we dig among the atheistic roots of Secular Humanism to discover why atheists do not believe in God, and we come up with four specific reasons. Our role as Christians, then, becomes helping these nonbelievers rethink their views by offering persuasive counter-arguments to their skepticism.

In chapter four, we explore the philosophical root of the secular worldview and how humanists answer questions related to reality and knowledge. We also note that Secular Humanism is a religious worldview, not a "neutral" one—a point of vital significance for contemporary education and politics.

Chapter five further examines how atheistic religion has infiltrated our educational system, especially where the subject of biology is concerned. Naturalistic evolution is the only viewpoint admissible in science classes, and we show this to be a religious view that contradicts the best and latest scientific evidence. It also contravenes the idea of providing a religiously "neutral" education for our children. Religion is being taught in schools, and it is the religion of Secular Humanism!

Finally, chapter six looks at the stranglehold humanists have on law and politics. We contrast secular positive law with biblical natural law and see that the first is built on sand compared with the solid foundation of God's laws which are the historical, philosophical underpinnings of the United States.

# CHAPTER 3

# The Theology
# of Secular Humanism

"Humanism is a philosophical, religious,
and moral point of view as old as human
civilization itself... What more pressing
need than to recognize in this critical age
of modern science and technology that,
if no deity will save us,
we must save ourselves?"[1]

—PAUL KURTZ

"It's my life. It's now or never. I ain't
gonna live forever. I just want to live
while I'm alive...like Frankie said,
'I did it my way.'"[2]

—JON BON JOVI

Through the words of one of his most popular hits, recording artist Jon Bon Jovi offers considerable insight into a Secular Humanist worldview. Similarly, in his band's signature song, "Tripping Billies," Dave Matthews encourages people to "Eat, drink, and be merry, for tomorrow we die; we're tripping Billies."[3] And both Jon and Dave are absolutely right: we answer to no one but ourselves and should seek to experience all the sensual pleasure this life has to offer if … there is no God who holds us accountable.

But that is the question, isn't it? Is there a God who judges mankind's actions? This question lies at the foundation of every worldview, and each offers an answer for this all-important issue. What a person believes about God has ramifications for what he or she thinks about every other aspect of life.

> Is there a God who judges mankind's actions? This question lies at the foundation of every worldview.

These popular musical expressions of man's independence from God follow naturally from a theology of atheism. By assuming there is no God and that this life is all there is, the best anyone can do is to live it "my way." These ideas, however, are not nearly as new as the music which touts them. Corliss Lamont, author of *The Philosophy of Humanism*, insists that humanism—"seeking man's fulfillment in the here and now of this world"—follows a long tradition of atheism, with proponents as far back as Democritus in ancient Greece and Lucretius in ancient Rome, continuing through to American John Dewey and Englishman Bertrand Russell in the twentieth century.

The first *Humanist Manifesto* formalized ideas reflected by Jon Bon Jovi and Dave Matthews when it confessed, "The quest for the good life is still the central task for mankind. Man is at last becoming aware that he alone is responsible for the realization of the world of his dreams, that he has within himself the power for its achievement."[4] And according to numerous articles and books by recognized humanists—including more than fifty years of *The Humanist* magazine—the weight of evidence is overwhelmingly in favor of atheism as the theological foundation of Secular Humanism.

## THEOLOGICAL BELIEFS OF SECULAR HUMANISTS

The theology of most Secular Humanists is remarkably dogmatic: the supernatural—including God, Satan, angels, demons, the souls, and conscience—does not exist. This theology is spelled out in all its certitude by various humanist leaders.

After pondering religion and the supernatural for three years, Bertrand Russell abandoned the notion of God. He later admitted, "I believed in God until I was just eighteen."[5] Russell, one of Secular Humanism's most famous international voices, maintains that the God is a conception derived from the ancient Oriental despotisms, and therefore concluded, "I am not a Christian… I do not believe in God and in immortality; and… I do not think that Christ was the best and wisest of men, although I grant Him a very high degree of moral goodness."[6]

> "As humanists we urge today, as in the past, that humans not look beyond themselves for salvation."
> —Humanist Manifesto 2000

Many humanists, including John Dewey, Roy Wood Sellers, and Edwin H. Wilson, signed *Humanist Manifesto I* in 1933, declaring, "the time has passed for theism." Writing several years later, in 1949, Lamont insisted there is no place in the humanist worldview for God. Instead of the gods creating the world and all there is, "the cosmos, in the individualized form of human beings giving rein to their imagination, created the gods."[8]

Then, in 1973, leading humanist thinkers published *Humanist Manifesto II* in which they reiterated, "We find insufficient evidence for belief in the existence of a supernatural; it is either meaningless or irrelevant to the question of the survival and fulfillment of the human race. As non-theists, we begin with humans not God, nature not deity." Hundreds of humanists signed this declaration of atheism, affirming, "…we can discover no divine purpose or providence for the human species. While there is much that we do not know, humans are responsible for what we are or will become. No deity will save us; we must save ourselves."[9]

The *Secular Humanist Declaration* of 1980 does not diverge from the earlier views of *Manifesto I & II*. Written by Paul Kurtz, Editor-in-Chief of *Free Inquiry*, the *Declaration* contends, "Secular Humanists… reject the idea that God has intervened miraculously in history or revealed himself to a chosen few, or that he can save or redeem sinners."[10]

Always ready to reflect changing social and cultural conditions, Secular Humanists once again updated their manifestos and declaration in the year 2000. This latest expression of humanist thought, titled *Humanist Manifesto 2000: A Call for a New Planetary Humanism* (also drafted by Paul Kurtz), does not deviate from the same theological tradition: "As humanists we urge today, as in the past, that humans not look beyond themselves for salvation. We alone are responsible for our own destiny…"[11]

## BERTRAND ARTHUR WILLIAM RUSSELL (1872-1970)

How do we know what we know?

The central question of epistemology, the study of knowledge, was also central to the career of mathematician and philosopher Bertrand Russell. He is considered one of the most important logicians of the 20th century, and foremost among his many works is the 3-volume *Principia Mathematica* which he co-authored with Alfred North Whitehead. Although some of his concepts have been revised since the books' publication in 1910-13, Russell's logic-based mathematics remains a foundation for much of modern math. "Russell's Paradox" is a famous conundrum of mathematical set theory he discovered early in his career as a math scholar.

Russell authored dozens of major books including *Why I Am Not a Christian* (1927), *Our Knowledge of the World* (1914), and *Marriage and Morals* (1929). In 1950, he was awarded the Nobel Prize for literature.

Strongly left-leaning in his social and political views, Russell was twice jailed for pacifist-oriented civil disobedience—once during World War I and after World War II for protesting nuclear weapons development. In 1955, he co-authored with Albert Einstein the *Russell-Einstein Manifesto* which called for the curtailment of nuclear weapons. Russell ran for the British Parliament three times although he was never elected (his grandfather, Lord John Russell had served as British Prime Minister), and he was the founding president in 1958 of the Campaign for Nuclear Disarmament.

His non-traditional views of marriage and sexuality perhaps were expressed through his personal life in that he was divorced three times, dying at the age of 97 while still married to his fourth wife. Although he traveled internationally, including spending much time in the United States, he was both born and died in Wales.

While many humanists boldly assert that God is a myth and does not really exist, others are more circumspect. One example is Isaac Asimov, the prolific

## ISAAC ASIMOV

A professor of biochemistry at Boston University for much of the 1950's, Dr. Isaac Asimov achieved unparalleled acclaim for the quality and proliferation of his writing, largely because of his ability to communicate difficult scientific concepts on a popular level. He authored more than 500 books between the time of his first publication in 1939 and his death in 1992.

Best-known for his science fiction classic *Foundation* trilogy, Asimov also wrote non-fiction works in physiology, astronomy, chemistry, geography, history, math, and other diverse subjects—including his 2-volume *Asimov's Guide to the Bible*. His *Guide*, though, belies his avowed atheism and concerted efforts to influence "thinking people" away from what he considers the multifarious myths of religions of all kinds. Asimov stipulates that it is always inappropriate to believe God exists since "God" is always a premature explanation for whatever is being considered.

Asimov's anti-religious crusading in the name of science and rationality is curious in light of his family of origin. He was born in 1920 to orthodox Jewish parents in the town of Petrovichi, Russia in the Soviet Union. His parents emigrated to the United States when Asimov was three, settling in New York City. There he helped his parents run a candy shop, even while attending college. He received bachelor, master's and doctoral degrees from New York's Columbia University.

His immense abilities as a writer and communicator made Isaac Asimov an especially convincing promoter of a variety of humanistic concepts: world government, population control, and a belief in the potential for rightly-used technology to solve the problems of mankind.

science fiction writer and popularizer of modern science, who served as the director of the American Humanist Association from 1989 to 1992. Writing in *Free Inquiry*, Asimov leaves no doubt regarding his personal belief about God, yet also makes a noteworthy admission:

I am an atheist, out and out. It took me a long time to say it. I've been an atheist for years and years, but somehow I felt it was intellectually unrespectable to say one was an atheist, because it assumed knowledge that one didn't have. Somehow it was better to say one was a humanist or an agnostic. I finally decided that I'm a creature of emotion as well as reason. Emotionally I am an atheist. I don't have the evidence to prove that God doesn't exist, but I so strongly suspect he doesn't that I don't want to waste my time.[12]

As Asimov points out, *proving* God does not exist is impossible, and thus, intellectually honest atheists find themselves in a quandary. How can one rationally claim to be an atheist if there is no absolute proof—theological, philosophical, historical, or scientific—of God's non-existence? Because of this problem, many humanists prefer to call themselves "skeptics" instead of atheists. "Skeptic" implies there is little, if any, solid evidence for God's existence; therefore, the humanist remains in unbelief unless and until better confirmation is produced. As Paul Kurtz contends in the *Secular Humanist Declaration* of 1980, "Secular Humanists may be agnostics, atheists, rationalists, or skeptics, but they find insufficient evidence for the claim that some divine purpose exists for the universe."[13] From Kurtz's comment one can construct a continuum representing the range of humanist theology, with those who do not *know* if God exists on one end (i.e., agnostics), those who do not *think* that God exists (skeptics) in the middle, and those who are *convinced* that God does not exist (atheists) at the other extreme.

Yet, no matter which label any given Secular Humanist prefers, humanist theology is based fundamentally on the denial of the existence of God and the supernatural. This rejection of a God-of-the-universe

leads the human-
ist to another nec-
essary theological
conclusion: man
is the Supreme
Authority, and
hence, the words
sung by Bon Jovi
and Dave Matthews
circumscribe our
reality. Of course,
it is possible that
h u m a n i s m ' s

*Columbia University professor Dr. Paul Kurtz is a leading humanist philosopher and writer of the Humanist Manifesto 2000.*

"deification" of man may have preceded the worldview's atheistic assumptions. At bottom, though, it is
of little importance whether the denial of God or the
deification of man was humanism's first theological
impulse; the crux of humanistic theology remains
anti-God. This is the heart and soul of Secular
Humanism: man setting himself in place of God (see
Jeremiah 17:5–8).

## HUMANISTIC THEOLOGICAL LITERATURE

Secular Humanism's primary publishing arm is
Prometheus Books of Buffalo, New York. One of
Prometheus' most doctrinaire publishing efforts
includes atheistic children's books such as *What About
Gods?* by Chris Brockman. This book coaches children
toward atheistic thinking with dogmatic projections
like, "Many people say they believe in a god. Do you
know what a god is? Do you know what it means to
believe in a god? A god is a mythical character.
Mythical characters are imaginary—they're not real.
People make them up. Dragons and fairies are two of
many mythical characters people have made up.

They're not real. . . ."[14]

Prometheus also publishes atheistic literature
geared toward adults. Paul Blanshard's *Classics of Free
Thought* was published "to keep atheism before the
public." *Critiques of God*, edited by Peter Angeles, provides 371 pages of support for humanist theology's
denial of God's existence. In *Critiques*, Angeles
announces that belief in the supernatural has all but
vanished from our culture. He says that God first lost
His spatial location as a monarch in heaven and then
His pre-existence to the universe as its Creator *ex
nihilo*. "It is not that God is being relegated to a
remote region," Angeles insists. "It is not that God has
become a bodiless abstraction (a sexless It). It is the
realization that there is no God left to which to relate.
Without God, what is left? Man and the Universe.
That should be enough. That has to be enough
because that is all there is."[15]

---

### JEREMIAH'S INDICTMENT OF MAN USURPING GOD
(JEREMIAH 17:5-8)

*This is what the Lord says:*
*⁵Cursed is the man who trusts in mankind,
who makes [human] flesh his strength and
turns his heart from the Lord.*
*⁶He will be like a juniper in the Arabah; he
cannot see when good comes but dwells in the
parched places in the wilderness, in a salt land
where no one lives.*
*⁷Blessed is the man who trusts in the Lord,
whose confidence indeed is the Lord.*
*⁸He will be like a tree planted by water: it
sends its roots out toward a stream, it doesn't
fear when heat comes, and its foliage remains
green. It will not worry in a year of drought or
cease producing fruit.*

A number of websites carry the Secular Humanist message. The Secular Web (www.infidels.org) is published by Internet Infidels, "an organization of unpaid volunteers dedicated to the growth and maintenance of the most comprehensive freethought web site on the Internet." Their stated mission is "to defend and promote Metaphysical Naturalism, a nontheistic worldview which holds that our natural world is all that there is, a closed system in no need of a supernatural explanation and sufficient unto itself." The site contains over 8,000 articles, reviews, and essays from the best secular authors and scholars. With more than 300,000 unique visitors per month, the Secular Web bills itself as "the largest and most heavily visited non-theistic web site on the Internet."[16]

Other humanist websites include Positive Atheism (www.positiveatheism.org) and The Council for Secular Humanism (www.secularhumanism.org), the organization that publishes *Free Inquiry*, the monthly magazine edited by Paul Kurtz. According to their website, The Council for Secular Humanism "cultivates rational inquiry, ethical values, and human development through the advancement of secular humanism" and seeks to "promote secular humanist principles to the public, media, and policy-makers."

# ARGUMENTS FOR GOD'S EXISTENCE

Secular Humanists maintain that the traditional arguments *for* God's existence are weak.[17] For example, the "argument from design" states the following (in simplified form):

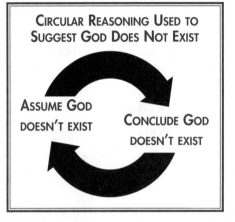

CIRCULAR REASONING USED TO SUGGEST GOD DOES NOT EXIST

ASSUME GOD DOESN'T EXIST

CONCLUDE GOD DOESN'T EXIST

1. Arrangements showing complex design require a designer.
2. Life evidences complex design.
3. Therefore, life must have a Designer, i.e., God.

The skeptic's rebuttal to this argument is that modern science has demonstrated that Darwinian natural selection can account for the apparent design we observe in living things; therefore there is no need to postulate a "Grand Designer."[18] Richard Dawkins' book, *The Blind Watchmaker: Why the Evidence of Evolution Reveals a Universe Without Design*, opens with the assertion that biology is the study of things which appear to have been designed for a purpose, but that this appearance is deceiving. According to Dawkins, natural selection produces complex living things over time, yet this is a blind process because it does not see ahead and has no purpose or intent. Darwin first suggested that nature supplies the creative force once attributed to God, and now Dawkins proclaims it is possible to be "an intellectually fulfilled atheist."

This line of reasoning, though, has a logical flaw. The skeptic *assumes* something is true about evolution without being able to prove it—namely, that evolution is a completely natural process that moves ahead without interference from any source outside of the material universe, without a Supernatural Designer. In other words, the skeptic *assumes* God does not exist in order to *conclude* that God does not exist! In formal logic, this is called the fallacy of "circular reasoning" or "begging the question." It assumes to be true the very thing that is under debate. It does not address the question at hand—does God exist? So the real question still goes begging for an answer.

If a skeptic takes this approach, the Christian can respond by pointing out two things that logically follow. First, God *could* have used natural selection as the means for producing design, in which case this line of argument does nothing to disprove God's existence. (Note: We don't think God *did* use evolution in this way for reasons that will be presented in chapter 5 on biology. We are simply demonstrating that the skeptic's reason does not *necessarily* lead to the conclusion he is defending.)

> Often the basis for non-belief in God is an assumed worldview rather than a clearly reasoned position.

Second, the skeptic has sidestepped the central topic—whether or not God exists—not whether or not evolution can produce complex living systems. By presupposing that evolution operates apart from God, the skeptic assumes an atheistic worldview in order to prove that God does not exist. But this, too, is circular reasoning—you cannot assume to be true what you're trying to prove to be true.

When it comes to the argument from design, two noted atheists actually acknowledge the preponderance of evidence of design in nature. In their book, *Rare Earth*, Peter Ward and Donald Brownlee reveal an astounding array of earth's (and indeed the solar system's) intricate designs for life. A Christian reading their book can readily say with the Psalmist, "The heavens declare the glory of God, and the sky proclaims the work of His hands" (Psalm 19:1).[19] However, in spite of the clear evidence before their eyes, Ward and Brownlee contend that all the manifestations of design are the result of chance, accident, luck and randomness.[20] Since they offer no explanation as to how that can be in the face of such manifest design, one can only conclude that it takes more faith to believe that *Rare Earth* happened by chance than that "In the beginning" God created it. Ironically, faith is supposedly the staple of the Christian's worldview, not the humanist's.

But even if the skeptic were to concede that design is undeniable, there remains the question of whether there are one or many designers, or what the nature of this God or gods might be. On this point, the Christian can build a case for God's revelation of Himself through the Bible. In, *Thinking Like A Christian*, we detailed arguments for the reliability of the Scriptures in the chapter on biblical Christian philosophy, and those will not be repeated here. For additional instruction on this point, Josh McDowell offers an extremely coherent apologetic in *The New Evidence That Demands a Verdict*.

The point here is not necessarily to persuade someone to believe in God, but rather merely to demonstrate that belief in God is reasonable and to show that often the basis for non-belief is an assumed worldview rather than a clearly reasoned position. The Apostle Paul, according to accounts of his missionary travels recorded in Acts, used rational arguments to try to persuade both

> **ACTS 17:2-3**
>
> *As usual, Paul went to them, and on three Sabbath days reasoned with them from the Scriptures, explaining and showing that the Messiah had to suffer and rise from the dead, and saying: "This is the Messiah, Jesus, whom I am proclaiming to you."*

Jews and Greeks to believe in Jesus as the Christ (see Acts 17–18). For example, Acts 17:2-3 uses three words to indicate Paul's evangelistic approach. He "reasoned," "explained" and "showed" that Christ had to suffer and rise from the dead.

Because of their worldview, skeptics have difficulty admitting the reasonableness of a God-centered biblical view. As Kenneth Boa and Robert Bowman observe, "non-Christians are unaware that they look at life through a certain set of worldview 'glasses.' Making them aware of this can *help non-Christians rethink some of their beliefs.*"[21] Taking their thought to the next step, these authors maintain that contrasting the biblical worldview with humanism can *"help non-Christians recognize the rationality of Christian beliefs given a theistic worldview."*[22] The Apostle Peter likewise admonishes his readers to "always be ready to give a defense to anyone who asks you a reason for the hope that is in you. However, do this with gentleness and respect" (1 Peter 3:15-6).

## THE PROBLEM OF PAIN

Skeptics not only argue from a *lack* of evidence for God's existence, but also present positive reasons for why they believe God does not exist.[23] One such argument is featured in the film, *Patch Adams*. Viewers are treated to one of the most powerful arguments for why skeptics believe God does not exist; it's called "the problem of pain." Halfway through the story, Patch (Robin Williams) is informed that the woman he loves has been murdered. The next scene shows Adams standing on the edge of a cliff expressing his grief to God. He begs, "So answer me, please, what are you doing?" Instead of waiting for an answer, Patch changes his demeanor, sets his jaw and continues, "Okay, let's look at the logic. You create man. Man suffers enormous amounts of pain. Man dies. Maybe you should have spent a few more brainstorming sessions prior to creation. You rested on the seventh day,

maybe you should have spent that day on compassion." As Patch contemplates throwing himself over the cliff, he looks toward the sky and concludes, "You know what? You're not worth it!" He then physically turns around—symbolically turning his back on God—walks away from the edge and returns to finish medical school. Patch's personal solution to pain becomes the use of humor as a part of his healing technique.

While a movie such as *Patch Adams* purports simply to be entertainment, in truth, it is a powerful educational tool for Secular Humanism. The climactic scene of the film presents an emotionally charged reason for why you should turn your back on God. Not surprisingly, during the rest of the film a theistic answer to the problem of pain is never addressed. Patch's condemnation of God is left for viewers to sort out on their own.[24]

Aside from popular expressions in music and emotional appeals from movies, the skeptic's more formal presentation of the problem of pain goes like this:

> If God is all-good and loving, as Christians claim, then He should *want* to alleviate human pain and suffering. And if God is all-powerful, as Christians claim, then He is able to alleviate pain and suffering. But humans still experience personal pain and suffering. This situation contradicts the character of the Christians' God; therefore, the Christian God must not exist.

Humanists assert this is an insurmountable problem for theists, dealing a knockout blow for believing in God.

Some humanists even go on the offensive by declaring that suffering is wholly consistent with an atheistic worldview. Suffering is the natural outgrowth of a blind, impersonal, random process of evolution-

> "You're not worth it!"
> —Patch Adams to God

ary natural selection. Therefore, according to humanists, pain and suffering provides better support for a Secular Humanist worldview than it does for a biblical Christian view. But here again the skeptic assumes evolution is true in order to defeat the Christian position, and as we noted above this is begging the question.

What atheists do not generally admit is that most pain and suffering are caused by mankind's mistakes, ignorance, or outright refusal to follow God's moral and/or physical order. War, manmade famine and, perhaps most notably, the AIDS epidemic, all carry great pain and suffering throughout the human community, and all are the result of man's choices.

Conspicuously, it has been *atheistic* worldviews that have caused the lion's share of human suffering during the past century. Fascism, Nazism, and Communism are all built on the humanist planks of atheism, socialism, and evolution. The outworking of these humanistic ideologies over most of the past century has been the torment and death of at least 170 million human beings—some estimates run as high as 320 million—more deaths in a single century than in all previous centuries combined![25] This pain and destruction has been caused by man's folly, not God's.

To deny God's existence because of mankind's corrupt activities is not a logical proposition. As Gene Veith sums up, "The confident project of rejecting the transcendent and putting in its place an immanent spirituality based upon human culture, human self-sufficiency, and a unity with nature led… to the construction of Auschwitz. The Holocaust was indeed a turning point for religious faith, not because it makes faith in God impossible, but because it makes faith in human beings impossible."[26] While many Secular Humanists decry Hitler's gas chambers and claim their worldview encompasses compassion for other humans, history bears out the undeniable fact that it is the atheist who is building his house upon the sand.

## RESPONDING TO THE PROBLEM OF PAIN

How can a Christian respond to atheistic theology in general, and to the problem of pain in particular? Regarding human pain and suffering, the thoughtful Christian can pinpoint a serious fallacy in logic. The skeptic's argument as reflected above makes a claim about the character of God—God is all-loving and all-powerful—which means the skeptic is arguing within a theistic framework. The skeptic supposes God exists and that He has certain characteristics. The problem, however, is that the skeptic *misrepresents* the character of God in order to prove his point. This is called a "straw man" argument—erecting a "man made of straw" that is easy to knock down. What is the "straw man" in the skeptic's argument? The skeptic limits his description of God to terms that fit his own purpose (God would want to do something about pain because He is loving and can do something about pain because He is all-powerful) but leaves out other

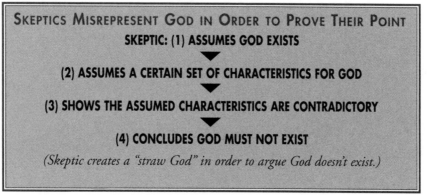

SKEPTICS MISREPRESENT GOD IN ORDER TO PROVE THEIR POINT

SKEPTIC: (1) ASSUMES GOD EXISTS

▼

(2) ASSUMES A CERTAIN SET OF CHARACTERISTICS FOR GOD

▼

(3) SHOWS THE ASSUMED CHARACTERISTICS ARE CONTRADICTORY

▼

(4) CONCLUDES GOD MUST NOT EXIST

*(Skeptic creates a "straw God" in order to argue God doesn't exist.)*

pertinent characteristics that do not support his argument, such as God's holiness, righteousness, patience (long-suffering), and justice.

> **JOB 42:5-6**
>
> *I had heard rumors about You, but now my eyes have seen You. Therefore I take back [my words] and repent in dust and ashes*

We should point out to our skeptical friends that when building a case using *our* worldview, they run into two problems. First, they assume God exists in order to prove God does not exist. But unbelievers can't have it both ways. If God exists, then He exists! The goal for skeptics should be to build an argument straightforwardly for the belief that God does not exist.

Second, if skeptics are going to operate within a theistic worldview, then they need to accept a complete view of God, not pick and choose only certain characteristics to make their case. According to an all-inclusive biblical theology, evil and suffering do have an explanation. While God is not the author of evil, God's plan and purpose for mankind include allowing evil, pain, and suffering for certain reasons that He has revealed to us, as well as for other reasons that have not been revealed. In the Old Testament, for example, we read that Job endured many hardships, including emotional anguish and physical pain, yet all of his suffering brought him to a point at which he gained a better understanding of God's person and power (see Job's response to God in Job 42:5-6).

Many skeptics find this explanation distasteful and complain that if it is true God uses suffering to draw people closer to Him, then it is analogous to a husband beating his wife so she will love him more; why would someone want to worship such a sadistic God? This again misrepresents God's character, and for an unbeliever to stand outside the biblical worldview and criticize it because he does not *like* the biblical explanation does not further his case in establishing that God does not exist. That is like someone looking at a house and complaining, "I don't like the color of that house, and therefore I'm not going to believe anyone lives inside." The truth may be that people do live inside, whether an outside observer likes the color of the house or not. An intellectually honest skeptic must come to terms with evidences and logic and not base unbelief on personal likes and dislikes. Whereas the first approach of the skeptic is to discredit the idea of God by assuming something to be true *outside* of biblical Christianity (evolution explains design in nature), this second tactic assumes something *inside* a theistic worldview. But as we have shown, both approaches fail.

> For an unbeliever to stand outside the biblical worldview and criticize it because he does not like the biblical explanation is like someone looking at a house and complaining, "I don't like the color of that house, and therefore I'm not going to believe anyone lives inside."

## CONCLUSION

While many atheists point to intellectual and philosophical reasons to disbelieve in God, some candidly reveal their true motives which have nothing to do with intellectual problems. They reject God because of their own personal moral preferences. Aldous Huxley frankly admits this:

*I had motives for not wanting the world to have*

*meaning*, consequently assumed that it had none, and was able without any difficulty to find satisfying reasons for this assumption…. For myself, as, no doubt, for most contemporaries, the philosophy of meaninglessness was essentially an instrument of liberation. The liberation we desired was simultaneously liberation from a certain political and economic system and liberation from a certain system of morality. *We objected to the morality because it interfered with our sexual freedom.*[27]

Or hear the words of New York University philosopher Thomas Nagel:

> *I want atheism to be true* and am made uneasy by the fact that some of the most intelligent and well-informed people I know are religious believers. It isn't just that I don't believe in God and, naturally, hope that I'm right in my belief. It's that *I hope there is not God. I don't want there to be a God; I don't want the universe to be like that.*[28]

This is why some people still do not accept God's offer of forgiveness and acceptance even when presented with legitimate counter-arguments to their skepticism. They *choose* not to believe. Recall that Jesus said some will not believe even if they see someone come back from the dead (Luke 16:31). So being presented with factual evidence—even of the miraculous —is not enough for the one who has his mind and heart set against God.

Yet, while some atheists are hardened in their beliefs, others who are skeptics may be open to God's truth. When we encounter an inquiring skeptic, we need to answer his or her questions to show that Christianity has a rational basis—the facts presented in the Bible concerning the historical life, death and resurrection of Jesus. To learn more about the debate over the existence of God and biblical responses to an atheist's arguments, you may want to read one or more of the books we recommend at the end of this chapter. Most people argue their point of view without analyzing the underlying ideas they assume to be true. That is why it is so important for Christians to be equipped to discuss these issues in the marketplace of ideas—with friends, associates at work or school, politicians, the media, and even over Sunday dinner.

## RECOMMENDED READING

Beisner, E. Calvin. *Answers for Atheists, Agnostics, and Other Thoughtful Skeptics: Dialogs About Christian Faith and Life.* Wheaton, IL: Crossway Books, 1993.

Boa, Kenneth D. and Robert M. Bowman, Jr. *Faith Has Its Reasons: An Integrative Approach to Defending Christianity.* Colorado Springs, CO: NavPress, 2001.

Geisler, Norman. *Baker Encyclopedia of Christian Apologetics.* Grand Rapids, MI: Baker Book House, 1999.

Glynn, Patrick. *God—The Evidence: The Reconciliation of Faith and Reason in a Postsecular World.* Rocklin, CA: Prima Publishing, 1999.

Lewis, C.S. *The Problem of Pain.* San Francisco, CA: Harper, 2001.

Moreland, J.P. *Scaling the Secular City.* Grand Rapids, MI: Baker Book House, 1987.

Moreland, J.P. and Kai Nielsen. *Does God Exist?* Amherst, NY: Prometheus Books, 1993.

Russell, Bertrand. *Why I am not a Christian: And other Essays on Religion and Related Subjects.* New York: Simon & Schuster, 1957.

## ENDNOTES

1.  Paul Kurtz, ed. *Humanist Manifestos I* and *II* (Buffalo, NY: Prometheus Books, 1973) p. 3-4.

2.  Jon Bon Jovi, "It's My Life," on the *Crush* CD, 2000.

3. Dave Matthews Bank, "Tripping Billies" on the *Live at Red Rocks* CD, 1997.

4. Kurtz. *Humanist Manifestos I* and *II*, p. 10.

5. Bertrand Russell, "My Mental Development," in *The Basic Writings of Bertrand Russell*, ed. Robert E. Egner and Lester E. Denonn (New York: Simon and Schuster, 1961), p. 40.

6. Russell, "Why I Am Not a Christian," in *The Basic Writings of Bertrand Russell*, p. 586. C.S. Lewis provided the best counter to Russell's acknowledgment of Jesus' "moral goodness." He points out that one cannot grant Jesus Christ moral goodness if He is a liar regarding his own being, namely, declaring Himself to be God. Lewis insists Jesus was a liar, a legend, a lunatic, or Lord.

7. Kurtz, ed. *Humanist Manifestos I* and *II*. p. 8.

8. Ibid., p. 145.

9. Ibid., p.16.

10. "A Secular Humanist Declaration," *Free Inquiry*, vol. 1, no. 1 (Winter 1980/81), p. 5.

11. Paul Kurtz. *Humanist Manifesto 2000: A Call for a New Planetary Humanism* (Amherst, NY: Prometheus Books, 2000), p. 63.

12. Isaac Asimov, " An Interview with Isaac Asimov," *Free Inquiry*, Spring 1982, vol. 2, no. 2, p. 9.

13. "A Secular Humanist Declaration," *Free Inquiry*, p. 5.

14. Chris Brockman, *What About Gods?* (Buffalo: Prometheus Books, 1978).

15. Peter Angeles, ed., *Critiques of God* (Buffalo: Prometheus books, 1976), p. xiii.

16. Quoted from "About Us" on the Internet Infidels website, www.infidels.org/infidels/index.shtml.

17. See Kai Nielsen's comments to this affect on pages 248-50 in J.P. Moreland and Kai Nielsen. *Does God Exist?* (Amherst, NY: Prometheus Books, 1993). Also, various arguments used to support the existence of God are rebutted at www.infidels.org/library/modern/theism/arguments.html.

18. Numerous writers have addressed this issue from a secular position. Several dozen views are available at www.infidels.org/library/modern/theism/design.html.

19. Specific evidences for design in nature will be discussed in Chapter 5. Our purpose here is to show how the skeptic's arguments do not hold up under logical scrutiny.

20. Peter D. Ward and Donald Brownlee, *Rare Earth*, (New York: Copernicus, 2000), p. 36, 37, 51.

21. Kenneth D. Boa and Robert M. Bowman, Jr., *Faith Has Its Reasons* (Colorado Springs, CO: NavPress, 2001), p. 148

(italics in the original).

22. Boa and Bowman, *Faith Has Its Reasons*, p.148.

23. For an overview of the range of arguments atheists use, the following website lists a couple of dozen articles: www.infidels.org/library/modern/nontheism/atheism/arguments.html.

24. One more detail is significant in recounting this scene. As Patch turns around, a butterfly lands on his shirt. The butterfly reminds him of Carin, his girlfriend. The viewer is expected to make this connection because earlier Carin had confided to Patch her childhood experience with sexual abuse and how she wished she could be a butterfly and fly away. She also wore butterfly earrings. One way of interpreting this scene is that the butterfly reminds Patch that Carin had given her life showing compassion to others as she and Patch worked in a free medical clinic for the poor. This memory motivates Patch to find purpose for his life by giving himself to helping others with the same passion and compassion that Carin had.

25. For details and statistics on the role of Fascism, Nazism, and Communisim in human destruction, see the following books: R. J. Rummel, *Death by Government* (New Brunswick, NJ: Transaction Publishers, 1994); Stephane Courtois, Mark Kramer (Translators), *The Black Book of Communism* (Harvard University Press, 1999); and Erwin W. Lutzer, Ravi Zacharias, *Hitler's Cross* (Moody Publishers, 1998).

26. Gene Edward Veith, *Modern Fascism* (St. Louis, MO: Concordia Publishing House, 1993) pp. 76-7.

27. Aldous Huxley, *Ends and Means* (London: Cahtto and Windus, 1969), 270, 273. Quoted in *That's Just Your Interpretation* by Paul Copan (Grand Rapids, MI: Baker Books, 2001), p. 21 (emphasis his).

28. Thomas Nagel, *The Last Word* (New York: Oxford University Press, 1997), 130. Quoted in *That's Just Your Interpretation* by Paul Copan, p. 21 (emphasis his).


(1) Paul Kurtz: From Countering Culture video (2004 Summit Ministries: Manitou Springs, CO)

# CHAPTER 4

# The *Real World* of Secular Humanism

"Humanism is naturalistic and rejects the
supernaturalistic stance with its postulated
Creator-God and cosmic Ruler."[1]
—ROY WOOD SELLARS

"Humanism is alive and well. And this
philosophical creed continues to be,
I would argue, the underlying reason
for walking away from faith."[2]
—RUTH A. TUCKER

"Here [in Secular Humanism] are
all the elements for a religious faith that
shall not be confined to sect, class, or race.
Such a faith has always been implicitly the
common faith of mankind. It remains
to make it explicit and militant."[3]
—JOHN DEWEY

In the action adventure, Kung fu-fighting, science fiction film, *The Matrix*, high-tech hacker Neo is rescued from a computer-generated world (the Matrix) through which machines have suppressed reality and dominated mankind.[4] Neo is brought into "reality" by a bold, revolutionary, *real* human leader named Morpheus. As part of Neo's training to save humanity from its slavery to Artificial Intelligence, he is introduced to the all-encompassing virtual reality of the Matrix. Neo is stunned to discover that he experienced his previous real-seeming, pseudo-life completely within a computer program. Coming to grips with this new understanding, he touches a chair and asks Morpheus, "This isn't real?" To which Morpheus responds, "What is real? How do you define 'real?' If by 'real' you mean what you can touch, smell, taste and see, then reality is simply electrical impulses interpreted by your brain."

> "If by 'real' you mean what you can touch, smell, taste and see, then reality is simply electrical impulses interpreted by your brain."
> —Morpheus in *The Matrix*

At this point in the film, what might otherwise pass as simple entertainment crosses the line and subtly *educates* the audience on a significant element of worldview. Morpheus' response is a classic definition of naturalism, the idea that nature is the only reality. To see this more clearly, one need only to consider a different possible answer to Neo's question. According to a Christian worldview, for example, nature (what you can touch, smell, taste, and see) is real, *and so is the supernatural* realm (what cannot be touched, smelled, tasted, or seen), including God. Since the supernatural dimension is left out of Morpheus' definition, the education that takes place during this scene is of a distinctly non-biblical nature.[5] This is just one example of worldview "education" that takes place all around us, and in light of this environment, Christians must continually discipline their minds not to be captured by these deceptive philosophies (Colossians 2:8).

## THE QUESTION OF PHILOSOPHY

Neo's inquiry surfaces a key worldview issue from the discipline of philosophy: What is real? There are basically three ways to answer Neo's question. One response is that only the non-natural realm exists. This is the Cosmic Humanist view. It means our current world we can touch, smell, taste and see is actually an illusion. The most real thing is the cosmic energy that pervades all and is all. We will explore more about the Cosmic Humanist view of reality in chapter 10.

The second way to answer the question is from a biblical standpoint. The Bible is clear that both the supernatural and natural realms are real (see Genesis 1:1).

The third way to respond is to say that only nature exists (the closest position to Morpheus'). Called naturalism, this view denies everything that is not of the material universe—things that do not exist in nature. This belief is

> **GENESIS 1:1**
> *In the beginning God created the heavens and the earth.*

foundational for Secular Humanism. As Corliss Lamont notes, "Materialism denotes the same general attitude toward the universe as Naturalism."[6]

# NATURALISM

*Humanist Manifesto II* summarizes the philosophical position of humanists: "Nature may indeed be broader and deeper than we now know; any new discoveries, however, will but enlarge our knowledge of the natural."[7] This belief is the essence of naturalism: whatever exists can be explained by natural causes; the supernatural cannot exist. As we noted in chapter 3, naturalists are especially unwilling to believe the universe exhibits design because design in nature could be construed as evidence for a Designer. Here, the humanist is admirably consistent within his own worldview. A theology of atheism implies a philosophy of naturalism, and vice versa. The naturalist can accept no Designer and no personified First Cause of the universe. As we will see in the next chapter, this naturalistic philosophy plays a major role in how science is taught in our public schools.

Lamont believes the fundamental principle of humanism—the principle that distinguishes it from all other worldviews—is that "Humanism . . . considers all forms of the supernatural as myth."[8] The supernatural, quite simply, "does not exist."[9] "Humanism," says Lamont, "in its most accurate philosophical sense, implies a worldview in which Nature is everything, in which there is no supernatural."[10] *Humanist Manifesto I* (1933) succinctly describes the universe as "self-existing and not created."[11]

Naturalistic humanism's denial of the supernatural gives rise to its over-arching philosophy of life, a worldview that we shall prove is religious to the core. Henry Miller plainly states, "To imagine that we are going to be saved by outside intervention, whether in the shape of an analyst, a dictator, a savior, or even God, is sheer folly."[12] Notice that Miller implies something about philosophy (nature is all there is) by making a statement about theology (it is folly to

believe in God) that has implications for psychology (we must "save" ourselves). Dr. Miller's position certainly reflectss worldview thinking!

Corliss Lamont also conveys a comprehensive worldview based on philosophical naturalism when he writes:

> To define naturalistic Humanism in a nutshell: it rejects all forms of supernaturalism, pantheism, and metaphysical idealism, and considers man's supreme aim as working for the welfare and progress of all humanity in this one and only life, according to the methods of reason, science and democracy."[13]

This definition is important from a philosophical perspective because it outlines both the Naturalist's metaphysics (which examines the nature of reality) and epistemology (the study of how we know things to be true).

# METAPHYSICS AND COSMOLOGY

Cosmology is a branch of metaphysics that refers to the philosophical study of the universe, especially its origin and nature. Secular Humanists believe the physical universe came into being by accident and that the physical universe is all that exists. Obviously, this belief rests on the denial of God and the supernatural. If there is no eternal God to do the creating, then matter itself must be eternal and must have the ability to spontaneously generate life and through an evolutionary process, ultimately to develop the human mind.

Carl Sagan, 1981 "Humanist of the Year," best sums up the cosmology of naturalism: "The Cosmos is all that is or ever was or ever will be."[14] For the humanist, no personal First Cause exists—only the cosmos. "Nature is but an endless series of efficient causes," Robert Ingersoll writes. "She cannot create but she eternally transforms. There was no beginning and there can be no end."[15] Of course, this understanding of nature is in lockstep with a humanist theology, since there is no need for a God to explain a

## CARL SAGAN

An audience estimated at more than 500 million viewers in 60 countries watched Carl Sagan's 1980 TV mini-series *Cosmos*, and the book on which the TV programs were based spent 70 weeks on the New York Times best-seller list—15 of those as the number one best-seller. Prior to the stunning success of his educational television series, Sagan in 1978 won a Pulitzer prize for his book, *The Dragons of Eden: Speculation on the Evolution of Human Intelligence.*

While Dr. Sagan's influence on popular thinking about science was dramatic, his professional influence was profound as well. For 25 years—most of his career—he was a professor of astronomy and space science at Cornell University. He also was an active member of the Council for Secular Humanism and a co-founder of the Committee for the Scientific Investigation of Claims of the Paranormal (CSICOP). In 1987, he received CSICOP's "In Praise of Reason" award, and in 1994, he was awarded the organization's first "Isaac Asimov Award" for his ability "to communicate achievements, methods, and issues of science to the public." His close associates included both Isaac Asimov and renowned humanist Paul Kurtz.

In December of 1996, at age 62, Sagan died of bone cancer, leaving behind a wife and five children. Taken from a *Parade* magazine interview with Sagan ("In the Valley of the Shadow," March 1996) nine months before his death, the following quote articulates Sagan's conclusions regarding life after death:

*But as much as I want to believe that [in an afterlife], and despite the ancient and worldwide cultural traditions that assert an afterlife, I know of nothing to suggest that it is more than wishful thinking.*

beginning that didn't happen.

To avoid God as the First Cause, humanists assume a different basis for the reality of the universe, a non-sequential group of first causes. Lamont calls these the "ultimate principles of explanation and intelligibility."[16] For the humanist, these ultimate principles are a sufficient source for the rest of reality. They are the fundamental facts assumed to be true and beyond which we cannot (and need not!) search further to understand the cosmos.

## EPISTEMOLOGY

"Epistemology" refers to one's theory of knowledge. It answers the question, "How much can one know about reality, and how does one obtain this knowledge?" Naturalism answers that everything in the physical world (which means *everything* since, to the naturalist, the physical world is all there is) is knowable, and science—or more specifically, the scientific method—is the proper means of knowing all there is to be known. Roy Wood Sellars goes so far as to say, "The spirit of naturalism would seem to be one with the spirit of science itself."[17] He further states, "Christianity, for example, had a supernaturalistic framework in a three-tier universe of heaven, earth and hell. . . . The Humanist argues that the traditional Christian outlook has been undercut and rendered obsolete by the growth of knowledge about man and his world."[18] Humanists thus consider their worldview more valid than the "older" Christian view because theirs is based on scientific knowledge and methods acquired over the last 400 years.

Most humanists agree with Sellars. *Humanist Manifesto II,* for instance, states, "Any account of nature should pass the tests of scientific evidence,"[19] which, of course, supernatural explanations could never do, since they are not measurable or observable. Naturalists, grounding their epistemology in science, will only believe what they can "touch, smell, taste and see." Any knowledge purporting to involve the supernatural is automatically rejected.

Humanists' epistemology shapes their metaphysics. Because humanists believe science tells us we are products of chance and that we have evolved over billions of years, they must act on that knowledge and formulate a worldview consistent with it—a worldview in which the universe is all that exists and ever will exist. Science (according to their view) has no means of obtaining knowledge about the supernatural, and therefore, the supernatural must not exist. But doesn't this grounding of belief in science as the ultimate means of perception require faith, just as the supernatural does? Doesn't Sagan's statement that "science has itself become a kind of religion"[20] admit that very self-contradiction? There is, after all, no reason (beyond the humanist assumption) to believe that nothing exists outside the purview of science.

Lamont acknowledges the charge as valid and answers it this way:

> It is sometimes argued that since science, like religion, must make ultimate assumptions, we have no more right to rely on science in an analysis of the idea of immortality than on religion. Faith in the methods and findings of science, it is said, is just as much a faith as faith in the methods and findings of religion. In answer to this we can only say that the history of thought seems to show that reliance on science has been more fruitful in the progress and exten-

> **Science, according to the humanist view, has no means of obtaining knowledge about the supernatural, and therefore, the supernatural must not exist.**

sion of the truth than reliance on religion.[21]

For the naturalist, science is the ultimate means of perception and therefore, the definitive means of gaining knowledge. As a result, it should be applied to every aspect of life (including the social and moral realms) so that we can better understand our world. The epistemology of the naturalist is inseparable from science and, indeed, mandates a faith in science as the only means by which we can know the world around us.

## THE MIND-BODY PROBLEM

The epistemology and metaphysics of naturalism present another very specific problem for humanist philosophy. This dilemma is traditionally referred to as the mind-body problem because it asks, "Does the mind exist solely within nature, just as the body does, or is the mind more than physical matter alone?"

Humanists believe the mind (or consciousness, personality, or soul) is simply a manifestation of the brain (for the sake of continuity, we shall refer to this phenomenon simply as the "mind"). The mind is merely an extension of the natural world, easily explainable in physical terms. This belief is required by their epistemology, again, in that science is our only way to obtain knowledge.

Since this view of the cosmos allows only for the existence of matter, the mind must somehow be a strictly physical phenomenon. Recall in *The Matrix* that Morpheus describes reality as simply "electrical impulses interpreted by your brain." This view is called "monism": there is only one aspect of reality—

the physical world. (The opposing view—the belief that the mind is both a conglomeration of matter as well as a non-material component—is called dualism.)

According to naturalist philosophy, the amazingly complex human mind is the result of evolutionary processes. Lamont says, "naturalistic Humanism… take[s] the view that the material universe came first and that mind emerged in the animal man only after some two billion years of biological evolution upon this material earth."[22]

# IMPLICATIONS OF THE MONISTIC VIEW

The monistic view of the mind leads to two additional, logically necessary conclusions for the humanist. The first answers the question, "Is man immortal?" Lamont recognizes this question, and accepts the only conclusion available to the naturalist: "If, on the other hand, the monistic theory of psychology is true, as Naturalism, Materialism, and Humanism claim, then there is no possibility that the human consciousness, with its memory and awareness of self-identity intact, can survive the shock and disintegration of death. According to this view, the body and personality live together; they grow together; and they die together."[23]

For the humanist, there can be no doubt that there is no life after death. In fact, the denial of the after-life is inescapable for the humanist worldview, so much so that accepting belief in the fundamental mortality of man is seen by Lamont as the first step in becoming a humanist. He writes, "The issue of mortality versus immortality is crucial in the argument of Humanism against supernaturalism. For if men realize

> **GENESIS 2:7**
> *Then the LORD God formed the man out of the dust from the ground and breathed the breath of life into his nostrils, and the man became a living being.*

that their careers are limited to this world, that this earthly existence is all that they will ever have, then they are already more than half-way on the path toward becoming functioning Humanists…."[24]

The second necessary conclusion for humanists results from their belief that mind evolved through

> For the humanist, there can be no doubt that there is no life after death.

natural processes. According to this view, there is no guarantee that mind is anything special at all. Some better mutation of mind could occur any day. In truth, many humanists believe a more efficient mind is in the process of being created today. Victor J. Stenger, author of *Not By Design*, claims, "Future computers will not only be superior to people in every task, mental or physical, but will also be immortal." He believes it will become possible to save human "thoughts which constitute consciousness" in these computer memory banks, as well as to program computers in such a way as to give them the full range of human thought. After all, he says, "If the computer is 'just a machine,' so is the human brain. . . ." So why shouldn't the computer become the next step in the evolutionary chain, the new, higher consciousness? Stenger sees this as a real possibility, and concludes, "Perhaps, as part of this new consciousness, we will become God."[25]

Does this sound like science fiction? Not to the humanist. In a naturalist, monistic worldview, it is not only a logical possibility, but also a likely one. Evolution created the human brain strictly out of matter; evolution and natural selection are still at work to improve that brain, and the computer is really nothing more than an incredibly efficient man-made brain. Conceivably, then, the computer does become the inevitable next step in the evolutionary chain. Perhaps *The Matrix* is not so far-fetched after all. When Morpheus says to Neo, "Welcome to the real world," humanists may someday have to ask, "*Whose* real world?"

# HOW TO RESPOND TO MONISM

What should be a Christian response to the humanist belief in monism? First of all, a biblical worldview portrays man as a physical body energized by a living soul (Genesis 2:7). This living soul exists apart from the body, and as a result, survives physical death (see 1 Kings 17:21-22). And in Matthew 10:28, Jesus makes

> **1 KINGS 17:21-22**
>
> *Then he stretched himself out over the boy three times. He cried out to the Lord and said, "My Lord God, please let this boy's life return to him!" So the Lord listened to Elijah's voice, and the boy's life returned to him, and he lived.*

it clear that man is more than mere matter when He says, "Don't fear those who kill the body but are not able to kill the soul; but rather, fear Him who is able to destroy both soul and body in hell."

From a biblical standpoint, the most fundamental aspect of human nature is the dimension that cannot be accounted for by simple electrical firings in gray matter. Something beyond the physical brain separates man from the rest of the animal kingdom. In their book, *Body and Soul*, Christian authors J.P. Moreland and Scott Rae define a version of dualism called substance dualism. They write, "Substance dualism is the view that the soul—I, self, mind—is an immaterial substance different from the body to which it is related.... [T]he substance dualist is committed to the claim that the soul is an immaterial entity that could, in principle, survive death and ground personal identity in the afterlife."[26] Elaborating on this definition, Moreland and Rae defend the idea that humans have a mental existence beyond the material. They write, "In general, mental states have some or all of the following features, none of which is a physical feature of anything: Mental states, like pains, have an intrinsic, raw conscious feel.... Mental states are inner, private and known by first-person, direct introspection."[27] Elsewhere, they continue, "The soul contains various mental states within it—for example, sensations, thoughts, beliefs, desires and acts of will. This is not as complicated as it sounds.... Water can be in a cold or a hot state. Likewise, the soul can be in a feeling or thinking state."[28] In other words, you have immediate access to your thoughts in ways that no one else does. Someone cannot cut open your brain and find a thought or emotion. Mental states are not physical in that sense—they are non-material—but to the one possessing them, very real.

John W. Cooper, Professor of Philosophical Theology at Calvin Theological Seminary, comments, "In an age when some educated Christians are selling out the soul for a mess of materialistic pottage, Moreland and Rae's *Body and Soul* is a significant restatement and cogent defense of the historic Christian teaching about human nature and responsibility...."[29] Cooper goes on to explain why it is imperative to have the right understanding of human nature. He continues, "The traditional view of persons as substantial souls is necessary for a robust Christian understanding of moral responsibility and our obligation toward the unborn, the dying, reproductive technology and genetic engineering.

Moreland and Rae defend dualism not so much to reassure us about what happens when we die as to guide us in how we should live." Cooper's is a worldview perspective, pointing out that one must have the correct belief (in this case, concerning the true nature of human beings) in order to pursue proper behavior (regarding issues such as abortion or genetic engineering). Thus, the thinking Christian cannot write off philosophy as unimportant to his worldview because philosophical ideas lead to practical actions.

This brings us back to the current cultural battles that we must be armed to face on every side. Why do humanists seem to be winning the culture war? To discover the answer, we must expose a key facet of Secular Humanism that has been kept off the public's radar screen: the fact that Secular Humanism is fundamentally *a religious worldview.*

## SECULAR HUMANISM'S DARK SECRET

Secular Humanists have a deep-seated interest in keeping the public in the dark as to the real nature of their worldview. If it were widely understood that Secular Humanism is a religion in the very same sense as Christianity, then it could not be taught in our public schools—hence, the gravity of the question "Is Secular Humanism a religion?"

Regarding the religious nature of Secular Humanism, Paul Kurtz explains that *Humanist Manifesto I,* "recommended first a form of nontheistic religious humanism as an alternative to the religions of the age…"[30] When the *Manifesto* was written in 1933,

> The thinking Christian cannot write off philosophy as unimportant to his worldview because philosophical ideas lead to practical actions.

the general consensus in America was that religion had a place in public life. Early twentieth-century humanists understood their role was to develop a "new religion"—one based on science and man, not on the supernatural and God. Charles Francis Potter, for example, a *Humanist Manifesto I* signatory, authored a book titled *Humanism: A New Religion.* Another signer, John Dewey, wrote *A Common Faith* in which he said, "Here are all the elements for a religious faith that shall not be confined to sect, class, or race."[31] Even the author of *Humanist Manifesto I,* Roy Wood Sellars, "apparently prevaricated over whether it was appropriate to use the term religion for a movement without belief in God, but opted in favor of the practice since a predominately religious world 'is more likely to swallow something called religion than atheism.'"[32] Clearly, these men acknowledged the religious nature

*Secular Humanist philosophy replaces God with man but retains its inescapably religious dimensions of thought.*

of their worldview.

By 1973, humanists recognized the need for a new manifesto. Kurtz explains that *Humanist Manifesto II* "left room for both naturalistic humanism and liberal religious humanism."[33] In the same year, Edwin H. Wilson wrote "...Humanism in a naturalistic frame is validly a religion..."[34] Again, humanists at this time were clear that theirs was a religious worldview.

However, by 1980, it came time to write yet another humanist statement, this time called *A Secular Humanist Declaration*. Explaining why this new statement was necessary, Kurtz reveals that the 1973 manifesto "had come under heavy attack" and had many critics who "maintained that secular humanism was a religion." The reason this "attack" was so significant for Kurtz and his fellow humanists was that the Supreme Court had ruled in 1962 and 1963 that religious exercises in public schools (specifically related to devotional Bible reading and prayer) is unconstitutional. The national mood had changed correspondingly during the 1970's, with a greater awareness and sensitivity toward keeping religious endorsement or promotion out of education under the guise of maintaining religious "neutrality."

In light of these developments, Kurtz discloses a change in strategy by the humanist community. Concerning the charge that Secular Humanism is a religion, he writes, "The *Declaration* responded that secular humanism expressed a set of moral values and a nontheistic philosophical and scientific viewpoint that could not be equated with religious faith. The teaching of the secular humanist outlook in no way was a violation of the separation principle. It defended the democratic idea that the secular state should be neutral, neither for nor against religion."[35] This is a very notable twist on the earlier humanist position. In the course of just seven years, Secular Humanism

Because the U.S. Supreme Court ruled against the practice of religion in public schools, contemporary humanists distance their philosophy from religion as a way to maintain its place in our education system—even though their counterparts in the early 1900's argued that humanism is a modern religion.

morphed from a "religious humanism" to a "nontheistic philosophical and scientific viewpoint" that no longer could be "equated with religious faith." This appears to be an attempt by Kurtz and his colleagues to obscure the facts by redefining their worldview.

To add to this appearance, in the preamble to the *Humanist Manifesto 2000*, Kurtz defines humanism as "an ethical, scientific, and philosophical outlook...."[36] Here, Kurtz takes the definition of Secular Humanism one final step, dropping the earlier "nontheistic" modifier just in case that term was too close to anything sounding even remotely religious. Yet, the fact remains, the basic tenets of Secular Humanism in the year 2000 are the same as in 1933. Their theology is atheism; their philosophy is naturalism, and their biology is evolutionism. Humanists maintain that ethics are *relative*. In sociology, they seek to redefine the family, and they continue to believe in positive (versus absolute) law. Then, as now, these components make up a total worldview, a set of dogmatic beliefs upon which to determine how life should be lived—

just as any religion does. Yet, the debate whether humanism is a religion continues, even among humanists. Robert Price describes the ongoing dialog this way:

> Is humanism an alternative *to* religion, or an alternative *kind of* religion? It is easy to find committed Humanists who'll give either answer. Those who call it a religion define the word *religion* broadly, as tantamount to any dedicated philosophy of life. Those who think humanism is not a religion would rather say simply that they embrace humanism as a philosophy instead, since they associate *religion* with the supernaturalist claims most traditional religions make. This is ultimately a semantic argument, and both usages make sense.[37]

Ian S. Markham edited a work on world religions and placed Secular Humanism among Hinduism, Buddhism, Chinese Religion, Shintoism, Judaism, Christianity, Islam, and Sikhism. Since Secular Humanism is atheistic, Markham admits it is not a religion in the traditional sense of the word. But it is a religion from a worldview standpoint. "So with modesty and for practical purposes," says Markham, "I offer a 'definition' of religion that both underlies and embraces the descriptions that follow in this book. Religion, for me, is a way of life (one which embraces a total worldview, certain ethical demands, and certain social practices)..."[38]

How can this issue be resolved? As it turns out,

> The debate whether humanism is a religion continues, even among humanists.

---

> In 1961, the Supreme Court specifically named Secular Humanism as one of the "non-theistic" religions.

the highest court in our land has weighed in on the matter. In their book, *Clergy in the Classroom: The Religion of Secular Humanism*, the authors describe a significant affirmation of the Supreme Court about the religious nature of Secular Humanism:

> In 1961 the Supreme Court handed down the *Torcaso v. Watkins* decision regarding a Maryland notary public who was initially disqualified from office because he would not declare a belief in God. But the Court ruled in his favor. It argued that theistic religions could not be favored by the Court over non-theistic religions. In a footnote it clarified what it meant by non-theistic religions: "Among religions in this country which do not teach what would generally be considered a belief in the existence of God are Buddhism, Taoism, Ethical Culture, Secular Humanism and others."[39]

In this decision the Court specifically named Secular Humanism as one of the "non-theistic" religions, recognizing that Secular Humanism functions in the same way all other religions do—as a personally held belief concerning the ultimate "religious" questions about God (theology) and reality (philosophy). To bring in the "worldview tree," these twin disciplines of theology and philosophy form the religious roots of every worldview, with each of the other categories (biology, psychology, ethics, sociology, law, politics, economics, and history) drawing nourishment from these roots. Every world-view, including Secular Humanism, is at root a religious view of life, and these religious roots bear fruit in every area of life.

If Secular Humanism is a religion, as claimed by the U.S. Supreme Court and countless humanists over the years,[40] why then, is it allowed in public schools

> If Secular Humanism is a religion, why is it allowed in public schools where there is to be no established religion?

where there is to be no established religion? This question has enormous implications for public education that will be explored in greater detail in the following two chapters.

## RECOMMENDED READING

Kurtz, Paul. *Humanist Manifesto 2000: A Call for a New Planetary Humanism.* Amherst, NY: Prometheus Books, 2000.

Moreland, J.P. and Scott B. Rae. *Body & Soul: Human Nature and the Crisis in Ethics.* Downers Grove, IL: InterVarsity Press, 2000.

Noebel, David A., J.F. Baldwin and Kevin Bywater, *Clergy in the Classroom: The Religion of Secular Humanism.* Manitou Springs, CO: Summit Press 2nd Edition, 2001.

Varghese, Roy Abraham, ed., *The Intellectuals Speak Out About God.* Dallas, TX: Lewis and Stanley, 1984.

## ENDNOTES

1. Roy Wood Sellars, "The Humanist Outlook," in *The Humanist Alternative,* ed. Paul Kurtz (Buffalo, NY: Prometheus, 1973), p. 135.

2. Ruth A. Tucker, *Walking Away from Faith* (Downer's Grove, IL: InterVarsity Press, 2002) p. 16.

3. John Dewey, *A Common Faith* (Yale University Press: 1999) p. 87.

4. We are not endorsing this R-rated movie, but we include it because some analysts consider this film to be the same cultural lighting rod for the current generation that *Star Wars* was in the 1970's. The story not only informs but also reflects the worldview of this generation. If that is the case, all Christians would do well to analyze what it is about this film that young people find so fascinating and to use that insight for building a bridge over which to lead them to the Gospel.

4. We understand that Morpheus framed his answer as a question, and there is much that could be said about the meaning of his words and the overall worldview found in *The Matrix.* Our purpose here is not to explore these larger issues but simply to point out that a worldview is being expressed, and Morpheus does, indeed, give a definition of what is real, even if that definition is not fully explained until later in the film. See our further comments on *The Matrix* in Chapter 10.

6. Corliss Lamont, *The Philosophy of Humanism* (New York: Frederick Ungar, 1982), p 28.

7. *Humanist Manifesto II* (Buffalo, NY: Prometheus, 1980), p.16.

8. Lamont, *The Philosophy of Humanism*, p.145.

9. Ibid., p. 14.

10. Ibid., p. 22.

11. Kurtz, ed. *Humanist Manifestos I* and *II.* p. 8.

12. Henry Miller, as cited in *The Best of Humanism*, ed. Greeley, p.149.

13. Corliss Lamont, as cited in *The Best of Humanism*, ed. Greeley, p.149.

14. Carl Sagan, *Cosmos* (New York: Random House, 1980), p.4.

15. Robert Green Ingersoll, as cited in *The Best of Humanism*, ed. Greeley, p.162.

16. Lamont, *The Philosophy of Humanism*, p. 170-1.

17. Roy Wood Sellars, *Evolutionary Naturalism*, (Chicago, IL: Open Court, 1922), p.5.

18. Roy Wood Sellars, "The Humanist Outlook," in *The Humanist Alternative*, p.133.

19. *The Humanist Manifesto II*, p. 16.

20. Carl Sagan, *UFO's—A Scientific Debate* (Ithaca, NY: Cornell University Press, 1972), p. xiv.

21. Corliss Lamont, *The Illusion of Immortality* (New York: Frederick Ungar, 1965), p. 124-5.

22. Corliss Lamont, *Voice in the Wilderness* (Buffalo, NY: Prometheus, 1975), p.82.

23. Lamont, *The Philosophy of Humanism*, p.82-3.

24. Ibid., pp. 82.

25. Victor J. Stenger, *Not By Design* (Buffalo, NY: Prometheus, 1988), p.188-9.

26. J. P. Moreland and Scott B. Rae, *Body and Soul: Human Nature and the Crisis in Ethics* (Downers Grove, IL: InterVarsity Press, 2000), p. 20.

27. Moreland and Rae, *Body and Soul,* p. 159-60.

28. Idid., p. 203.

29. In the introduction to the hardback edition of *Body and Soul.*

30. Paul Kurtz, *Humanist Manifesto 2000: A Call for a New Planetary Humanism.* (Amherst, NY: Prometheus Books, 2000), p. 8-9.

31. John Dewey, *A Common Faith.* (New Haven and London: Yale University Press, 1934), p. 87.

32. Frank L. Pasquale, *Free Inquiry,* Winter, 2002/3, p. 67.

33. Kurtz, *Humanist Manifesto 2000.* p. 9.

34. Quoted in *Clergy in the Classroom.* p. 85.

35. Kurtz, *Humanist Manifesto 2000,* p. 10-11.

36. Ibid., p. 7

37. Robert M. Price, "Religious and Secular Humanism, What's the Difference?" *Free Inquiry Magazine,* Volume 22, Number 3.

38. Ian S. Markham, *A World Religions Reader,* 2nd Revision edition (Blackwell Publishers; 2000), p. 5-6.

39. David A. Noebel, J.F. Baldwin and Kevin Bywater, *Clergy in the Classroom: The Religion of Secular Humanism* (Manitou Springs, CO: Summit Press 2nd Edition, 2001), p. 7.

40. According to an ad in the "Guide Star Page" in *Free Inquiry* magazine, the American Humanist Association "is not required to file an annual return with the IRS because it is a religious organization." (See the Fall 2002 issue, p. 40). For a definitive expose' on the religion of Secular Humanism, see David A. Noebel's *Clergy in the Classroom,* available in both book and video format. The book contains 53 exhibits that demonstrate the religious nature of humanism.


(1) U.S. Supreme Court building: From Countering Culture video (2004 Summit Ministries: Manitou Springs, CO)

# CHAPTER 5

# Evolving Ideas
# in Science

"Humanism cannot in any fair sense of the word apply to one who still believes in God as the source and creator of the universe."[1]
—PAUL KURTZ

"But Secular Humanism is more than science, because it proceeds to make all kinds of inferences about the human condition and human possibilities that are not, in any authentic sense, scientific. Those inferences are metaphysical and in the end theological…"[2]
—IRVING KRISTOL

"If God is real, then a naturalistic science that insists on explaining everything is out of touch with reality; if God is imaginary, then theologians have no subject matter."[3]
—PHILLIP E. JOHNSON

Many people today have the impression there is a war between modern science and religion, and that science has won the day. But is that really the case? Are scientific knowledge and religious ideas incompatible? Has science replaced religion as the means for understanding life and mankind's place in the universe? Dr. Ian Hutchinson, Professor at MIT, traces much of the blame for the current hostility between these two disciplines to Andrew Dickson White, former president of Cornell University. In 1898, White wrote a book entitled *A History of the Warfare of Science with Theology in Christendom.* White's preface stated outright that he intended the book to support his battle against the church's control of higher education. Hutchinson comments, "White contended that all true knowledge was scientific, thereby creating a wall—an artificial one—between scientific knowledge and religious faith. And his book marked a profound change in how we viewed science and Christianity."[4] Further, according to Hutchinson, White's book was not an attempt at objective analysis but "a tactical maneuver to gain secular independence for universities."[5]

Nancy Pearcey and Charles Thaxton elaborate on the initiation of this modern "war" between science and religion when they write,

> In late nineteenth-century England, several small groups of scientists and scholars organized under the leadership of Thomas H. Huxley to overthrow the cultural dominance of Christianity—particularly the intellectual dominance of the Anglican church. Their goal was to secularize society, replacing the Christian worldview with scientific naturalism, a worldview that recognizes the existence of nature alone. Though secularists, they understood very well that they were replacing one religion by another, for they described their goal as the establishment of the "church scientific." Huxley even referred to his scientific lectures as "lay sermons."[6]

Thomas Huxley's grandson, Julian Huxley, continued in the steps of his grandfather. One incident in his life reveals a moment of inspiration:

> One day while browsing through a library in Colorado Springs, [Julian] Huxley came across some essays by Lord Morley in which he found these words: "The next great task of science will be to create a religion for humanity." Huxley was challenged by this vision. He wrote, "I was fired by sharing his conviction that science would of necessity play an essential part in framing any religion of the future worthy of the name." Huxley took up Morley's challenge to develop a scientific religion. He called it "Evolutionary Humanism."[7]

> "The next great task of science will be to create a religion for humanity."
> —Julian Huxley

## THE FOUNDATION OF EVOLUTION

A worldview perspective allows us to see the larger implications of science. At the popular level, most people today believe science and religion are two separate realms of knowledge, but the studied humanist knows better. Humanism's worldview, as we've seen, begins with atheistic theology and naturalistic philosophy. These "roots" provide nourishment to the branch of biology which produces the fruit of Darwinian evolution. In the humanist worldview, it is almost as if the fruit and root support each other. Without the theory of evolution, the humanist would have to rely on God as the explanation for life, which would undermine atheism as a viable system of thought and hence, humanism as a whole. As a result, Secular Humanists embrace the theory of evolution.

*To preserve its naturalistic foundation and its corresponding atheistic theology, humanism asserts evolution as the explanation of origins.*

*Humanist Manifesto I* states, "Humanism believes that man is a part of nature and that he has emerged as the result of a continuous process."[8] This belief is echoed in *Humanist Manifesto II*, which claims "science affirms that the human species is an emergence from natural evolutionary forces."[9]

For humanists, atheistic evolution is not one option among many but rather the only option compatible with their worldview. That is why any form of Creationism is considered an enemy of science, despite the fact that the Christian worldview had far more to do with the founding of modern science than did humanism.

## SCIENTISM—NOT JUST SCIENCE ANYMORE

According to the latest humanist pronouncement, "The unique message of humanism on the current world scene is its commitment to scientific naturalism."[10] While this statement may sound innocuous to the casual reader, it is packed with worldview implications. To understand the significance of the phrase "scientific naturalism," we need to read a little further in *Humanist Manifesto 2000*, where we are told, "Scientific naturalism enables human beings to construct a coherent worldview disentangled from metaphysics or theology and based on the sciences."[11]

As we saw in the last chapter, humanism relies on science as its basic source of knowledge. The humanistic interpretation of science excludes any supernatural explanation for events occurring in nature, including the origin of life. For humanists, the lesson of science is that whatever takes place in nature is "natural" not supernatural. Humanists believe that, for science, "supernatural" is a meaningless word.

This view that knowledge is attainable only through science is called "scientism." However, there is a major problem with scientism as the means of obtaining knowledge. Paul Kurtz

> For humanists to explain origins, atheistic evolution is not one option among many but rather the only option compatible with their worldview.

stumbles over this problem when he writes that scientific naturalism requires that "all hypotheses and theories must be tested experimentally by reference to natural causes and events."[12] The problem is this: the belief that the scientific method is the only way to know what is true about our world cannot itself be tested scientifically! In other words, scientism fails to meet its own standard of verifying what is truth. This point is so critical it can hardly be emphasized enough. To put it bluntly, scientism is the humanist's dogmatic belief, grounded in a religion-like faith in the *non*-existence of God.

From a worldview perspective, biology (how one answers the question of the origin of life) is intimately connected with theology (the way one answers the ultimate question concerning the existence of God). But when it comes to what should be taught in public schools about the origin of life, the religious foundation of science is regularly overlooked.

> The belief that the scientific method is the only way to know what is true about our world cannot itself be tested scientifically! Scientism fails to meet its own standard of verifying what is truth.

## THE EDUCATION CONNECTION

Battles are being fought today over what kinds of knowledge teachers should encourage their students to acquire. Thomas Sowell exposes the influence Secular Humanists exert on education when he writes, "Advocates of secular humanism, for example, have been quite clear and explicit as to the crucial importance of promoting their philosophy in the schools, to counter or undermine religious values among the next generation....While the organized secular humanist movement might seem to be a small fringe group, its impact on education is out of all proportion to its size."[13]

To see the humanist influence on education, we need look no further than how science is taught in our public schools. Evolutionists cry "Foul!" when anyone suggests that a Creator should be introduced into a science class during the study of the origin of life. Kurtz complains, "We decry the efforts of a few scientists... to impose transcendental interpretations upon natural phenomena."[14] Kurtz is echoing the sentiment of various other humanist education watchdogs who insure the current dogma is not challenged. For example, Roger DeHart, a biology teacher at Burlington-Edison High School outside Seattle, Washington, was barred from teaching his students about recent scientific discoveries that bring into question several standard evidences for evolution presented in biology textbooks. He attempted to use articles, not from any religious publications but from scientific journals such as *Scientific American* and *The Scientist.* Yet the A.C.L.U. threatened the local school board with a lawsuit if DeHart presented this material in class.[15]

Worldview analysis shows the fallacy in this approach to education. To use only one example (from numerous that could be cited), consider the opening statement we noted earlier from Carl Sagan's

> "Scientific credence, when evaluated without an overwhelming bias toward materialism, does not support that Darwinian creation story that has effectively become the state supported religion in modernist culture."—Phillip Johnson

science series, *Cosmos*: "The Cosmos is all that is or ever was or ever will be." Stop and reflect on that statement for a moment. Is this a statement of scientific fact? Clearly, it is not. How can we know through scientific experimentation that nature (the Cosmos) is "all that is," i.e., the only reality? Sagan is not making a scientific statement here but projecting a philosophical assumption regarding the nature of reality—an assumption which is both unproved and unprovable by any known method of science.

Nevertheless, most science teachers allow this kind of rhetoric to go unchallenged in their classes, not realizing they have introduced a *religiously* held belief of Secular Humanism. Therefore, when children in school are exposed only to the teaching of scientific naturalism in science class, they are being indoctrinated into a basic tenet of Secular Humanism. And as we are witnessing across our land, this religion is a jealous one when it comes to allowing any rivals in the classroom.

Still, humanists insist that evolutionary theory is scientific, and Intelligent Design theory is not. Just how closed-minded humanists are toward the idea of a Creator is summed up by Isaac Asimov: "To those who are trained in science, creationism seems like a bad dream, a sudden reliving of a nightmare, a renewed march of an army of the night risen to challenge free thought and enlightenment."[17] And Huxley claims, "The first point to make about Darwin's theory is that it is no longer a theory, but a fact. . . . Darwinianism has come of age so to speak. We are no longer having to bother about establishing the fact of evolution."[18]

These statements would not be so alarming if humanists were simply claiming that evolution within a species (microevolution) is a fact. Microevolution is a readily observable phenomenon. But both Asimov and Huxley are promoting the belief that macroevolu-

## "WHAT IS THE ACLU?"

The 400,000-member American Civil Liberties Union is a private organization founded in 1920 with the stated goal of guarding against various forms of government oppression and "the tyranny of the majority." The organization calls itself "our nation's guardian of liberty" although the causes it supports are distinctively left-leaning. As offered on its website, www.aclu.org, the ACLU's 1999 position paper includes the following causes among those it supports:

➤ Abortion rights that favor a woman's right to choose over the rights of a fetus

➤ The right of gay couples to adopt children

➤ The governing of the majority through democratically elected representatives but with power limited so as to protect individual rights

➤ These protected groups: native Americans, people of color, lesbians, gay men, bisexuals, transgendered people, women, mental patients, prisoners, people with disabilities, the poor.

tion—the transmutation of one species into another—is a scientific fact. Humanists do not just claim that science has proved dogs can change or "evolve" into faster or bigger breeds. They claim that all dogs—indeed all mammals—evolved from reptiles which evolved from amphibians which evolved from fish, and so on back to the first speck of life. They wholeheartedly believe Darwin's conclusion that since microevolutionary changes occur within species (Darwin bred pigeons and saw such changes; dog and cattle breeders likewise see such changes), these changes can accumulate until macroevolution occurs, but this has never been observed nor has any fossil evidence ever been uncovered to support this conclusion.

Macroevolution can only be embraced as a fact by those who have enough faith to deny all possibility of the supernatural. Phillip Johnson opened the door to the fact that Darwinists were hiding their religious motivations behind the guise of "science." Referring to his book, the *Wedge of Truth*, Johnson says, "Our bold claim was that scientific credence, when evaluated without an overwhelming bias toward materialism, does not support the Darwinian creation story that has effectively become the state supported religion in modernist culture."[19]

In accord with its faith, humanist biology clings dogmatically to numerous ideas that are not grounded in scientific fact. The following discussion outlines these ideas.

# SPONTANEOUS GENERATION

The first idea humanist biology accepts is that life arose spontaneously from non-living matter by natural, random processes. Without this concept, humanism would have to postulate a supernatural force to explain the development of the first life on earth. The existence of any supernatural force would contradict humanism's atheistic theology and naturalistic philosophy. Therefore, humanists are left with the pre-scientific theory of spontaneous generation. We say "pre-scientific" because one of the early milestones of the modern scientific method was to disprove this

## THE SIX BASIC TENETS OF HUMANIST BIOLOGY

1. Life arose spontaneously from non-living matter by natural, random processes.

2. Natural selection is the mechanism that naturally and randomly allows to live and reproduce only those life forms best suited to survive.

3. Life forms best equipped to survive will win the struggle for existence.

4. Mutations among species occurring over millions of years supports natural selection.

5. Adaptation explains why different species evolve specialized abilities that allow them to survive in their particular environmental niches.

6. The fossil record provides an accurate account of the transmutation of species—macroevolution.

centuries-old belief. As we learn from Benjamin Wiker, "Modern evolutionary theory is not modern—we find it full–blown in the first century B.C. in the Roman Epicurean poet-philosopher Lucretius—and its rise was assured with the victory of materialism in the seventeenth century.... There is an entire cosmological framework that Darwinism presupposed, and it can be traced all the way back to Epicurus."[20] Thus, the so-called "modern" theory of evolution is grounded in the ancient Epicurean philosophy of materialism.

The idea of spontaneous generation is so fraught with difficulties that few scientists consider it science at all. Yet, faith in spontaneous generation is essential as the starting point for evolution as described by the humanist. Listen to the blind faith revealed in Matthew D'Agostino's article:

> Based on current knowledge we can only assume that life is one of the many inherent capabilities that matter happens to possess, a capability that actualized or developed under some still largely unknown set of initial conditions. We're not absolutely sure what life looked like once the process was fully underway: something like algae, the biologists suggest a foamy blue-green pond scum. Note, however, that we can already begin to answer those catechism-type questions: Q. "Who or what are you?" A. "I am a descendant of a blue-green algae."[21]

Note that "catechism-type questions" historically have been religious in nature—a catechism is a statement of belief, not a recounting of proven facts. D'Agostino is free to "assume" certain "largely unknown" initial conditions that led to "not absolutely sure" results, but these are not the assurances of science. They are statements of philosophy that represent a blatant attempt to indoctrinate his readers into a naturalistic worldview.

Ironically, not even Charles Darwin was willing to postulate a theory that hinged on spontaneous generation. Rather, he wrote, "Probably all the organic beings which have ever lived on this earth have descended from some one primordial form, into which life was first breathed."[22] Darwin himself felt the need to rely on some supernatural force to explain the existence of life—but humanists cannot afford such a concession. The existence of the supernatural has disastrous consequences for the Secular Humanist worldview.

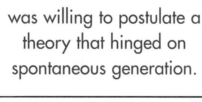

Not even Charles Darwin was willing to postulate a theory that hinged on spontaneous generation.

## NATURAL SELECTION

The second idea humanists embrace in biology is natural selection. Natural selection is the mechanism proposed by Darwin that—through competition and other factors such as mutations, predators, geography, and time—naturally and randomly allows to live and reproduce only those life forms best suited to survive. Through reproduction, slight variations occur that reform existing molecules, cells, plants, or animals into new molecules, cells, plants, and animals. A sort of self-creation takes place. Related to this theory are the notions of the "survival of the fittest" and the struggle for existence, which we will examine shortly. Carl Sagan insists, "Natural selection is a successful theory devised to explain the fact of evolution."[23]

Darwin relied on natural selection as the mechanism for his theory of evolution largely because he felt it was something man had already observed artificially through breeding. When one breeds horses to create faster offspring, Darwin reasoned, one is selecting a beneficial trait for that horse and synthesizing a microevolutionary process. Darwin was convinced that, given enough time, nature could use a similar means of selection to evolve all forms of life from the single original life form.

Indeed, Darwin believed that "natural selection is daily and hourly scrutinizing . . . every variation, even the slightest; rejecting that which is bad, preserving and adding up all that is good; silently and insensibly working. . . at the improvement of each organic being."[24] While a breeder purposely (i.e., not randomly) controls selection so that each generation of animal contains the best improvements, Darwin believed that random variations, influenced by environmental factors, were responsible for such improvements in nature. As Richard Dawkins puts it, "Natural selection, the blind, unconscious, automatic process which Darwin discovered, and which we now know is the explanation for the existence and apparently purposeful form of all life, has no purpose in mind. It has no mind and no mind's eye. It does not plan for the future. It has no vision, no foresight, no sight at all. If it can be said to play the role of watchmaker in nature, it is the *blind* watchmaker."[25] Since natural selection is the most convincing idea anyone has proposed to "drive" evolution, most humanists accept it with the same faith modeled by Darwin.

> "Natural selection, the blind, unconscious, automatic process which Darwin discovered, and which we now know is the explanation for the existence and apparently purposeful form of all life, has no purpose in mind."
> —Richard Dawkins

## STRUGGLE FOR EXISTENCE AND SURVIVAL

The notion that life forms best equipped to survive will win the struggle for existence is inherent in the concept of natural selection. This allegedly explains why various life forms have become better equipped to survive as time passes.

Humanistic biologists accept this concept although they are usually circumspect about acknowledging it. Corliss Lamont, however, is not bashful: "The processes of natural selection and survival of the fittest, with the many mutations that occur over hundreds of millions of years, adequately account for the origin and development of the species."[26]

At least one reason most humanists are more cautious than Lamont lies in the ethical implications of survival of the fittest: it suggests that the only moral good is survival. The sole value born out by the struggle for existence is existence itself, and whatever it takes to survive is "good." What makes this an uncomfortable position is that, to put it bluntly, survival of the fittest is bloodthirsty. It does not care for the weak or the poor. In fact, it disdains them both. Hitler's Aryan policies and Engels' Marxism followed natural selection to its logical outcome and concluded that, not only *would* the fittest survive, only the fittest *should* survive. Their social policies were a grotesque reflection of the natural process, and, as noted earlier, these two atheistic worldviews have produced the most efficient political killing machines in the history of man.

Another embarrassment for Darwinian evolution is found in the new field of evolutionary psychology, which claims that evolution explains the development not only of the human body but also of human behavior. In their book, *The Natural History of Rape*, authors

## THE REALITY OF MICROEVOLUTION AND MACROEVOLUTION

**MICROEVOLUTION —**
Observed by researchers
(Fossil evidence shows this happened)

*VS.*

**MACROEVOLUTION —**
Never been observed by anyone
(No fossil evidence exists to suggest this happened)

> Hitler's Aryan policies and Engels' Marxism followed natural selection to its logical outcome and concluded that, not only *would* the fittest survive, only the fittest *should* survive.

Randy Thornhill of the University of New Mexico and Craig Palmer of the University of Colorado advance the startling thesis that rape is an evolutionary adaptation—a strategy for maximizing reproductive success. Just like "the leopard's spots and the giraffe's elongated neck," rape is "a natural, biological phenomenon that is a product of the human evolutionary heritage."[27] Nancy Pearcey goes on to explain that:

> Thornhill insisted… that since evolution is true, it MUST also be true that "Every feature of every living thing, including human beings, has an underlying evolutionary background. That's not a debatable matter." Accept evolution, and the reasoning is axiomatic. This explains why other proponents of evolutionary psychology have "discovered" an evolutionary advantage in jealousy, depression, and even infanticide."[28]

Humanists also recognize yet another problem with survival of the fittest. Asimov describes it this way: "In the first place, the phrase 'the survival of the fittest' is not an illuminating one. It implies that those who survive are the 'fittest,' but what is meant by 'fittest'? Why, those are 'fittest' who survive. This is an argument in a circle."[29] In other words, when you say "survival of the fittest," you really aren't saying anything of consequence. It is a tautology—an explanation that includes its own definition.

Obviously, the humanist biologist would like to avoid discussing the struggle for existence whenever possible, but at the same time, humanism needs it to explain natural selection as a mechanism for evolution.

## ADAPTATIONS

Combining mutations with the theory of natural selection provides an explanation for adaptation, yet another concept humanists endorse. "Adaptation" is used to explain why different species evolve specialized abilities that allow them to survive in their particular environmental niches.

Of course, in accepting adaptation as part of the mechanism of evolution, the humanist must overlook (or explain away) all the apparently meaningless adaptations that exist in our world. Darwin admits, "I did not formerly consider sufficiently the existence of structures which, as far as we can . . . judge, are neither beneficial nor injurious, and this I believe to be one of the greatest oversights as yet detected in my work."[30] Huxley attempts to solve this problem for Darwin by explaining seemingly harmful or meaningless adaptations in such a way that

> "The phrase 'survival of the fittest' is not an illuminating one. It implies that those who survive are the 'fittest,' but what is meant by 'fittest'? Why, those are 'fittest' who survive. This is an argument in a circle."
> —Isaac Asimov

they can actually be labeled as beneficial. His attempt becomes absurd, however, when he describes schizophrenia as a useful adaptation. He claims, "genetic theory makes it plain that a clearly disadvantageous genetic character like this cannot persist in this frequency in a population unless it is balanced by some compensating advantage. In this case it appears that the advantage is that schizophrenic individuals are considerably less sensitive than normal persons to histamine, are much less prone to suffer from operative and wound shock, and do not suffer nearly so much from various allergies."[31] Huxley does not say whether he would rather be schizophrenic or suffer from allergies.

## THE FOSSIL RECORD

The final plank on which the theory of evolution rests is the claim that the fossil record gives an accurate account of the transmutation of species, or, macroevolution. "Evolution is a fact," says Sagan, "amply demonstrated by the fossil record."[32] The fossil record is crucial for the evolutionist because it is the only means available by which to observe steps in the evolutionary process. In Darwin's day, the fossil record was incomplete and as a result, there was no fossil evidence that any of the major divisions of nature—plants, fish, amphibians, reptiles, mammals—had been crossed.

More than 150 years ago, Darwin wrote, "The geological record is extremely imperfect and this fact will to a large extent explain why we do not find intermediate varieties, connecting together all the extinct and existing forms of life by the finest graduated steps.

He who rejects these views on the nature of the geological record will rightly reject my whole theory."[33] When Darwin made this claim, he was correct in asserting that the geological record, as scientists knew it then, was imperfect. He was also more objective in his assessment of what a complete fossil record would mean to his theory than are contemporary evolutionists. A century and a half later, the geological record has been thoroughly recovered and scrutinized, and rather than confirming Darwin's theories, the fossils condemn them.

One reason the fossil record undermines evolutionary theory is that many complex life forms appear in the very earliest rocks without any incidence of forms from which they could have evolved. Finding that there were creatures who did not have ancestors necessarily implies special creation. As Brown says, "The evolutionary tree has no trunk."[34]

The explosion of complex life, though, is not the only way in which the fossil record condemns evolution. The lack of fossils supporting the transitional phases between species is perhaps the single most embarrassing topic for evolutionists. And yet, this absence of transitional fossils is undeniable. And it is grudgingly acknowledged by leading evolutionists. David Raup, a geologist, admits, "The record of evolution is still surprisingly jerky and, ironically, we have even fewer examples of evolutionary

> The geological record has been thoroughly recovered and scrutinized, and rather than confirming Darwin's theories, the fossils condemn them.

transition than we had in Darwin's time." [35]

The problem in the evolutionist's inability to produce transitional fossils is made clear by Brown: "If [Darwinian] evolution happened, the fossil record should show continuous and gradual changes from the bottom to the top layers and between all forms of life. Actually, many gaps and discontinuities appear throughout the fossil record."[36] An evolutionary tree with no trunk (no life forms earlier than the already very complex ones in Cambrian rocks) and no branches (no transitional forms) can hardly be called a tree at all.

> The lack of fossils supporting the transitional phases between species is perhaps the single most embarrassing topic for evolutionists.

## A SECOND REVOLUTION

By the late 1800's, Darwin's book had caused a revolution in the way scientists explained the origin and diversity of life. By the mid-1900's, Darwinism had become the accepted scientific theory of origins in academia. The theistic idea that design in nature leads to a Designer was replaced by Darwin's "god" of natural selection.

During the 1950's, however, a few vocal scientists expressed grave doubts concerning the merits of Darwin's theory. Whitcomb and Morris (*The Genesis Flood*) led the debate but, because of their "young earth" leanings, were rebuffed as religious fundamentalists by much of the scientific community.

However, with the 1986 publication of Michael Denton's *Evolution, A Theory in Crisis*, the emphasis was placed not on the biblical interpretation of origins but squarely on the lack of credible scientific evidence for the Darwinian view. Denton's devastating critique, along with Thaxton and Bradley's *The Mystery of Life's Origin*, exposed severe difficulties in the possibility of a naturalistic explanation for life. By arguing that DNA contains highly specified information, Thaxton and Bradley successfully revealed the marks of intelligent origin and boldly reintroduced into meaningful scientific discussion the concept of "design."

In the 1990's, law professor Phillip Johnson took up the challenge of dismantling Darwin's dominance over science by arguing logically through the scientific weaknesses of the Darwinian paradigm in *Darwin on Trial*. His subsequent book, *Reason in the Balance*, further revealed the unfounded naturalistic assumptions of Darwinism.

In a growing movement now known as "design theory", a number of other scientists and philosophers have joined Johnson in researching and writing on the topic.[37] Their aim is to open a broader discussion of the positive scientific examples of complex design in order to bolster the premise that intelligence is responsible for the diversity of life on earth. Michael Behe's *Darwin's Black Box*, for example, reveals a biochemist's-eye-view of life's aston-

> Systems essential to all life forms are "irreducibly complex," meaning that gradual Darwinian style build-up from simpler parts cannot account for their origin.

ishingly complex biomolecular systems that stands as a rebuttal to Dawkins' "blind watchmaker" thesis. With examples from blood clotting and the human immune system to the synthesis of nucleotides (the building blocks of DNA), Behe explains how these systems are "irreducibly complex," meaning that a gradual Darwinian style build-up from simpler parts cannot account for their origin.

In addition, William Dembski points out that searching for design is not new to the scientific enterprise, since the entire government-funded SETI Project (Search for Extra-Terrestrial Intelligence) is based on the notion that an intelligent agent beyond our earth can be detected if we receive a coded, specified message from space.[38] Using this same logic, called information theory, scientists seek to uncover evidences of specified "messages" inherent in biological systems. The clearest example is the genetic code—foundational for all living things. Scientists compare the genetic code to language, where different letters are assembled to make words, which are strung together into sentences to convey meaning. In a similar way, protein bases (like letters of the alphabet) combine to make genes that provide a meaningful sentence structure for living systems. Some scientists suggest that a single cell contains more coded information than all 30 volumes of the *Encyclopedia Britannica*.[39] With the advent of information theory, theists are once again taking the high ground in the origins debate.

# CONCLUSION

Secular Humanist biology rests its case for evolution on six specific planks: spontaneous generation, natural selection, struggle for existence, beneficial mutations, adaptations, and the fossil record. And yet, Jonathan Wells, who holds a PhD. in molecular and cell biology, draws attention to the inadequacies of the major "evidences" for macroevolution. In *Icons of Evolution*, Wells examines ten examples used to support evolu-

tion found in most biology textbooks, including such well-known items as the evolutionary "tree of life," common ancestry from similar bone structures, pictures of similarities in early embryos, peppered moths resting on tree trunks, the size of beaks on Darwin's finches, and fruit fly experiments. Using recent studies published in peer-reviewed scientific journals, Wells reveals how each of these "icons" of evolution misrepresent the truth. Take "Darwin's Finches," for example. Darwinists claim that the different species of finches Darwin studied on the Galapagos Islands represent evidence of nature selecting for the size of their beaks. The problem is, more recent studies of the finches reveal that the size of finch beaks fluctuate during severe weather conditions such as drought, and go back when more normal weather patterns return. So there is no movement in any certain evolutionary direction, but variation around a norm. In addition, we start with finches and end with finches; there is no movement toward a different *kind* of animal, which macroevolution demands if the Darwinian theory is true. Wells concludes, "This is not science. This is not truth-seeking. This is dogmatism, and it should not be allowed to dominate scientific research and teaching."[40]

Humanism relies on macroevolution for much more than a theory about the origin of life. The Secular Humanist trusts evolution as a "fact" worthy of being the foundation for many humanistic ideas about theology, philosophy, ethics, and even social and political ideals for the future. In truth, the humanist considers evolution the correct foundation for every individual's worldview and believes that the world can be properly understood only from this perspective. For this reason, humanists encourage teaching evolution as "fact" throughout our educational system—thereby relegating the supernatural, especially God, to the world of literature and mythology. The humanist does not expect evolution to be taught as a theory just in the biology classroom, but rather believes, in the words of Julian Huxley, that "it is essential for evolution to become the central core of any educational system, because it is evolution, in the broad sense, that links inorganic nature with life, and the stars with earth, and matter with mind, and animals with man. Human history is a continuation of biological evolution in a different form."[41]

However, as we have briefly demonstrated in this chapter, an objective scientific method does not support Darwinian evolution. Instead, we have shown how macroevolution rests squarely on philosophical naturalism, a religiously held dogma of Secular Humanists. And since naturalistic evolution is the only theory allowed in public schools—to the exclusion of other viable scientific theories such as intelligent design—then we have affirmed the fact that Secular Humanism is the established religious view when it comes to teaching biology. That being the case, we agree with biologist H. P. Yockey when he says, "Since science has not the vaguest idea how life originated on earth . . . it would be honest to admit this to students . . . . Leaders in science . . . should stop polarizing the minds of students and younger creative scientists with statements for which faith is the only evidence."[42]

**What can you do to remedy this situation?** Some school districts are trying to provide a more balanced approach to teaching about the origin of life. For example, the State Board of Education for Alabama provides a sticker to be placed in each biology textbook explaining to students the difference between scientific facts and theory, micro- and macroevolution, and several areas that the theory of macroevolution does not explain. The text of this sticker is provided below. As an action point, you may want to check into how the issue of origins is taught in your school district and, if evolution is the only theory discussed, approach your local school board to suggest that a more broad-minded, unbiased, and balanced approach be considered.

## A MESSAGE FROM THE ALABAMA STATE BOARD OF EDUCATION

*(Adopted by the Board on November 9, 1995, printed on stickers, and affixed inside public high school biology textbooks)*

This textbook discusses evolution, a controversial theory some scientists present as a scientific explanation for the origin of living things, such as plants, animals and humans.

No one was present when life first appeared on earth. Therefore, any statement about life's origins should be considered as theory, not fact. The word, "evolution" may refer to many types of change. Evolution describes changes that occur within a species. (White moths, for example, may "evolve" into gray moths.) This process is microevolution, which can be observed and described as fact. Evolution may also refer to the change of one living thing to another, such as reptiles into birds. This process, called macroevolution, has never been observed and should be considered a theory. Evolution also refers to the unproven belief that random, undirected forces produced a world of living things.

There are many unanswered questions about the origin of life which are not mentioned in your textbooks, including:

• Why did the major groups of animals suddenly appear in the fossil record (known as the Cambrian Explosion)?

• Why have no new major groups of living things appeared in the fossil record in a long time?

• Why do major groups of plants and animals have no transitional forms in the fossil record?

• How did you and all living things come to possess such a complete and complex set of "instructions" for building a living body?

Study hard and keep an open mind. Someday you may contribute to the theories of how living things appeared on earth.

## RECOMMENDED READING

Behe, Michael J., *Darwin's Black Box: The Biochemical Challenge to Evolution.* New York: The Free Press, 1996.

Richard Dawkins, *The Blind Watchmaker: Why the Evidence of Evolution Reveals a Universe Without Design.* W.W. Norton and Company, Reissue, 1996.

Dembski, William A. *Intelligent Design: The Bridge Between Science and Theology.* Downers Grove, IL: InterVarsity Press, 1999.

Denton, Michael. *Evolution: A Theory in Crisis: New Developments in Science Are Challenging Orthodox Darwinism.* Bethesda, Md.: Adler and Adler, 1986.

Wells, Jonathan. *Icons of Evolution: Science or Myth? Why Much of What We Teach About Evolution is Wrong.* Washington, DC: Regnery Publishing, 2000.

Witham, Larry. *By Design: Science and the Search for God.* San Francisco, CA: Encounter Books, 2003.

## ENDNOTES

1. Paul Kurtz, "Is Everyone a Humanist?," in *The Humanist Alternative*, ed. Paul Kurtz (Buffalo: Prometheus Books, 1973), p. 177.

2. Irving Kristol, *Commentary.* August 1991.

3. Phillip E. Johnson, *Reason in the Balance* (Downers Grove, IL: InterVarsity Press, 1995), p. 103.

4. Charles Colson, *Wagging the Dog: The Invented War between Science and Christianity* ("BreakPoint" Radio Commentary, August 30, 2002), www.breakpoint.org/Breakpoint/ChannelRoot/FeaturesGroup/BreakPointCommentaries/Wagging+the+Dog.htm

5. Charles Colson, *Wagging the Dog.*

6. Nancy R. Pearcey and Charles B. Thaxton, *The Soul of Science,* (Wheaton, IL: Crossway Book, 1994) p. 19.

7. Norman L. Geisler, *Baker Encyclopedia Of Christian Apologetics,* (Grand Rapids, MI: Baker Book House, 1999), p. 346.

8. *Humanist Manifesto I* (Buffalo: Prometheus Books, [1933] 1980), p. 8.

9. *Humanist Manifesto II* (Buffalo: Prometheus Books, [1973] 1980), p. 17.

10. *Humanist Manifesto 2000* (Amherst, NY: Prometheus Books, 2000), p. 24.

11. *Humanist Manifesto 2000*, p. 24.

12. Ibid.

13. Thomas Sowell, *Inside American Education*, p. 59.

14. *Humanist Manifesto 2000*, p. 26.

15. Nancy R. Pearcey, "Creation Mythology: Defenders of Darwinism resort to suppressing data and teaching outright falsehoods." (*World* Magazine, June 24, 2000).

16. Carl Sagan, *Cosmos* (New York: Random House, 1980), p. 4.

17. Isaac Asimov, in *Science and Creationism*, ed. Ashley Montagu (Oxford: Oxford University Press, 1984), p. 183.

18. Julian Huxley, "At Random," a television preview on Nov. 21, 1959. Also, Sol Tax, *Evolution of Life* (Chicago: University of Chicago Press, 1960), p. 1.

19. Phillip E. Johnson, *The Right Questions*, p. 79-80.

20. Benjamin Wiker. *Moral Darwinism: How We Became Hedonists* (Downers Grove, IL: InterVarsity Press, 2002) p. 25-6.

21. S. Matthew D'Agostino, *Free Inquiry*, Winter 2001/2, p. 39.

22. Darwin, *The Origin of the Species*, cited in Sagan, *Cosmos*, p. 23.

23. Carl Sagan, *The Dragons of Eden* (New York: Random House, 1977), p. 6.

24. Charles Darwin, *The Origin of the Species* (London: John Murray, 1859), p. 84.

25. Richard Dawkins, *The Blind Watchmaker: Why the Evidence of Evolution Reveals a Universe Without Design* (W.W. Norton and Company, Reissue, 1996).

26. Corliss Lamont, *The Philosophy of Humanism*, rev. ed. (New York: Frederick Ungar, [1949] 1982), p. 120.

27. Quoted in Nancy Pearcey, "Darwin's Dirty Secret," *World* (March 13, 2000), from Randy Thornhill and Craig Palmer, *The Natural History of Rape* (MIT Press, 2001).

28. Nancy Pearcey, "Darwin's Dirty Secret."

29. Isaac Asimov, *The Wellsprings of Life* (London: Abelard-Schuman, 1960), p. 57.

30. Charles Darwin, as cited in Norman Macbeth, *Darwin Retried* (Boston: Gambit, 1971), p. 73.

31. Julian Huxley, *Essays of a Humanist* (New York: Harper & Row, 1964), p. 67.

32. Sagan, *The Dragons of Eden*, p. 6.

33. Charles Darwin, *The Origin of Species*, reprint of sixth edition (London: John Murray, 1902), pp. 341-2.

34. Brown, *In the Beginning*, p. 3.

35. David Raup, "Conflicts Between Darwin and Paleontology," *Field Museum of Natural History Bulletin*, January 1979, p. 25.

36. Brown, *In the Beginning*, p. 3.

37. See Michael Behe's *Darwin's Black Box*, William Dembski's *Mere Creation* and *Intelligent Design*, or for a simplified and entertaining reading, try Robert Newman and John Wiester's *What's Darwin Got to Do with It?*

38. William Dembski and Michael Behe, *Intelligent Design: The Bridge Between Science and Theology* (Downers Grove, IL: InterVarsity Press, 1999).

39. Evolutionist Richard Dawkins uses this analogy in his book, *Climbing Mount Improbable*. While Dawkins acknowledged the incredible complexity in each cell, he still clings to the idea that small mutations selected by nature can account for a step-by-step progress up the mountain called evolution. To counter Dawkins' premise, read Michael Behe's *Darwin's Black Box*, where Behe offers numerous biological examples to demonstrate the improbability of this ever happening without the aid of a Supernatural Mind.

40. Wells, Jonathan. *Icons of Evolution: Science or Myth? Why Much of What We Teach About Evolution is Wrong* (Washington, DC: Regnery Publishing, 2000), p. 248.

41. Julian Huxley, "At Random," a television preview on Nov. 21, 1959.

42. H. P. Yockey, "Self Organization Origin of Life Scenarios and Information Theory," *Journal of Theoretical Biology*, vol. 91 (1981), p. 29.


(1) Evolution of Man graphic: From Countering Culture video (2004 Summit Ministries: Manitou Springs, CO)


(2) ACLU sign: From Countering Culture video (2004 Summit Ministries: Manitou Springs, CO)

# CHAPTER 6

# Mixing Religion and Politics

"Humanists everywhere have defended the
separation of religion and state.
We believe that the state should be secular,
neither for nor against religion."[1]
—PAUL KURTZ

"It is secular humanism that is the orthodox
metaphysical-theological basis of the two
modern political philosophies—
socialism and liberalism."[2]
—IRVING KRISTOL

"In this [university] arena, it is not
Protestantism, Catholicism, or Judaism which
will emerge the victor, but secular humanism, a
cultural force which in many respects is stronger
in the United States than any of the major
religious groups or any alliance among them."[3]
—LEO PFEFFER

When Wisconsin public high school senior Rachel Horner provided the school faculty with the lyrics of a song she planned to sing at her graduation ceremony, they came "unglued." The reason? The song mentions God three times. The school principal told Rachel that "God" might offend some of the audience and would violate the "separation of church and state." The principal suggested Rachel replace references to "God" with "He," "Him" and "His."

> "By prohibiting students from uttering 'God,' the school is stifling religious freedom, not advancing it."
> —David Limbaugh

When Miss Horner filed a federal lawsuit, the school reversed its decision concerning the song but nevertheless insisted she not mention God in the introduction to her performance. David Limbaugh remarks that "in their obsession to achieve total church-state separation through the First Amendment Establishment Clause in the name of fostering religious freedom, the separationist zealots are suppressing religious freedom, which is also protected by that same First Amendment. By prohibiting students from uttering 'God,' the school is stifling religious freedom, not advancing it."[4]

In another instance, first grader Zachary Hood was not allowed by his teacher to read a story titled "A Big Family" from his own copy of *The Beginner's Bible.* Although the teacher rewarded students' reading proficiency by allowing them to bring from home and read to the class a story of their choice, and even though Zachary's selection does not mention God, the teacher refused to allow him to read it "because of its religious content."[5]

How have we gotten to the point where public school officials are afraid of having the word "God" mentioned in public places? Does this represent the correct way to apply the concept of "separation of church and state"? Or is this a gross misunderstanding of the founder's intent regarding the role of religion and government? To better understand why we are experiencing restrictions on religious freedom, we must first understand the influence of Secular Humanism in law, politics, and education.

## WHAT HUMAN RIGHTS?

Charles Darwin's evolutionary theory profoundly changed our understanding of law. "There proceeded during the 19th Century," says Huxley, "under the influence of the evolutionary concept, a thoroughgoing transformation of older studies like . . . Law."[6] A commentary by Oliver Wendell Holmes, Jr., appointed to the Supreme Court in 1902, epitomizes this transformation in attitude toward law: "I see no reason for attributing to man a significance different in kind from that which belongs to a baboon or a grain of sand."[7]

It is no small matter when a U.S. Supreme Court justice proclaims a sea change in the understanding of mankind and our innate rights. What we think of our significance as humans reverberates through the way we govern ourselves. Holmes' statement is stunning in

> If laws and morality evolve, could certain rights which we assume today evolve out of existence tomorrow?

*"I see no reason for attributing to man a significance different in kind from that which belongs to a baboon...," observed Oliver Wendell Holmes, Jr. (U.S. Supreme Court Justice, 1902-32).*

itself, but even more so when the worldview it reflects is traced to its root. The outworking of Justice Holmes' philosophy in the area of law is organically connected to his view of psychology—man is not special in any way, but simply a part of nature. This psychology stems from the assumption of biological evolution which, as we noted in the last chapter, draws nourishment from the roots of philosophical naturalism and theological atheism. Yet, the belief that man is an evolving animal on par with the baboon creates a moral and legal dilemma: why should man enjoy rights not enjoyed by other animals? Morris B. Storer puts the question this way:

> What is there that's different about a human being that dictates the right to life for all humans (unarguably in most circumstances) where most people acknowledge no such right in other animals? That justifies equal right to liberty where we fence the others in, equal justice under law where the other animals are not granted any trial at all.[8]

Further, if laws and morality evolve, why don't rights evolve? Could certain rights which we assume today

evolve out of existence tomorrow? Answers to such questions are, at best, difficult to deduce when God is removed from the equation. Nevertheless, the humanist makes many bold claims about, and even champions, "human rights." Kurtz conjures a baseless conclusion when he declares, "There are common human rights that must be respected by everyone."[9] Humanists accept the existence of certain rights as indisputable. But how can they be so convinced of rights worthy of protection by law when their source is man, the evolving animal?

## THE LOSS OF NATURAL LAW

The phrase "natural law" was coined in the 1700's to describe God's design built into the nature of things, including the physical, moral, and civil realms. The corollary, "natural rights," is enshrined in the famous phrase from the Declaration of Independence, "all men are created equal, and are endowed by their Creator with certain unalienable rights." These twin concepts of natural law and natural rights became the bedrock for a new form of civil government—a constitutional republic. The philosophical underpinnings of the United States of America produced a land of freedom and opportunity unprecedented in the history of mankind.

However, in recent years, America's experiment in ordered liberty has drifted frighteningly toward a micro-managed system of "Big Brother" knows best. This has come about because the concepts of natural

> "When, one wonders, in evolutionary history did hominids first acquire natural rights?"
> —Delos McKown

law and natural rights have been systematically removed from our law schools and replaced with a humanist view of legal theory that, in turn, has born fruit in the political arena where our laws are made.

Humanism is incompatible with the theory of natural law and natural rights. Humanist writer, Delos McKown, makes this clear when he asks the pointed question, "When, one wonders, in evolutionary history did hominids first acquire natural rights?"[10] The humanist must abandon natural law to develop a legal theory consistent with the basic assumptions

> Legal positivism is the concept that governing laws are derived not from pre-existing natural law but from human judgments of what renders the most functional operation of society.

of his evolutionary worldview. Again, Paul Kurtz offers the logically consistent humanist position: "Am I not bringing in a doctrine of natural rights that are prior to political policy? No, I reject any such fiction."[11] Indeed, Kurtz sees rights as recently evolved through human systems: "Most . . . rights have evolved out of the cultural, economic, political, and social structures that have prevailed."[12]

Kurtz also denies the existence of natural law: "How are these principles [of equality, freedom, etc.] to be justified? They are not derived from a divine or natural law, nor do they have any special metaphysical status. They are rules offered to govern how we shall behave. They can be justified only by reference to their results."[13] Here, then, is a statement attempting to create a coherent humanist approach to law. Kurtz believes that laws are derived not from natural law but

from human judgments of what renders the most functional operation of society. This approach to legal theory is known as legal positivism.

## POSITIVELY HUMANIST LAW

Legal positivism (or positive law) claims that the state is the ultimate authority for creating law. Since God is a mythical being and the idea of natural law is legal fiction, man must rely on his reason to discern what is legal, and those who determine the law are those in power—in

> Legal positivism claims that the state is the ultimate authority for creating law.

government. Max Hocutt is one humanist who understands the need to abandon natural law, thereby making mankind responsible for the creation of all laws: "Human beings may, and do, make up their own rules. All existing moralities and all existing laws are human artifacts, products of human society, social conventions."[14] If this is true, then government is the final source of legal truths since it is the state that enacts—or in the humanist model, creates—laws. There is no Creator upon whose laws to base our own.

Legal positivism spills over into the realm of rights as well. The state becomes the source of all human rights which can no longer be referred to as natural, only constitutional. McKown says, "Natural human rights exist only among human beings; that is, one holds natural rights only against other natural rights holders. Maintaining this point, however, begs the question of natural rights and leaves us wondering how such rights differ from constitutional or legal rights."[15] McKown concludes that if the concept of natural rights is simply question-begging, then legal rights are all that exist: "Our eyes and our idealism ought to be focused, rather, on the only kind of rights that can be realized: legal rights . . ."[16]

The philosophy of positive law produces an arbitrary legal code. When one combines positivism with the humanist position that mankind and his laws are in a continuing state of evolution, humanist legal theory grows strangely capricious. Just how much this is so is made clear by Kurtz, who declares, "Laws, however, provide us only with general guides for behavior; how they work out depends upon the context."[17]

Arbitrary law is a dire house of cards. "Rights" created by humanist legal theory are in mortal danger from the government's potential to take advantage of its position as the ultimate source of legal truth. Rights granted by nothing other than governmental edict can also be removed by edict. Some humanists recognize this danger: "If there were no moral, humanistic foundations for the legal rights we ought to have," says Tibor Machan, "we would face the prospect of governments that exist without any limits, without any standards by which to ascertain whether or not they are just and morally legitimate."[18] This is the heart of the problem created by humanist legal theory: the state is given the authority of a god. "Big Brother" wields all power. The individual is merely a cog in the machinery of the state.

> When one combines positivism with the humanist position that mankind and his laws are in a continuing state of evolution, humanist legal theory grows strangely capricious.

## RESULTS OF POSITIVE LAW

The shift in our understanding of law is reflected in a number of legal decisions handed down over the past half century. In 1963(*Abington v. Schempp*), the Supreme Court ruled that Bible reading before classes in school was contrary to the First Amendment's Establishment Clause. While the Court ruled only "devotional" Bible reading unconstitutional, many school districts have gone far beyond the court's ruling and even prohibit teachers from having a Bible on their desks!

In the 1973 *Roe v. Wade* decision, the Court ruled 7-2 that a woman has the freedom to abort her unborn child based on a constitutional "right to privacy." Oddly, this right had gone unrecognized by previous courts for almost 200 years! And in *Stone v. Graham* (1980), the Justices ruled the Ten Commandments could not be displayed on public school walls for fear students might read them and feel compelled to obey them—even though the Decalogue is etched in stone behind the bench of the very Supreme Court justices who handed down this ruling.

In *Planned Parenthood v. Casey* (1992), the majority court wrote, "At the heart of liberty is the right to define one's own concept of existence, of meaning, of the universe and of the mystery of human life. Beliefs about these matters could not define the attributes of personhood were they formed under compulsion of the State." Upholding a woman's right to abort her child, this ruling reached a new level of postmodern moral relativism. This section of the opinion, known as the "mystery clause," opens the way to unbounded personal freedom to define one's "own concept of existence." Subjectivism of this magnitude leaves little room to outlaw any kind of behavior, no matter how immoral, since individuals can claim their bizarre behavior defines the "mystery of human life" for them.

## THE 10 COMMANDMENTS—Exodus 20:1-17

*Then God spoke all these words:*

*²I am the Lord your God, who brought you out of the land of Egypt, out of the place of slavery.*

**#1** *³Do not have other gods besides Me.*

**#2** *⁴Do not make an idol for yourself, whether in the shape of anything in the heavens above or on the earth below or in the waters under the earth. ⁵You must not bow down to them or worship them; for I, the Lord your God, am a jealous God, punishing the children for the fathers' sin, to the third and fourth [generations] of those who hate Me, ⁶but showing faithful love to a thousand [generations] of those who love Me and keep My commands.*

**#3** *⁷Do not misuse the name of the Lord your God, because the Lord will punish anyone who misuses His name.*

**#4** *⁸Remember to dedicate the Sabbath day: ⁹You are to labor six days and do all your work, ¹⁰but the seventh day is a Sabbath to the Lord your*

*God. You must not do any work—you, your son or daughter, your male or female slave, your livestock, or the foreigner who is within your gates. ¹¹For the Lord made the heavens and the earth, the sea, and everything in them in six days; then He rested on the seventh day. Therefore the Lord blessed the Sabbath day and declared it holy.*

**#5** *¹²Honor your father and your mother so that you may have a long life in the land that the Lord your God is giving you.*

**#6** *¹³Do not murder.*

**#7** *¹⁴Do not commit adultery.*

**#8** *¹⁵Do not steal.*

**#9** *¹⁶Do not give false testimony against your neighbor.*

**#10** *¹⁷Do not covet your neighbor's house. Do not covet your neighbor's wife, his male or female slave, his ox or donkey, or anything that belongs to your neighbor.*

Truth becomes what is true for the individual. Based on this legal reasoning, it is but a tiny step to legalizing infanticide and euthanasia.

More recently, the *Lawrence v. Texas* case of 2003 restated the above "mystery clause" in striking down a Texas law against homosexual sodomy. This action opened the floodgates for homosexuals to force acceptance of their lifestyles on the public—including the rights of homosexuals to marry and adopt children—thus overturning the precedent in more than two millennia of Western Culture and undermining the family as the only stable foundation for sustaining society.

# SEPARATING CHURCH AND STATE

Another result of positive law and the corresponding secularization of politics has been an increasingly hostile relationship between church and state. The concept of "separation of church and state" has taken on a radically different meaning than was originally intended. Chuck Colson explains the background:

Radical separationists see themselves as heirs of Thomas Jefferson. During his presidency,

Jefferson wrote a letter to a Baptist group in Danbury, Connecticut, in which he described the First Amendment as having set up a "wall of separation" between church and state.

That is the origin of the "wall of separation" metaphor: not the Constitution, or any of its amendments; not the Declaration of Independence—just a letter from a president to the Danbury Baptists. He wrote the letter to assure them that the federal government could not set up a state church and thereby disenfranchise those, like Baptists, who would be unwilling to join that state church. This had been the history of Baptists in England, and they were concerned. The president's letter put their minds at ease by assuring them that, as religious believers, they had a place in the public square that could not be taken away from them.

Regrettably, the Supreme Court took up the "wall" metaphor and misapplied it. Thus the phrase that Jefferson used to reassure religious people became the instrument of radical separationism—government, that is, cannot help religion at all.[19]

Because it is repeated so often, the idea of separation of church and state has become like an urban legend that takes on a life of its own. This misapplied notion has led to bizarre incidents such as the ones mentioned at the beginning of this chapter, where in a nation founded on religious liberty, a high school senior is intimidated for trying to sing about her belief in God at her high school graduation or a child is kept from reading a Bible story to his classmates.

> Because it is repeated so often, the idea of separation of church and state has become like an urban legend that takes on a life of its own.

Yet, the truth is quite different from the current myth of separation. The founders of this nation never intended that religious ideas would be eradicated from public discourse and political deliberations, nor even the education of our children. Even the late president John F. Kennedy understood the connection between religion and government. He prepared the following words for a speech:

> We in this country, in this generation, are by destiny rather than choice the watchman on the walls of world freedom. We ask therefore, that we may be worthy of our power and responsibility, that we may exercise our strength with wisdom and restraint, and that we may achieve in our time and for all time the ancient vision of peace on earth, goodwill toward men. That must always be our goal. For as was written long ago, "Except the Lord keep the city, the watchman waketh but in vain."

Kennedy never delivered these words. The day was November 22, 1963, and as his motorcade wound through the streets of Dallas, Texas, an assassin's bullet took his life. Yet his words echo another statesman from 174 years earlier, Benjamin Franklin, inventor and public servant from Pennsylvania. Franklin was 80 years old when he attended the Constitutional Convention that gave birth to the United States. After several weeks of bickering between the delegates, Franklin rose to speak. As a hush came over the room, the most senior delegate addressed his remarks to the President of the Convention, George Washington:

I have lived, Sir, a long time, and the longer I live, the more convincing proofs I see of this truth—that God governs in the affairs of men. And if a sparrow cannot fall to the ground without His notice, is it probable that an empire can rise without His aid? We have been assured, Sir, in the sacred writings, that 'except the Lord build the House they labour in vain that build it.' I firmly believe this.

Franklin went on to recommend to the delegates that they begin each day in corporate prayer. George Washington, in his Farewell Address after his second term in office, said, "Of all the dispositions and habits which lead to political prosperity, religion and morality are indispensable supports.... Virtue or morality is a necessary spring of popular government."[20] Similarly, our second president, John Adams, wrote "religion and morality are the only foundations... of republicanism and of all free governments."[21] And we even find the following words of Thomas Jefferson etched into the memorial dedicated to him in Washington, D.C.: "God who gave us life gave us liberty. And can the liberties of a nation be thought secure when we have removed their only firm basis, a conviction in the minds of the people that these liberties are of the Gift of God?" We could cite hundreds of similar comments made by those who formed our government, as well as

> The founders of this nation never intended for religious ideas to be eradicated from public discourse and political deliberations, nor even the education of our children.

later political leaders, Supreme Court Justices, and historians.[22]

As is evident from these examples, there has been a sea change in how our politicians and public officials approach religious liberty. Unless Christians wake up soon, they will find themselves engulfed in a Secular Humanist society that no longer tolerates any expression of religion—public or private. It has happened as recently as this past century under Marxist and Nazi governments, and it could happen again.

## THE EVOLUTION OF LAW

Trusting the state as the absolute basis for law also leads to legal *relativism* since governments themselves change. Sidney Hook expands upon the implications of legal relativism: "The rights of man depend upon his nature, needs, capacities, and aspirations, not upon his origins. Children have rights not because they are our creatures but because of what they are and will become. It is not God but the human community that endows its members with rights."[23] This is the height of relativism! Since human nature itself is always in evolutionary flux and the needs and capacities of every individual differs from fellow human beings, it follows that each generation's and each individual's rights must vary in proportion to these differences. What are the possibilities here? That I have fewer rights than a concert pianist since he is more capable than I? Do I have more (or less?) rights than needy people in Ethiopia? Will some who evidence further evolutionary development than others be entitled to a greater share of human rights? Clearly, founding rights on human characteristics or governmental policies is a dead end street. Rights and laws not based on the character of God will with certainty be arbitrary.

An example of the extreme to which relativism

can lead is provided by the recent concern some humanists' have cultivated for animal rights. Kenneth L. Feder and Michael Alan Park write:

> [T]here is no objective rationale for elevating our species into a category separate from the rest of the animals with whom we share the presence of a nervous system, the ability to feel pain, and behaviors aimed at avoiding pain. Thus, the fundamental rights we accord ourselves must be equally applicable to any other organism with these same characteristics.[24]

The result has been an entirely new approach to law, including the inclusion of "animal law" as a course of study in many law schools. The study of animal law, in some cases, seeks to take certain rights that were once reserved for Homo sapiens and extend them to some animals. For example, "The Great Ape Legal Project" seeks to secure for gorillas, chimpanzees, and orangutans "the right to life, the protection of individual liberty, and the prohibition of torture."[25] Consistent with their evolutionary bias, Secular Humanists see no distinction between humans and the rest of the animal kingdom. Men and rats are viewed as equals, with no favoritism displayed in the realm of rights. This view strips man of his dignity as created in the image of God and denies God's will for mankind over His creation (Genesis 1:28), thus rendering human

rights as transitory and meaningless. Toads and Tasmanian devils are as deserving of rights as we are.

We must seriously consider: do lions

> **GENESIS 1:28**
>
> *God blessed them, and God said to them, "Be fruitful, multiply, fill the earth, and subdue it. Rule the fish of the sea, the birds of the sky, and every creature that crawls on the earth."*

have the right, according to the Secular Humanist view, to pursue happiness, even if that entails depriving jackals (or humans!) of their right to life? Will we bestow rights on plants as well, thereby starving the human race for fear of "murdering" a fellow living, evolutionary organism? The absurdity is apparent—as obvious as the absurdity that some animal rights advocates display more affection for bald eagles in the shell than for human babies in the womb. But the absurdity follows necessarily from worldviews that base human rights on temporal, changeable institutions and ideologies. The danger of legal relativism should be obvious to all. It is little exaggeration to say that under positivist law, an individual could one day awaken to find that old people have been decreed illegal and thus fit for execution. When the state is the only basis for law, any law may be conceived.

Hitler, Stalin, and many others used positive law to murder millions, passing laws to eliminate Jews, gyp-

*Memorials to great leaders of the past are a reminder of what they believed that made them—and us—great.*

## DECLARATION ON GREAT APES

*(See www.greatapeproject.org)*

We demand the extension of the community of equals to include all great apes: human beings, chimpanzees, bonobos, gorillas and orangutans.

The community of equals is the moral community within which we accept certain basic moral principles or rights as governing our relations with each other and enforceable at law. Among these principles or rights are the following:

### 1. The Right to Life

The lives of members of the community of equals are to be protected. Members of the community of equals may not be killed except in very strictly defined circumstances, for example, self-defense.

### 2. The Protection of Individual Liberty

Members of the community of equals are not to be arbitrarily deprived of their liberty; if they should be imprisoned without due legal process, they have the right to immediate release. The detention of those who have not been convicted of any crime, or of those who are not criminally liable, should be allowed only where it can be shown to be for their own good, or necessary to protect the public from a member of the community who would clearly be a danger to others if at liberty. In such cases, members of the community of equals must have the right to appeal, either directly or, if they lack the relevant capacity, through an advocate, to a judicial tribunal.

### 3. The Prohibition of Torture

The deliberate infliction of severe pain on a member of the community of equals, either wantonly or for an alleged benefit to others, is regarded as torture, and is wrong.

sies, the sick, landowners, Christians, or anyone they had an urge to destroy—which generally means anyone who stood in the way of their absolute domination of every person and action in society. In America, laws that many people considered inconceivable a few years ago now provide standards by which we must live. Abortion has been legalized because, suddenly, the state decided that a baby in the womb may not be a baby after all. Perhaps one day, infanticide will be legalized because the state will have decided that a baby is not a human being until it can walk or talk. And with the legalization of sodomy (in the Lawrence v. Texas case cited above) many commentators predict the next logical move of the courts is to legalize pedophilia, incest, polygamy, and even bestiality! The distinction between right and wrong is tenuous in a society that subscribes to atheistic legal positivism.

Conversely, natural law applied to society results in practical and just legal structures. Based on a belief in the character of God, a moral order, man created in the image of God, and the coming of Jesus Christ in the flesh, the Christian worldview has produced the concept of common law, the Magna Carta, the Declaration of Independence, and the Constitution of the United States. The Magna Charta resulted in a just government in England; likewise, the application of biblical and natural law to the U.S. Constitution shaped America's legal structure. Because her founding

> Hitler, Stalin, and many others used positive law to murder millions, passing laws to eliminate Jews, gypsies, the sick, landowners, Christians, or anyone they had an urge to destroy.

fathers apprehended the nature of man correctly and divided power appropriately, America instituted a system of law that protects human rights and individual dignity and is historically the envy of much of the world. "There is no country in the whole world," said Alexis de Tocqueville, "in which the Christian religion retains a greater influence over the souls of men than in America; and there can be no greater proof of its utility, and of its conformity to human nature, than that its influence is most powerfully felt over the most enlightened and free nation of the earth."[26]

Contrast such legal history with the history of positive law in the first fifty years of the twentieth century: "No half-century ever witnessed slaughter on such a scale," said Robert Jackson, "such cruelties and inhumanities, such wholesale deportations of peoples into slavery, such annihilations of minorities." Ideas have consequences. And the consequences of legal positivism are catastrophic.[27]

## THE EDUCATION CONNECTION

Secular Humanists have used the club of "separation" to change the face of education. As Charles Potter stated over 70 years ago, "Education is the most powerful ally of Humanism, and every American public school is a school of Humanism. What can the theistic Sunday Schools, meeting for an hour once a week, and teaching only a fraction of the children, do to stem the tide of a five-day program of humanistic teaching?"[28] Potter's words ring true. As non-humanist William F. Buckley observes, "The most influential educators of our time—John Dewey, William Kilpatrick, George Counts, Harold Rugg, and the lot—are out to build a New Social Order... There is not enough room, however, for the New Social Order and religion [Christianity]... The State prefers a secure monopoly for itself. It is intolerably divisive to have God and the State scrapping for disciples."[29]

While "tolerance" and "diversity" are now the hallmarks of educational philosophy, inclusiveness is not extended to the biblical Christian worldview. Instead, the worldview infused in practically every subject in our schools is Secular Humanism (with a smattering of Cosmic Humanism and Marxism thrown in the mix). For example, in religion classes in most universities (and, if it is taught at all, in public schools), the Bible is not considered a holy book that presented to mankind by God but one authored sim-

### WHAT IS THE MAGNA CARTA?

The Magna Carta, or "Great Charter," was a statement of civil rights adopted in England in 1215 A.D. Its 63 specific provisions support fundamental freedoms such as the right to trial by jury of peers and the citizens' redress of grievances. While the charter also addresses particular needs of the political situation of its time, the first provision introduces the concept of essential freedoms:

*In the first place we have granted to God, and by this our present charter confirmed for us and our heirs forever that the English Church shall be free, and shall have her rights entire, and her liberties inviolate; and we will that it be thus observed; which is apparent from this that the freedom of elections, which is reckoned most important and very essential to the English Church, we, of our pure and unconstrained will, did grant, and did by our charter confirm and did obtain the ratification of the same from our lord, Pope Innocent III, before the quarrel arose between us and our barons: and this we will observe, and our will is that it be observed in good faith by our heirs forever. We have also granted to all freemen of our kingdom, for us and our heirs forever, all the underwritten liberties, to be had and held by them and their heirs, of us and our heirs forever.*

ply by men. When it comes to science, naturalism is the philosophical starting point and naturalistic evolution is the only theory allowed as an explanation for the origin of life. Anthropology and sociology assume cultural evolution. Economics and business courses are devoid of biblically based moral principles. Instead, business ethics are taught from a pragmatic standpoint. And history textbooks have systematically omitted the positive contributions of Christians over the centuries, leaving the impression that biblical faith has had little positive influence in shaping culture. Courses in law and political science no longer include a serious study of natural law as the foundation for law. In psychology, only noted Secular Humanists are studied, and children are no longer assured they are created in God's image but are told they have evolved from blue-green algae—ordinary pond scum. How inspiring! No wonder "self-esteem" education has become the rage in recent years!

Is there any hard evidence that the humanist educational agenda is reaching its intended audience? According to a nationwide survey by researchers at the University of California, Los Angeles, "More college freshmen today describe themselves as politically liberal than at any time since the Vietnam War." As the *LA Times* reports:

> A resurgence of liberalism among the freshmen also is reflected in their attitudes on a range of political and social issues.... "It's a real change, a broad-based trend toward greater liberalism on almost every issue we look at," said Alexander Astin, an education professor at UCLA who started the survey, the nation's largest, in 1966. The researchers measured liberalism by asking students to describe their political views and take positions on certain benchmark issues. For instance, a record percentage—57.9 percent—think gay couples should have the legal right to marry. The highest portion in two decades—32.2 percent—say the death penalty should be abolished. And more than one-third—the highest rate since 1980—say marijuana should be legalized.... while 29.9 percent—the highest figure since 1975—say they are liberal or "far left."[30]

It seems that students are learning their liberal, secular lesson well. The point here is that education does not take place in a worldview vacuum, and since all worldviews are inherently religious, it is impossible to separate religious ideas from the educational enterprise. This is not to say that teachers are intentionally teaching Secular Humanism to their students. For instance, a biology teacher simply may be teaching out of the textbook when it comes to the chapter on evolution. But while an individual teacher's intent may not be secular humanist instruction, the cumulative effect of students being exposed to only a humanist viewpoint on practically every subject comes down to a thorough-going Secular Humanist indoctrination.

Although committed Christians are sprinkled throughout our public schools, colleges, and universities, it is an unfortunate fact that a biblical Christian worldview—once the foundation of education in America—has been replaced with a different religion, Secular Humanism. What is surprising is that Christians have allowed this to happen right under their noses, and while some have recently become

> "Education is the most powerful ally of Humanism, and every American public school is a school of Humanism."—Charles Potter

aware of the problem, countless others are still in denial.

For more on Secular Humanism as the predominant religious viewpoint in public education, see *Clergy in the Classroom: The Religion of Secular Humanism.* It provides over 50 exhibits, mostly from humanist writings, and two extended articles detailing the religious nature of this worldview and its stranglehold on the classroom.

What does the future hold for law, politics, and education in America? It is always risky to predict the future, but one thing is clear: the philosophy presented in the classrooms of today will certainly be the predominate worldview of the leaders of tomorrow. For Christians to regain the intellectual and political high ground, we must be diligently involved in these culture-shaping institutions.

*Having displaced the Christian worldview that fueled educational thought for more than 1500 years, Secular Humanism is now the dominant philosophy behind contemporary Western education.*

## WHERE DO WE GO FROM HERE?

As we watch our society steadily move away from biblical morality in law, politics, education, and general culture, what should be our response as Christians? Some, like Chuck Colson and Nancy Pearcey, call on Christians to confront the culture in two ways. One way is to become personally involved in the lives of others, seeking to win them to the Gospel. Second, we should work to shape the public arena through the application of godly principles. In both cases, Christians must be armed with knowledge, in accord with the theme of this book, so as to go forward with confidence.

In their book, *How Now Shall We Live?*, Colson and Pearcey list numerous ideas for nurturing a better society. For example, they tell how a group of pastors in a crime-ridden area of Boston have rescued inner-city kids from gangs and drugs. Their churches started after-school tutoring programs and Bible studies, formed neighborhood patrols, and counseled juveniles on probation. Within a few years, the crime rate dropped 70 percent, and the desperate neighborhood had turned around.

This kind of "hands-on" work by Christians is what is meant by the "cultural mandate" given in Genesis 1:26-28. Colson and Pearcey urge Christians to carry the lordship of Christ into every area of society: "in the home and the school, in the workshop and the corporate boardroom, on the movie screen and the concert stage, in the city council and the legislative chamber."[31] Practically speaking, for whom will Christians vote if there are no moral candidates running for office? And what does it take in a democracy to run for political office? Money must be raised and issues debated. In fact, that is the way the founders designed our republic to operate, with free and open

| U.S. COLLEGE FRESHMEN ATTITUDES TOWARDS ISSUES THAT DEFINE CONSERVATIVE/LIBERAL VIEWS | | |
|---|---|---|
| **Issue** | **View Held By** | **Historical Precedent** |
| Gay couples should have legal right to marry | 57.9% | All-time high |
| Death penalty should be abolished | 32.2% | Highest in 20 years |
| Marijuana should be legalized | 33% | Highest since 1980 |
| Self-described liberal or "far left" | 29.9% | Highest since 1975 |

public discussion of issues so people can make an informed, intelligent decision on who will represent them in office.

Our nations' political structure is designed to work with the corporate effort of its citizens, Christians included. And if Christians are not involved in the process, including raising money, registering people to vote, and expounding on the issues with a moral viewpoint, our society will slip into a moral abyss for lack of our participation. In fact, this is what has been happening in many Western nations. We have disobeyed the biblical mandate to fill and subdue the earth (Genesis 1:28) and to be the salt and light for the rest of society (Matthew 5:13-16). The case can be made that, as Christians withdrew from the political and educational arenas beginning in the early 1900's, people of a humanist worldview eagerly and easily filled the vacancies. The resulting effect on our society has been predictable—increased illiteracy, crime and immorality, a poverty class dependent on the government dole, a bloated bureaucracy, and a burgeoning code of laws and regulations that encroach on individual freedoms.

God has given those of us living in the United

States and committed to the Gospel of Christ an unprecedented opportunity not only to share the Gospel but also to maintain a government that reflects God-ordained principles of morality and justice. By appealing to God's Law written on the hearts of every man, we can proceed to enact civil laws in keeping with His moral law for the betterment of all mankind. Christians should not miss this chance to be involved on both fronts—spiritually and politically. What an incredible time to be alive!

## BELIEVERS ARE SALT AND LIGHT
*(Matthew 5:13-16, from Jesus' Sermon on the Mount)*

"You are the salt of the earth. But if the salt should lose its taste, how can it be made salty? It's no longer good for anything but to be thrown out and trampled on by men.

"You are the light of the world. A city situated on a hill cannot be hidden. No one lights a lamp and puts it under a basket, but rather on a lampstand, and it gives light for all who are in the house. In the same way, let your light shine before men, so that they may see your good works and give glory to your Father in heaven."

## RECOMMENDED READING

Bastiat, Frederic. *The Law.* Irvington-on-Hudson, NY: 1998.

Budziszewski, J. *The Revenge of Conscience: Politics and the Fall of Man.* Dallas, TX: Spence Publishing Co, 1999.

Eakman, B. K. *Cloning of the American Mind: Eradicating Morality Through Education.* Lafayette, LA: Huntington House, 1998.

George, Robert P. *In Defense of Natural Law.* Oxford University Press, 1999.

Noebel, David A., J. F. Baldwin, and Kevin J. Bywater. *Clergy in the Classroom: The Religion of Secular Humanism* (2nd edition). Manitou Springs, CO: Summit Press, 2001.

Neuhaus, Richard John, Gen. Ed. *Democracy and the Renewal of Public Education.* Grand Rapids, MI: Eerdmans, 1987.

## ENDNOTES

1.  Paul Kurtz, *Humanist Manifesto 2000* (Prometheus Books, 2000) p. 30.

2.  Irving Kristol, *Commentary*, August 1991.

3.  Leo Pfeffer, *Journal of Church and State*, Vol. 19, Spring 1977, p. 211.

4.  David Limbaugh, "A Partial Victory For Religious Freedom." Online commentary at http://www.townhall.com/columnists/davidlimbaugh/dl2003 0607.shtml.

5.  George F. Will, "The Censoring of Zachary," *Newsweek*, March 20, 2000, p. 82.

6.  Cited in John W. Whitehead, *The Second American Revolution* (Elfin, IL: David C. Cook, 1982), p. 46.

7.  Richard Hertz, *Chance and Symbol* (Chicago: University of Chicago Press, 1948), p. 107.

8.  Morris B. Storer, "A Factual Investigation of the Foundations of Morality," in *Humanist Ethics*, ed. Morris B. Storer (Buffalo: Prometheus Books, 1980), p. 291.

9.  Paul Kurtz, *Eupraxophy: Living Without Religion* (Buffalo: Prometheus Books, 1989), p. 158.

10. Delos B. McKown, "Demythologizing Natural Human Rights," *The Humanist*, May/June 1989, p. 22.

11. Paul Kurtz, *The Fullness of Life* (New York: Horizon Press, 1974), p. 162.

12. Paul Kurtz, *Forbidden Fruit* (Buffalo: Prometheus Books, 1988), p. 196.

13. Kurtz, *The Fullness of Life*, p. 162.

14. Max Hocutt, "Toward an Ethic of Mutual Accommodation," in *Humanist Ethics*, ed. Storer, p. 137.

15. McKown, "Demythologizing Natural Human Rights," p. 23-4.

16. Ibid, p. 34.

17. Kurtz, *The Fullness of Life*, p. 163.

18. Tibor R. Machan, "Are Human Rights Real?" *The Humanist*, Nov/Dec 1989, p. 28.

19. Charles Colson, "Historic Preservation: The Wall of Separation," BreakPoint Commentary #030708, 07/08/2003.

20. George Washington, "Address of George Washington, President of the United States... Preparatory to his Declination" (Baltimore: George and Henry S. Keatinge, 1796), p. 22-3.

21. John Adams, *Works*, Vol. IX p. 636, to Benjamin Rush on August 28, 1811.

22. For additional resources on the original intent of the founders concerning their understanding of religion and government, see David Barton's well-researched book, *Original Intent*, or search his website at www.wallbuilders.com.

23. Sidney Hook, "Solzhenitsyn and Secular Humanism: A Response," *The Humanist*, Nov/Dec 1978, p. 6.

24. Kenneth L. Feder and Michael Alan Park, "Animal Rights: An Evolutionary Perspective," *The Humanist*, July/August 1990, p. 44.

25. Quoted in the online article, "Personhood, Property and Legal Competence," by Gary L. Francione, http://www.animal-law.org/library/ape.htm. For more information pertaining to animal rights, see the following Web sites: Psychologists for the Ethical Treatment of Animals (http://www.psyeta.org), or the Great Ape Project (http://www.greatapeproject.org).

26. Alexis de Tocqueville, *Democracy in America*, two volumes (New Rochelle, NY: Arlington House, n.d.), vol 1, p. 294.

27. Cited in John Warwick Montgomery, *Human Rights and Human Dignity* (Dallas, TX: Probe Books, 1986) p. 107.

28. Charles Francis Potter, *Humanism: A New Religion* (New York: Simon and Schuster, 1930), p. 128.

29. William F. Buckley, *Let Us Talk of Many Things* (Prima Publishing), p. 9, 10.

30. "College Freshmen More Liberal, Less Apathetic, Poll Finds," *Los Angeles Times*, January 28, 2002.

31. Charles Colson and Nancy Pearcy, *How Now Shall We Live?* (Wheaton, IL: Tyndale House, 1999), p. 296-7.

(1) Baboon: From ClipArt.com

(2) Mt. Rushmore: Photo by Gregory Webster (The Gregory Group: Lynnville, TN)

(3) Students and computers in classroom: From ClipArt.com

# SECTION III
# POSTMODERN MARXISM

While Secular Humanists have initiated many battles in the culture war, it is Postmodern Marxists who have introduced guerrilla tactics into the theater of conflict. If Christian students are to survive behind enemy lines on today's college campuses, and if Christ's followers are to have any influence in the larger society, they must be armed and equipped to engage Postmodern ideas aimed at their minds and seeking to capture their hearts.

The implications of Postmodern Marxism are most profound for economics, education, sociology, and law. Each of these areas provides a focus for the three chapters here in Section 3.

In chapter seven, we discuss why some people hate America. It is because of what our country stands for—God and a free market economy—both of which are anathema to Marxists. We review the development of Marx's ideas into four different strands, with Postmodernism being the predominate component at today's universities.

Chapter eight makes clear the connections between Marxism, multicultural education and feminism. These radical elements have launched vicious attacks on western, Judeo-Christian culture and its foundational unit, the family.

Chapter nine offers an expose' of the Marxists favorite tool for manipulating culture to achieve their utopian goals: political power. The result at many colleges has been the imposition of speech codes that punish politically incorrect words and even gestures. Marxist-inspired power plays also have fueled the diversity movement as a vehicle for propelling the homosexual agenda, including the right for gays to marry.

# CHAPTER 7

# Why Some People Hate America

"As humanism in its development became
more and more materialistic, it made itself
increasingly accessible to speculation and
manipulation, at first by socialism
and then by Communism. So that
Karl Marx was able to say in 1844 that
'Communism is naturalized humanism.'"[1]
—ALEKSANDR SOLZHENITSYN

"America is caught in the cross hairs of those
who hate this land, hate what we stand for, and
hate what we've accomplished. Her people have
been sold down the river by the socialist liberals
who worship at the altar of secular humanism
and multiculturalism."[2]
—MICHAEL SAVAGE

"If Christians are to minister effectively in the
postmodern world and avoid its temptations,
they must understand the spirit of the age."[3]
—GENE EDWARD VEITH

In March of 2003 at an anti-Iraq-war "teach-in" on the campus of Columbia University, anthropology professor Nicholas De Genova railed, "Peace is not patriotic. Peace is subversive, because peace anticipates a very different world than the one in which we live— a world where the U.S. would have no place…. We have to believe in the victory of the Iraqi people and the defeat of the U.S. war machine." The crowd of over 3,000 students and faculty erupted into applause.[4]

Why would anyone make such a statement?

While we can't presume to know Professor De Genova's motives, an understanding of worldviews allows us to uncover the possible reason behind rhetoric such as his. Jesus said, "You'll recognize them by their fruit."[5] As we've said in earlier chapters, a tree bears fruit by the nourishment drawn from its roots, and a person's ideas, statements and actions are the result of underlying worldview assumptions. When De Genova announced, "peace anticipates…a world where the U.S. would have no place," he is not simply arguing against the war with Iraq but is also lashing out against the United States. Why would someone hate the U.S.? One answer is because of what the U.S. represents—a worldview in conflict with the professor's.

## A CLASH OF RELIGIOUS WORLDVIEWS

Belief in a Creator, as expressed in America's founding document, the *Declaration of Independence* (which pays respect to the God of the universe), is the heritage of western civilization, rooted in a biblical Christian worldview. While there is a legitimate ongoing debate about whether or not America is a "Christian" nation, one thing is certain, a biblical Christian worldview

provided the ideas that went into this "experiment in freedom"—God-given natural rights, man's fallen nature, personal responsibility, and limited government with checks and balances. In stark opposition to this theistic worldview is Marxist atheism. According to *The Atheist's Handbook*, "The Communist Party has always taken and continues to take a position of militant atheism and of an implacable aggressive ideological struggle against religious befuddlement."[6] This aggressive, militant atheism is reflected in De Genova's words.

> "The Communist Party has always taken and continues to take a position of militant atheism…"
> —The Atheist's Handbook

Second, the U.S. economy is based on the free and peaceful exchange of goods and services, a system known as a free market economy. But a Marxist worldview holds that free markets—Marxists prefer the term "capitalism"—breed exploitation of the proletariat (non-property class), leading to crime and social unrest. Moreover, a nation's economic system controls to a significant degree the direction of every other institution in that society. Therefore, for the Marxist, a peaceful society is possible only when capitalism is replaced by socialism (an economic system run by the ruling government class). Marx and Engels wrote, "In proportion as the exploitation of one individual by another is put to an end, the exploitation of one nation by another will also be put to an end."[7] According to the *Statement of 81 Communist Workers Parties*, "Communism assures people freedom from the threat of war; it brings lasting peace, freedom from imperialist oppression and exploitation, and from unemployment and poverty."[8] De Genova implies the same sentiment when he advocated a world where the "U.S. would have no place."

## MARXISM, ALIVE AND WELL

David Horowitz, a 1960's Marxist who organized the first anti-Vietnam War rally at the University of California–Berkley, offers additional insight into De Genova's comments. Concerning his own involvement in the 60's anti-war effort, Horowitz writes, "We didn't want peace in Vietnam. We wanted a revolution in America."[9] Why? Because, as detailed above, America stands for the two things Marxists hate most: religion and capitalism.

Horowitz, who has since turned from his Marxist ideology, goes on to detail the background of many who demonstrated against the Iraqi conflict. All are Marxists such as Professor Eric Foner, the head of Columbia University's history department, who organized and spoke at the same rally as Professor De Genova.[10] But Columbia's anti-war "teach-in" was only one of many similar campus demonstrations.

> America stands for the two things Marxists hate most: religion and capitalism.

On March 5, 2003, the National Youth and Student Peace Coalition organized student protests at more than 230 colleges and universities across the U.S., rallying around the slogan "Books not Bombs!"[11] While the sentiment in the slogan may have popular appeal, the coalition's Web site reveals an agenda objectionable to many. The NYSPC is opposed to any military spending and considers the blame for the conflict in the Middle East to rest squarely on U.S. foreign policy. A look at the groups comprising the coalition reveals a virtual

### National Youth & Student Peace Coalition Member Organizations

Young Communist League

Young Democratic Socialists

Young People's Socialists League

180/Movement for Democracy and Education

Black Radical Congress-Youth Division

Campus Greens

Muslim Students Association of the US and Canada

National Youth Advocacy Coalition

Not With Our Money

Student Environmental Action Coalition

Student Peace Action Network

Students United for a Responsible Global Environment

Students Transforming and Resisting Corporations

United Students Against Sweatshops

United States Student Association

(Source: Web site for National Youth & Student Peace Coalition—www.nyspc.net)

"Who's Who" of Marxist/socialist/communist student organizations.

We recognize, of course, that some protestors against the war with Iraq may have different motives stemming from other worldviews.[12] But even so, there is evidence that many, if not most, are reflecting a straightforward Marxist understanding of the clash between oppressors and oppressed, theism and atheism, capitalism and socialism. By stirring up discontent and fostering resentment toward the United States, contemporary Marxists use the war as a platform from which to undermine support for American values and thus bring the world one step closer to the Marxist goal of world-wide communism administered by a one-world government. Calling for peace is a critical strategy in reaching this goal, for in their minds socialism is the only way to bring real and lasting peace. To understand why this is so, we need to know something about the views of Karl Marx on theology and economics and how Marx's ideas continue to influence people today under the guise of Postmodernism.

## THE THEOLOGY OF KARL MARX

After growing up in a Jewish home, Karl Marx attended the University of Berlin and studied the philosophies of Prometheus, Hegel, Strauss, and Feuerbach. In a circle of radical young Hegelians that included Ludwig Feuerbach, Moses Hess, and eventually Friedrick Engels, Marx became an atheist. "Philosophy makes no secret of it," said Marx. "Prometheus's admission: 'In sooth all gods I hate' is its own admission, its own motto against all gods,

> Marx determined to change all social institutions and re-establish them on atheistic foundations.

heavenly and earthly, who do not acknowledge the consciousness of man as the supreme divinity. There must be no god on a level with it."[13]

Marx believed man controls reality and must shape it to his specifications. "The philosophers have only interpreted the world, in various ways;" says Marx, "the point, however, is to change it."[14] Since the institutions of modern society have traditionally rested on a foundation of theism, Marx determined to change all social institutions and re-establish them on atheistic foundations. To this end, Marx and Engels, in the *Communist Manifesto*, called for the "forcible overthrow" of all existing social conditions.

It is important to note that this call was based on Marx's dogmatic atheism, not on dispassionate social observation. Marx's economic theories—and, indeed, his entire worldview—were tailored to fit his theology.

## THE ECONOMICS OF MARX

For Marx, a society's economic system determines the laws enacted, the type of government, and the role each plays in day-to-day life as well. While everyone would grant that economics influences these realms to some degree, Marx claimed that economic principles dictate exactly what each should be.

Working from this premise, Marxists draw the conclusion that undesirable economic systems create backward, undesirable societies. They point to the evils in capitalist society, such as greed and exploitation of workers, and conclude that capitalism is an evil economic system. For the Marxist, capitalism must be replaced with a more humane economic system. According to Karl Marx, the overriding problem with capitalism is that it breeds exploitation. In capitalist society, the bourgeoisie (property-owners) equate personal worth with exchange value, and this leads to "naked, shameless, direct, brutal exploitation"[15] of the non-property class.

So, how have Marx's ideas energized his present-day disciples to change the world? The answer to that question requires understanding the different paths Marxism has taken over the past 100 years.

## THE FOUR FACES OF MARXISM

While all Marxists hold to the same presuppositions regarding God and the evil of capitalistic exploitation, they also exhibit significant differences in their methodologies for solving the problems of mankind. And this warrants closer scrutiny of their views. Thus, we will explore the four "faces" of Marxism.

One face of Marxism comes from those who embrace a gradual approach to replacing capitalism with socialism. Many early Marxists, including Friedrick Engels, held this classical view, called "social-democratic" Marxism. They believed Marxism is compatible with democracy and political freedom. Those of this stripe represented the Menshevik party in Russia in the early 1900's. In Great Britain, the Fabian Socialists emerged in the late 1890's, also teaching that Marx's ideals could be realized through peaceful means such as democratic elections. The Fabians established their own university, The London School of Economics, and formed a political party to influence Parliament. Since World War II, this form of Marxism has dominated most of the nations of Western Europe and has made inroads in U.S. politics—reflected in many planks of the Democratic Party platform. While many U.S. Democrats would not consider themselves followers of Marx, they have unknowingly (or knowingly) bought into a Marxist interpretation of economics and politics.

The second face of Marxism is Marxism-Leninism. This interpretation of Marx was the official position of V. I. Lenin who led the Bolsheviks in the Russian revolution of 1917, which marked the founding of the Soviet Union. Lenin, like Marx, was a militant atheist and became convinced that violent overthrow of the capitalist system by the proletariat class was the best solution to the inequality and oppression set up, according to Marx's theory, by capitalism. Lenin's success in Russia led to similarly inspired revolutions in other countries. Civil wars were initiated around the world by the Comintern (Communist International) and backed by Soviet Communists. After World War II,

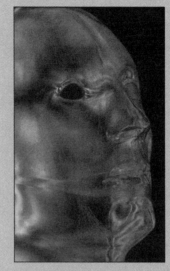

## PUT ON A MARXIST FACE

**Face #1:** Social Democratic Marxism. Marxist ideas can be integrated peacefully through democratic processes.

**Face #2:** Marxism-Leninism. Violent overthrow (a la Lenin in Russia, 1917) of capitalist systems is necessary.

**Face #3:** Neo-Marxism or Humanistic Marxism. Spread of Marxist philosophy through sociological and economic thought, including Liberation Theology.

**Face #4:** Postmodern Marxism. Liberation of all "oppressed" classes (not just the working class) through progressive social policies regarding gender, race, and sexual orientation that will result in cultural change.

Communists infiltrated, armed, and supervised the overthrow of nations throughout central Europe, including Albania, Poland, Czechoslovakia, Hungary, Bulgaria, Romania, East Germany, and Yugoslavia. They also took control of Malaysia, Laos, Korea, Vietnam, Cuba, and many nations of the Middle East, Central and South America, and Africa. China, the world's most populous nation, fell to Mao's revolutionary Marxism in 1949.

Neo-Marxism, or Humanistic Marxism, represents

*From the end of World War II until 1989, the Berlin wall separating Communist-dominated East Germany from free West Germany epitomized the repression brought by Marxism-Leninism.*

another variant of Marx's teaching. Humanistic Marxism emphasizes capitalism's role in causing alienation in the worker in four areas: from his work, from what he produces, from other workers, and from himself. This form of Marxism has become wedded to Christianity and is taught in many Christian colleges, especially in the areas of sociology and economics. According to Ron Nash and Jeff Myers, Tony Campolo, a well-known Christian speaker and professor of sociology at Eastern College, provides an example of Humanistic Marxist influence. In one of his books, "Campolo spends many pages praising Marx for a number of his ideas, including those related to the claims about human alienation."[16]

Nash and Myers critique Campolo's views by pointing out:

> Strangely missing from the discussions of alienation by Campolo and other Christian fans of Marx is any recognition of a fifth variety of human alienation, a type that Marx

also conveniently ignored. Scripture teaches that every member of the human race is *alienated from God*. In fact, the Bible proclaims that all forms of human alienation that concern neo-Marxists result from man's more fundamental alienation from his Creator.[17]

And by the way, this assessment is equally valid for Marxism in general.

Humanistic Marxism in Christian circles is better known as liberation theology. According to Ronald Nash:

> In its most narrow sense, liberation theology is a movement among Latin American Catholics and Protestants that seeks radical changes in the political and economic institutions of that region along Marxist lines. There also exist other versions of liberation theology which relate to feminist (the liberation of women) and racial concerns (black liberation).[18]

Liberation theology has been the primary means of introducing the Marxist worldview into many Latin American countries. Once peasants are taught the "Christian version of Marx by their own priests or pastors," the "initial opposition to [revolutionary] Marxism is worn down, [and] efforts can be made to win the new Marxist converts to the more radical views of Marxism-Leninism."[19] According to Nash, "Liberation theology becomes the Trojan Horse by which Marxism-Leninism gains access to nations that would otherwise have rejected it on religious grounds."[20]

This Marxist Trojan horse has not only entered many Latin American countries but many Christian colleges as well. For instance, a missionary couple to Mexico decided to send their son through the

Christian College Coalition's Latin American Studies Program. They were not aware that the reading assignments for the program included texts that denigrate western culture and free markets and elevate the cause of the poor and socialist/communist economic systems.[21]

Within a few weeks, their son was sending home comments from San Jose, Costa Rica like: "The Bible teaches socialism, not capitalism," "The kingdom of heaven is here and now," "The Bible was written for the poor,"

> "Liberation theology becomes the Trojan Horse by which Marxism-Leninism gains access to nations that would otherwise have rejected it on religious grounds."—Ron Nash

"I'm working with the Marxist Sandinista party in a school development project. They are doing so much to help the poor," The Bible can't be accurate because there have been so many translations," and "Our Father or Mother God."

While we agree that Jesus taught His followers to help the poor, the point here is to highlight the approach taken by this program. Instead of initiating a biblically based means of ministering to the poor, the Christian Coalition program is initiating unsuspecting students into a Marxist perspective of the problem, to replace free markets with socialism administered by a Marxist political system.

Finally, during the past twenty years or so, Marxism has morphed into what we refer to as Postmodern Marxism. Postmodernism focuses on the plight of the oppressed—hence its Marxist roots—except the focus has shifted from the struggle of the oppressed *working* classes to the struggle of those oppressed because of their gender, race, or sexual orientation. Whereas traditional Marxists interpreted the problem of mankind to be centered in economics, Postmodern Marxists point to culture as the source of oppression. They teach that inequalities have come about through the supremacy of a white, male,

heterosexual dominated social structure fostered by western civilization and the biblical Christian worldview. Thus, to remedy the situation—to grant equality to women, minorities, and homosexuals—the current system must be overturned. As a result, Postmodern Marxists have shifted their priorities from changing the economic structure to changing social norms. "The new Marxists," says Gene Veith, "following the teaching of the Italian Communist Antonio Gramsci, teach that cultural change must *precede* socialism." Veith goes on to elaborate:

> Today's left wing shows little concern for the labor movement and economic theory, unlike the Marxists of the last generation. Instead, the Left emphasizes *cultural change*. Changing America's values is seen as the best means for ushering in the socialist utopia. This is why the Left today champions any cause that undermines traditional moral and cultural values and why leftists gravitate to culture-shaping institutions—education, the arts, and the media.[22]

## POSTMODERN EDUCATION

Since Marxism promotes an idealistic utopian vision and many college students are at an idealist stage in life, Postmodern Marxists favor universities as their primary recruiting grounds. To be most effective at training radicals for cultural change, Marxists realized early on they had to control what was learned in the classroom. When it comes to education, whoever controls

> In today's Postmodern climate, most universities have replaced the study of western civilization with courses focused on minorities, women, and the undeveloped countries of the world.

the content of the curriculum, the "canon," controls the outcome produced in the lives of the students. This is why Jesse Jackson led the chant "Hey, Hey, ho, ho, western civ has got to go!" while seeking to stir up unrest among the students at Stanford University in 1987. He and his radical co-horts were agitating to remove the standard course in western civilization because of its emphasis on white, European males and on a biblically based worldview. And go it did. No longer are students introduced to the timeless ideas expressed by Aristotle, Plato, St. Augustine, Dante, Shakespeare and other great figures of western culture. Instead, these are replaced by what David Horowitz describes as a course designed to "indoctrinate students into the peculiar Marxoid worldview that [has] come to characterize the academic Left."[23]

Horowitz further points out that at Columbia University, the new canon is "an attempt to establish an orthodoxy out of the very intellectual tradition that history has refuted.... The required texts are exclusively by left-wing intellectuals... Communists... violent racialists... [and] second-rate ideologues."[24] In today's Postmodern climate, most universities have

replaced the study of western civilization with courses focused on minorities, women, and the undeveloped countries of the world.

The graphic below illustrates the range of approaches to education. The key issue, the fulcrum, is the content of the curriculum, or the "canon". The far right, or conservative end, formulates the canon around a biblical worldview and the great minds of Western Civilization that grew out of that worldview, with an emphasis on training the student to be a moral citizen. Moving to the left of center is the liberal approach of the Secular Humanist, those who seek to remove the Bible, negate the soul, and focus on utilitarian job training. The far left, or Marxist end of the spectrum, takes the basic canon of the humanists and radicalizes it by segmenting society into various factions with the goal of egalitarianism.

Taking its cue from Greek philosophers, the Bible, and particularly the Reformers, education in early America was viewed as primarily a moral exercise, seeking to produce godly young people of knowledge, character and wisdom. Yet, during the early 1900's, those of a Marxist persuasion influenced our teachers' colleges and began training a new generation of educators who saw their role as shapers of society instead of molders of character. As a result, the content, emphasis and approach to public education in America changed to fit the new socialist agenda.

In her book, *Cloning of the American Mind: Eradicating Morality through Education*, B. K. Eakman traces this shift in educational philosophy. "Perhaps the best place to begin," writes Eakman, "is in Europe

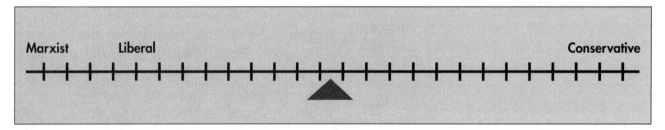

Marxist     Liberal                                            Conservative

in the 1920s, with the career of A.S. Neill, author of *Summerhill: A Radical Approach to Childrearing…*"[25] *Summerhill* wasn't published in America until 1960, but by 1970 it had become a best-seller with over 2 million copies sold "primarily to schools of education in colleges and universities, where it was frequently a required text for student teachers."[26] A leading education historian, Lawrence Cremin, the president of Teacher's College at Columbia University from 1974 to 1984, wrote that Neill's book brought about a "change in climate in educational opinion."[27] What did the change involve? Eakman writes, "Basically, *Summerhill* redefined the term 'freedom.' When Neill used that term, he didn't mean 'liberty'; he meant 'rebellion against authoritarianism,' and you will find that this theme is the glue that holds together the cast of characters in the ensuing education drama."[28]

That drama includes Karl Marx, Friedrick Engels, Erich Fromm, Sigmund Freud, plus numerous other men and women whose names most Americans would not recognize. However, these committed Marxists, according to Eakman, "were the source of today's obsession with early sex education, the rejection of the paternal family, the denigration of authority, the eradication of religion, and the overthrow of the character ethic."[29]

Other Marxists in the education drama include Georg Lukacs, who in 1923 founded the Frankfurt School in Frankfurt, Germany. "'[The] worldwide overturning of values cannot take place without the annihilation of old values and the creation of new ones by the revolutionaries," Lukacs said."[30] Another key figure in the Frankfurt School was Italian Marxist Antonio Gramsci, cited above, who "observed after the Bolshevik Revolution of 1917, that the same kind of revolution could not be brought about among Western workers because of the close alignment between their form of government and their Christian and Jewish idealism. Public opinion, he said, would first

have to be turned against biblical injunctions and precepts before a change of worldview could be inculcated."[31]

The Frankfurt School also produced Herbert Marcuse, influential, as Eakman notes, in America's cultural shift of the 1960's:

> If you like the sixties, you can thank Marcuse for the memories. Marcuse's *Eros and Civilization* was published in 1955, with funding from the Rockefeller Foundation, and became the founding document of the sixties counterculture. It was pressed into the hands of student anti-war activists, bringing the Frankfurt School's messianic revolutionary mission to all the American colleges and universities, beginning with Columbia's Teacher's College.[32]

We opened this chapter with the example of a 2003 anti-war rally at Columbia University. Notice from Eakman's commentary that we are back again at Columbia University, where it all began. Understanding the school's Marxist tilt since the 1960's helps explain why today's professors are seeking to foment distrust, even hatred, of American society in the hearts and minds of their students. These professors learned their lessons well from their Marxist mentors and are simply expressing the worldview they were taught as the true picture of reality. Eakman summarizes:

> thus the larger agenda of the Frankfurt School… was (1) the 'abolition of culture,' as Lukacs termed it, so as to undermine the Judeo-Christian value structure, and (2) to introduce a 'new barbarism'—new cultural icons and ideas that would be sure to divide the population and increase alienation between the younger and older generation.[33]

As we noted in the last chapter and expanded in this chapter, the liberal agenda is entrenched in all levels of American education. Richard Rorty, a Postmodern professor of comparative literature at Stanford University, confirms this when he writes, "I, like most Americans who teach humanities or social science in colleges and universities… try to arrange things so that students who enter as bigoted, homophobic, religious fundamentalists will leave college with views more like our own."[34] Rorty elaborates on his role as an educator and molder of ideas:

> The Fundamentalist parents of our fundamentalist students think that the entire 'American liberal Establishment' is engaged in a conspiracy….These parents have a point…. When we American college teachers encounter religious fundamentalists… we do our best to convince these students of the benefits of secularization….I think these students are lucky to find themselves under… people like me, and to have escaped the grip of their frightening, vicious, dangerous parents.[35]

The reality is this: if a child goes through twelve years of government-funded public education and four years of a state-supported college with no other educational influences from parents, church, or other counterbalancing sources, chances are good he or she will graduate as a liberal with a Secular Humanist outlook on life. If this same twenty-two year old goes on to three years of graduate school, he or she will more than likely become a leftist liberal (Marxist). And by the time this student completes a year or two of post-graduate training, he or she will be a full-fledged radical leftist liberal—a Postmodern Marxist. Ideas have consequences, and humanist/Marxist/Postmodernist ideas leave an indelible mark on those who are trained

in them.

This overview explains some of the reasons why public schools downplay America's early history, denying soul and spirit, denigrating capitalism, revising history, promoting feminism and the homosexual agenda, pushing sex education, and dumbing down the curriculum with an emphasis on multiculturalism and radical feminist studies. It also provides insight into why courts are seeking to eradicate all forms of the Christian religion from the public square.[36] It's a worldview issue—always has been and always will be.

# COUNTERING POSTMODERN MARXISM

In theory and practice, all faces of Marxism reflect an atheistic base. To be the best Postmodern Marxist is to see atheism as part of the materialistic, socialistic world outlook and to strive to eradicate all theistic religious sentiment, and to strive to realize the utopian vision of peace and the good life for all humanity, regardless of what it takes to bring about this new world order.

However, theists recognize, as did Fedor Dostoievski, that "The problem of Communism is not an economic problem. The problem of Communism is the problem of atheism."[37] As Irving Kristol comments:

> One need not have known a great deal about the theory of free-market economics to have been convinced that Soviet religious doctrine—described, somewhat redundantly but accurately enough, as 'godless, atheistic materialism'—could never sink roots among the Russian people. All people, everywhere, at all

*Russian novelist Fedor Dostoievski recognized the fundamental problem of Communism is not its economic philosophy but its atheism.*

times, are 'theotropic' beings, who cannot long abide the absence of a transcendental dimension to their lives. The collapse of Soviet Communism vindicates this truth."[38]

The "problem of atheism" leads to a skewed anthropology and psychology (man is merely matter in motion without soul or spiritual value) and from there, an unrealistic theory of economics. Socialism is based on the idea that people come into the world as blank slates to be shaped by their economic environments. But the history of mankind, and most dramatically during the past 75 years, has shown this view to be false. Everywhere socialism has been tried, it has failed to elevate men to a higher moral plane. It has failed even to provide the basic necessities of life for the people living under its grip. That is why the standard of living in the former Soviet Union was far below that of the U.S., and why even today, many Cubans are desperate to flee their soviet-style Marxist "utopia" seeking the shores of North America. Another way of putting this is to ask the simple question, "If you observe a boatload of people paddling furiously between Cuba and Florida, what direction are they headed?" The answer

is obvious, people are "voting with their feet" (or in this case oars) to reach a land of freedom and opportunity. Socialism does not offer the freedom to determine one's own direction in life.

The plight of the poor comes not from economic poverty, but a poverty of ideas being promulgated by those in academia—ideas that history has demonstrated to be false. After working for over 30 years among the poor and prisoners of England and personally interviewing over 10,000 people who had attempted suicide, British psychiatrist Theodore Dalrymple concluded that the poor underclass has not emerged as a result of economic, genetic, or racial determinism— the causes promoted by the academic and political left—but the answer is to be found in the "realm of ideas." He continues with these insightful comments:

> Human behavior cannot be explained without reference to the meaning and intentions people give to their acts and omissions; and everyone has a ... worldview, whether he knows it or not. It is the ideas my patients have that fascinate—and, to be honest, appall— me: for they are the source of their misery.[39]

Dalrymple places the blame for all this misery squarely on liberal ideas stemming from a humanist or Marxist orthodoxy. He concludes, "In fact most of the social pathology exhibited by the underclass has its origin in the ideas that have filtered down from the intelligentsia.... The

> "The problem of Communism is not an economic problem. The problem of Communism is the problem of atheism."
> —Fedor Dostoievski

climate of moral, cultural, and intellectual relativism—a relativism that began as a mere fashionable plaything for intellectuals—has been successfully communicated to those least able to resist its devastating practical effects."[40]

On the other hand, according to a biblical Christian worldview, evil does not reside in any system of economics, but in the heart of man. And accordingly, peace comes not from a change in economic policy, but from a change in heart. To effect that change, the Bible explains how God became a man, dwelt among us in the person of Jesus, suffered a cruel death for our sins, and was raised from the dead so we might join Him in newness of life, for here and for eternity.

Given this added dimension of the Christian worldview, we can agree with the Marxists when it comes to the need to help those living in poverty. It's just that we would suggest a very different way to relieve their distress. And we might even agree with the anti-war protestors that the world would be a more peaceful place with less bombs and more books (if we knew what books they had in mind!), but a realistic assessment of human nature leads to the conclusion there are times when evil men must be removed from power in order for peace to be a possibility, and the greatest peace is the peace of mind that comes with the assurance of eternal life in God's loving presence. Thus, the issues of peace, poverty, and prosperity are all ultimately *worldview* issues that find their roots in how one answers the question of theology—What about God?

## RECOMMENDED READING

Eakman, B. K., *Cloning of the American Mind*, Lafayette, LA: Huntington House Publishers, 1998.

Theodore Dalrymple, *Life at the Bottom: The Worldview that makes the Underclass*, Chicago: Ivan R. Dee, 2001.

Nash, Ronald H., *Poverty and Wealth: Why Socialism Doesn't Work*, Richardson, TX: Probe Books, 1986.

Schwarz, Dr. Fred C., *You Can Trust The Communists (to be Communists)* For a free online copy, go to http://www.schwarzreport.org/.

Veith, Gene Edward, Jr., *Postmodern Times*, Wheaton, IL: Crossway Books, 1994.

## ENDNOTES

1. Aleksandr Solzhenitsyn, *A World Split Apart*, (HarperCollins, 1979) p. 12.

2. Michael Savage, *The Savage Nation*, (WND, 2003) p. 152.

3. Gene Edward Veith, Jr. *Postmodern Times* (Wheaton, IL: Crossway Books, 1994), p. 20.

4. As quoted in the Columbia University student newspaper, *The Columbia Spectator*. See entire article at www.columbiaspectator.com/vnews/display.v/ART/2003/03/31/3e8820b855697?in_archive=1. *The Chronicle of Higher Education* has an interview with Professor De Genova concerning his remarks at http://chronicle.com/free/v49/i32/32a05601.htm. Or see the *New York Times* article: "At Columbia, Call for Death of U.S. Forces Is Denounced," www.nytimes.com/2003/03/29/education/29PROF.html. For a wealth of information on Marxist goals, history, current strategies, and an online copy of *You Can Trust The Communists (to be Communists)* by Dr. Fred C. Schwarz, a leader in the effort to inform Americans about the global expansion and deceitful tactics of Marxists, go to http://www.schwarzreport.org/.

5. Matthew 7:16.

6. Quoted in *Understanding the Times*, David A. Noebel, p. 68.

7. Karl Marx and Friedrick Engels, *The Communist Manifesto* (New York, Pocket Books: 1964), p. 90.

8. Quoted in *Understanding the Times*, p. 681.

9. "Moment of truth: For the Anti-American Left," David Horowitz: www.townhall.com/columnists/davidhorowitz/dh20030331.shtml

10. Ibid. Foner, by the way, later denounced De Genova's comments as "idiotic."

11. See the NYSPC Web site for details and a list of the national Marxist organizations that make up the coalition: http://nyspc.net/home.html.

12. Some are pacifists for theological reasons while others against the war claim a politically conservative or libertarian bent (such as the group sponsoring http://anti-war.com).

13. Karl Marx and Friedrich Engels, *On Religion* (New York: Schocken Books, 1974), p. 15.

14. Marx, Theses on Feuerbach, in Marx, *On Historical Materialism* (New York: International Publishers, 1974), p. 13.

15. Karl Marx and Friedrich Engels, *Collected Works*, forty volumes (New York: International Publishers, 1976), vol. 6, p. 487.

16. Ron Nash and Jeff Myers, *A Summit Ministries Guide to Choosing a College* (Manitou Springs, CO: Summit Press, 1995), p. 149.

17. Nash and Myers, *A Summit Ministries Guide*, p. 149 (emphasis theirs).

18. Ronald H. Nash, *Poverty and Wealth: Why Socialism Doesn't Work* (Richardson, TX: Probe Books, 1986), p. 103.

19. Nash, *Poverty and Wealth*, p. 100.

20. Ibid., p. 100.

21. This example and quotes are taken from David Noebel's article in Summit Ministries' *Journal*, September, 1999.

22. Gene Edward Veith, Jr. *Postmodern Times*, p. 161.

23. David Horowitz, *The Politics of Bad Faith: The Radical Assault on America's Future* ( New York: The Free Press, 1998), p. 35.

24. Horowitz, *The Politics of Bad Faith*, p. 33-34.

25. B. K. Eakman, *Cloning of the American Mind*, (Lafayette, LA: Huntington House Publishers, 1998) p. 111.

26. Eakman, *Cloning of the American Mind*, p. 111.

27. Ibid., p. 112.

28. Ibid., p. 112.

29. Ibid., p. 110.

30. Ibid., p. 147.

31. Idid., p. 148.

32. Ibid., p. 153.

33. Ibid., p. 155.

34. Robert B. Brandon, Editor, *Rorty and His Critics*, (Malden, MA: Blackwell Publishers, 2000), p. 21.

35. Brandon, *Rorty and His Critics*, p. 21-2.

36. For examples of how the highest court in our land is changing the social, moral and religious landscape of our nation, consider the following Supreme Court decisions: 1962 – prayer is ruled out of schools; 1963 – devotional Bible reading is ruled out of schools; 1973 – Killing a child in the womb is legalized; 1980 – The Ten Commandments is ruled out of schools; 1987 – The concept of a Creator is ruled out of science classes; 2003 – Sodomy is legalized.

37. Whittaker Chambers, *Witness* (New York: Random House, 1952), p. 712.

38. Irving Kristol, "Countercultures," *Commentary*. New York: Dec 1994. Vol.98, Issue 6; pg. 35.

39. Theodore Dalrymple, *Life at the Bottom: The Worldview that makes the Underclass* (Chicago: Ivan R. Dee, 2001), p. ix.

40. Dalrymple, *Life at the Bottom*, p. x-xi.


(1) Marxist face: From ClipArt.com

 (2) Berlin Wall: From ClipArt.com

(3) Dostoievski: From Countering Culture video (2004 Summit Ministries: Manitou Springs, CO)

# CHAPTER 8

# Class Warfare
# for the 21st Century

"Multiculturalists, influenced by Marxist
thinking, appear to want America to
become a divided country."[1]

—Alvin Schmidt

"[Socialism] lacks a central principle of virtue.
Instead, it proposes a whole set of virtues,
the 'liberal' virtues—toleration, pluralism,
relativism—which, one might say, construct a
supermarket of possible good and decent lives.
This is a prescription for moral anarchy, which
is exactly what we are now experiencing."[2]

—Irving Kristol

"Most Christians do not perceive the Church
to be in the midst of the most severe struggle
it has faced in centuries."[3]

—George Barna

Friedrich Nietzsche and Michel Foucault may well be the philosophical bookends of the last century. Both were brilliant, yet tragic, figures. German-born Nietzsche died in 1900 at age 54 after battling venereal disease and insanity. Foucault was a leading French intellectual who, by virtue of a promiscuous homosexual lifestyle, died of AIDS in 1984. And yet, at the dawn of the twenty-first century, both Nietzsche and Foucault are hugely popular on college campuses. Given their unsavory lifestyles, why the popularity? The answer lies in how their ideas have fueled the postmodern mindset of our current age.

According to philosophy Professor Lawrence Cahoone, Nietzsche coined the phrase, "God is dead," to signify the "waning of Christianity in an increasingly secular Europe."[4] Nietzsche wrote, "The most important of more recent events—that 'god is dead', that the belief in the Christian God has become unworthy of belief—already begins to cast its first shadows over Europe.... In fact, we philosophers and 'free spirits' feel ourselves irradiated as by a new dawn by the report that the 'old god is dead'; our hearts overflow with gratitude, astonishment, presentiment and expectation."[5] But, for Nietzsche, God's death ushers in the realization that we are alone in the universe with no one higher than ourselves to rely on. Cahoone continues, "Nietzsche's radical critique of metaphysics, the unity of the self, even of truth itself, and his conception of all reality and all values as expressing the 'will to power,' make him the grandfather of postmodernism."[6]

Foucault, having embraced the writings of Marx and Nietzsche, wrote "'Truth' is linked in a circular relation with systems of power which produce and sustain it..."[7] That is to say, what is considered "true"

> The important thing for the postmodernist is to use whatever power structure is available to change society.

for any particular society is an expression of what those in power (politicians, scientists, the military, or the media) say it is. Therefore, any idea or statement is not true in any absolute sense but, instead, is defined by the particular culture in which it is communicated. Marx and Engels, in *The Communist Manifesto*, said it plainly, "The ruling ideas of each age have ever been the ideas of its ruling class."[8] To the Postmodern Marxist, all "truth" is relative. Today we hear this philosophy echoed in the phrase, "That's just *your* interpretation."[9]

In our postmodern condition—which associates truth with whomever is in authority—the only determinant of right and wrong that remains is the "politics of power." The important thing for the postmodernist, then, is to use whatever power structure is available—whether the state, the school administration, or the media—to change society. Those who have been on the margins (by the Marxist's definition) are brought to center stage. As a result, they promote the rights of "oppressed" groups such as women, racial minorities, and homosexuals. An aggressive agenda to bring about social change is evident everywhere we look, from the classroom to the boardroom. Because the influence is so pervasive, we must understand a Postmodern Marxist approach to sociology, focusing especially on its affect on our educational institutions and our concept of the family.

## EDUCATION, POSTMODERN STYLE

Writing from their background in education and experience of ministering in a postmodern culture, Gary DeLashmutt and Roger Braund state, "No area of society has been more influenced by postmodern thought than education."[10] The postmodern idea that truth is not objective but is simply a social construct has specific implications for how race, gender and sexuality is currently taught in school, from kindergarten through graduate level.

To glimpse the influence of Nietzsche and Foucault's worldview on higher education, we need only look at the course offerings of our major universities. Young America's Foundation compiled course titles and descriptions from fifty of the most prestigious universities in the United States. Their annual publication,

*U.S. college campuses are the primary battleground over ideas that undermine our culture.*

*Comedy and Tragedy: College Course Descriptions and What They Tell Us About Higher Education Today*, documents the depths from which academia has drunk of the well of postmodernism. According to an article by Don Feder, these courses reveal politically correct indoctrination coupled with antagonism toward traditional religion, all at taxpayer expense! Feder explains:

> Moving on to hard-core indoctrination, …with the exception of Princeton, every Ivy League school now offers more courses in women's studies than economics. Cornell's "The Social Construction of Gender" "emphasizes the social psychology processes by which the culture transforms male and female newborns into 'masculine' and 'feminine' adults….Courses simultaneously advancing two or more isms are popular. Examples include 'Black Marxism' at University of California at Santa Barbara, 'Eco-Feminism' (Villanova) and 'Chicana Lesbian Literature' (UCLA)….Traditional religions are popular targets. Thus a course at the University of Pennsylvania, 'The Historical Origins

of Racism: Views of Blacks in Early Judaism, Christianity and Islam,' indicts these faiths for racial hatred. Dartmouth's Women and Religion: New Explorations' 'documents sexism…in the canonical writings and institution forms of Judaism and Christianity.' And Harvard offers 'Feminist Biblical Interpretation.[11]

After that last course title, Feder dryly comments, "A course on 'Christian Interpretation of Feminism' would be unthinkable."

But his remark raises a central question: Why is a course on a Christian critique of feminism "unthinkable"? The answer reveals the deeply entrenched postmodern mindset in academia. The postmodernist considers Christianity the focal problem in society because it has been a dominant force in Western culture over the past 1600 years. Its white, European, male-dominated social structures are seen as oppressing women and people of other cultures.

That is why battle lines are drawn and postmodern troops rally around the flag of liberation for these supposedly besieged fringe groups. The classic Marxian struggle for economic equality of the oppressed class, originally understood to be the proletariat (non-property owners), has now become the struggle for equality of gender, race, and sexual preference. Marx's

> "No area of society has been more influenced by postmodern thought than education."
> —Gary DeLashmutt and Roger Braund

> The postmodernist considers Christianity the focal problem in society because it has been a dominant force in Western culture over the past 1600 years.

underlying hatred for God makes the worldview connection between theology and another discipline, sociology, with its sweeping impact on American education.

Traditional education in America included rigorous study of philosophy (including logic), language, history, theology, and rhetoric. In fact, in the 1600's and 1700's, in order to pass the *entrance* exam for Harvard University, a student needed a working knowledge of both Latin and Greek. Yet, during the past century, standards such as these have been lowered throughout our American educational system.

This "dumbing down" of curriculum was not done in a worldview vacuum. Marxist educators understand that to convince the majority of people that the Postmodern Marxist worldview is correct, students must first be re-educated away from the traditional values and religious instruction they learned at home and in church. Only then will students accept uncritically the dictates of their social handlers. This strategy comes right out of the Marxist playbook. As B. K. Eakman points out:

> Most Americans believe that Russian education [under Communism] was highly academic despite its political propagandizing. They would be surprised to learn that one of Lenin's first official acts was to eliminate examinations, home work, failure and punishment, as well as to collectivize (consolidate) the schools. Even more remarkably, he

began disseminating the works of [John] Dewey! By 1924, Soviet education theorists were saying that holding the correct viewpoints, including a "collective spirit," was more important than substantive knowledge. Indeed, the first Communist Five-Year Plan in 1927 included several education provisions aimed at building the "new socialism" that was going to usher in a worker's paradise. Today, experts in America say something similar, that it will usher in a new era of competitiveness, prosperity and lead to less world conflict. New promises; same old collective philosophy.[12]

# MULTICULTURALISM AND DIVERSITY

Multiculturalism is another offspring of the marriage of atheism and radical social equality. According to Richard Bernstein, multiculturalism was "inspired by the ideas of French philosopher Michel Foucault, the jargon represent[ing] the reformulation of basic nineteenth-century Marxist ideas that have been borrowed by generations of intellectuals bent on showing that the world as it exists is the creation (the 'social construction') of the groups that hold power...."[13] Alvin Schmidt agrees with Bernstein when he writes, "Marxism flourishes in the ideology and politics of present-day multiculturalism."[14]

Whereas *multicultural* education introduces students to societies different from their own (a positive approach that broadens students' understanding and appreciation for people who are different from them), *multiculturalism* is the view that all societies are culturally equal. That is, no one social system is to be considered superior to any other. In practice, this translates into emphasizing the evils of Western culture while at the same time elevating the virtues of non-western societies. In the late 1980's at Stanford University, for example, traditional Western Civilization courses were replaced with an eight-track series called *Culture, Ideas, and Values* (*CIV*). Alvin Schmidt gives an account of what multiculturalism looks like under this new liberal ideology:

> The president, Donald Kennedy, and advocates of the *CIV* deceptively announced that little had really changed vis-à-vis the previous offerings. They stated that selections from Plato and from the Bible were still being read, but what they did not tell the students or the alumni was that some of the *CIV* sections taught that Genesis was rife with sexism and made St. Paul politically correct by saying that he may have been a homosexual. Shakespeare is still studied, but *The Tempest* is now viewed from a "slave's perspective" and is made to serve as an instructive lesson in Western imperialism.[15]

Changing the minds of students is appreciably easier if they arrive at college already prepared for indoctrination. Hence, multiculturalism is not confined to the university setting. Public school texts paint rosy pictures of other cultures while emphasizing the negative aspects of Western societies. For instance, in one high school text, the ancient Maya are described as people who "built great cities" and had a "remarkable history." We are told that "religion played an important

> Whereas multicultural education introduces students to societies different from their own, multiculturalism is the view that all societies are culturally equal—no one social system is superior to any other.

part in city life" and that priests performed "elaborate rituals for their gods."[16] What is left out of this telling is that the elaborate Mayan rituals included human sacrifice. We are dependant on outside sources, such as Howard La Fay, to tell us in *National Geographic* that in these "elaborate rituals a priest ripped open the victim's breast with an obsidian knife and tore out the still-beating heart," or "cut holes in their [prisoners'] tongues and drew rope festooned with thorns through the wound to collect blood offerings."[17]

The similarly cruel history of the Central American Aztecs is glossed over. One history textbook mentions, almost in passing, "The Aztec believed that the sun needed human blood to survive. Without this sacrifice, it would stop shining and all life would perish. The king and his high priests had the sacred task of preventing this disaster from occurring. Throughout the year, captives were led up the steps of the Great temple to be sacrificed."[18] The next paragraph demurely concludes, "Year after year, the sun continued to rise and set. The Aztec continued their traditional ways unaware that other worlds lay on the other side of the oceans."[19]

There is no mention that tens of thousands of human sacrifices were offered at the "Great temple," where, like

> Public school texts paint rosy pictures of other cultures while emphasizing the negative aspects of Western societies.

the Mayas, slaves, children of conquered tribes, and captured warriors had their hearts ripped out of their

*Multiculturalism often whitewashes the grisly details of non-western cultures, such as glossing over the fact that ancient rituals sometimes involved human sacrifice.*

living bodies while a leg or arm was removed to be eaten by the Aztec warrior and his family in a ritual feast.[20] Neither do we read in this text of the brutal patterns of everyday life for these people. Thomas Sowell fills in the gaps:

> Many conquered peoples were reduced to being serfs tied to land controlled by their Aztec overlords. An even worse fate could await conquered areas that later rebelled, which could lead to a wholesale slaughter of the population. Wonton brutality was not the whole story however. The Aztecs... used terror as a weapon to demoralize their enemies and keep the subjugated peoples in line.[21]

The same is true when detailing the spread of Islam in the 700's. A section title of one high school history book simply says that "Islam expanded east and west" and explains how "the Arabs were passionate in their new faith. The Koran taught that wars fought for God were just. A warrior killed in a jihad (jih-HAHD), or holy war, was promised immediate

entry into paradise. With this belief, Muslims rushed fearlessly into battle."[22] The text even adds, "The Arabs proved tolerant rulers."[23] Again, one has to go to an outside source to discover how ruthless and heartless Mohammad and his band of mercenaries actually were in their dealings with surrounding tribes. Historian Robert Payne paints a more accurate picture with this episode:

> Muhammad ordered an attack on the treacherous Bani Quraiza in their towers of refuge. He was in no mood to show mercy.... For twenty-five days the fortresses were besieged, while Muhammad debated with himself what he would do to the traitors.... When the starved defenders in their fortresses were seeking peace at any cost, Muhammad offered to allow them to surrender on condition that the Aus, their supposed allies, should decide their fate....The chief of the Aus...Sa'd ibn Muadh....said: "I condemn the men to death, their property to be divided by the victors, their women and children to be slaves!" There was a long silence followed by a torrent of objections, and then Muhammad said: "Truly Sa'd has declared the judgment of God from beyond the Seventh Heaven!"
>
> The terrible judgment was carried out to the last detail, with Muhammad himself superintending the general massacre, even helping to dig the trenches in the marketplace. The next morning the Jews, with their hands tied behind their backs, were taken out in batches of five or six at a time and forced to sit on the edge of the trench; then they were beheaded, and their bodies were tumbled into the trench.[24]

While the same public school text cited earlier is coy about revealing the unsightly side of the Mayas, it is *not* shy about describing blood and gore when it

*To say, as some public school texts assert, Mohammed was a "tolerant" ruler is arguably an exaggeration.*

comes to *Christian* endeavors. Recalling the Christian Crusaders who reached Jerusalem in 1099 A.D., the *World History* text explains:

> A dreadful slaughter followed, as Muslim men and women were chased through the streets and murdered. The Jews of the city were rounded up, herded into a temple, and burned to death. One eyewitness reported: "Piles of heads, hands, and feet were to be seen in the streets of the city… But these were small matters compared to what happened at the Temple of Solomon [where] men rode in blood up to their knees and bridle reins.[25]

We use these examples to show that those who teach multicultural*ism* are not so interested in providing a

balanced view of past cultural extremisms as they are in creating the impression that Western civilization in general and biblical Christianity in particular are the prime sources of the world's oppression, misery, and intolerance.

# CLASS WARFARE, FEMINIST STYLE

"The social construction of race, class, or gender creates the premise that it is socially 'oppressed,'" writes former Marxist David Horowitz. "Thus women have been historically excluded from certain roles not as a result of biological realities—for example, the hazards of childbirth before the development of modern medical techniques—but because 'patriarchal society' has *defined* their roles in order that men can oppress them."[26] If men are the oppressors, as radical feminists claim, then women must take it upon themselves to instigate a revolution to overthrow male domination. According to a Postmodern Marxist worldview, this is the only sensible and right thing to do.

B. K. Eakman traces the idea of gender oppression back to Marx. She writes:

> Most people don't realize the extent of anti-family bias in the philosophy of Marx and his close colleague Friedrich Engels. But it was part and parcel of their radical economic theory, the family's eradication was key to the "worker's paradise" they envisioned. Engels devoted an entire book to the subject, *Origin of the Family*, in which he advocated its "liberation"—ostensibly so that women would be "free." Engels wrote: "the first condition for the liberation of the wife is to bring the

whole female sex back into public industry, and this in turn demands the abolition of the monogamous family as the economic unit of society.[27]

Margaret Sanger is one who picked up on Engels' theme in the early 1900's. An early feminist, Sanger founded Planned Parenthood and heralded her cause

> If men are the oppressors, as radical feminists claim, then women must take it upon themselves to instigate a revolution to overthrow male domination.

by publishing a paper called *The Woman Rebel*. George Grant writes, "It was an eight-sheet pulp with the slogan 'No Gods! No Masters!' emblazoned across the masthead. She advertised it as 'a paper of militant thought,' and militant it was indeed. The first issue denounced marriage as a 'degenerate institution,' capitalism as 'indecent exploitation' and sexual modesty as 'obscene prudery.'"[28] Sanger also started a newspaper in which she admitted "Birth control appeals to the advanced radical because it is calculated to undermine the authority of the Christian churches. I look forward to seeing humanity free someday of the tyranny of Christianity no less than Capitalism."[29]

Sanger had learned her atheistic socialism and commitment to sexual freedom while attending meetings organized by various radical groups, including lectures on Nietzsche's moral relativism, during her one-year stay in England (where she had fled to avoid standing trial in the U.S. for including lewd and indecent articles in her paper). Planned Parenthood's attack on the church, began by Sanger one hundred

years ago, continues to this day. Grant comments, "In its advertisements, in its literature, in its program, and in its policies, the organization makes every attempt to mock, belittle, and undermine biblical Christianity."[30] Those who follow in the footsteps of Sanger understand the real issue is not women's liberation or sexual freedom, but whether God is "there and not silent" (to use Francis Schaeffer's phrase) about His design for our sexual expression.

One of Sanger's followers and the chief architect of the modern feminist movement is Betty Friedan, author of the groundbreaking book, *The Feminist Mystique.* In her book, Friedan presents herself as a typical suburban housewife "not even conscious of the woman question" before she began work on her manuscript. Yet, according to David Horowitz, a recent biography of Friedan reveals "nothing could be further from the truth."[31] Horowitz continues:

> Under her maiden name, Betty Goldstein, the record shows that Friedan was a political activist and professional propagandist for the Communist left for nearly thirty years before the 1963 publication of *The Feminist Mystique....* Friedan, from her college days and until her mid-thirties, was a Stalinist Marxist (or a fellow traveler thereof), the political intimate of leaders of America's Cold War fifth column.... Not at all a neophyte when it came to "the woman question" (the phrase itself is a Marxist construction), she was certainly familiar with the writings of Engels, Lenin and Stalin on the subject and had written about it herself as a journalist for the official publication of the Communist-controlled United Electrical Workers union.[32]

Simone de Beauvoir, another feminist, regards the

radical alteration of parenting as more than a utopian fantasy. In his book, *Feminism and Freedom*, Michael Levin, writes that de Beauvoir:

> finds it "easy to visualize" a world "where men and women would be equal," for "that is precisely what the Soviet Union promised: women trained and raised exactly like men...[M]arriage was to be based on a free agreement that the spouses could break at will; maternity was to be voluntary; pregnancy leaves were to be paid for by the State, which would assume charge of the children, signifying not that they would be taken from their parents, but that they would not be abandoned to them." De Beauvoir is so far from alone among feminists in admiring Marxist-Leninism that this admiration, together with hostility to "capitalism," can be considered virtually a further distinguishing mark of feminism....a great many well-known feminists... identify themselves as socialists or Marxists of some sort.[33]

Feminism is evident on campuses across the United States. According to the *Chronicle of Higher Education*, among the 350 best universities in the nation, 41 per cent of the literature courses are taught from a Marxist perspective, and 61 per cent approach the subject from a feminist point of view. Phyllis Schlafly indicates there are over 900 women's studies courses taught nationwide. Regarding one such program, she writes, "At the women's studies program at the University of South Carolina, students must acknowledge the existence of racism, classism, sexism, hetero-

> **B. K. Eakman traces the idea of gender oppression back to Marx.**

sexism and other institutional forms of oppression of women before being permitted to participate in class discussions."[34] She goes on to reveal that "The textbooks in women's studies programs teach that women are the victims of a male-dominated society, that marriage is an 'instrument of oppression,' and that fathers are 'foreign male elements' who stand between mothers and daughters. This was the conclusion of an Independent Women's Forum review of five of the most widely used textbooks and 30 course outlines from major universities."[35]

Elementary students also are targeted by the feminist agenda. *The Washington Times* reviewed a book by research associate Sandra Stansky at the Harvard Graduate School of Education. The *Times* writes:

> Mrs. Sandra Stotsky's analysis of the history and civics readers used in elementary schools is also important. Feminists and multicultualists, she contends, have cleansed fifth grade textbooks. The result: children will learn nothing about inventors, explorers, soldiers and all presidents except for Abraham Lincoln. "Stories about the great achievements in American science, technology and political life in the past 200 years are m i s s - ing," she writes, "and they are missing it seems simply because stories about them would call attention to a white male."[36]

The feminist attack on the family is evidenced throughout society in the changing attitudes of the general public as well as our elected politicians. The resulting affect on public policy is noteworthy as Irving Kristol points out:

> ...it remains true that one of the inherent weaknesses of even moderate socialist movements and

governments is this ingrained hostility to the family. We are coming to recognize that this hostility, now cloaked as indifference, is a major factor in the political torment of what we still call "liberalism" in the United States. That the hostility there is revealed by the complaisance of liberalism before the assaults on the family by contemporary radical feminism and the "gay-rights" movement. All liberal politicians today feel it necessary to speak highly of the family, but they cannot bring themselves to defend it against its enemies.

We are not suggesting that everything feminists call for should be discarded. For example, a case can and should be made for "equal pay for equal work" regardless of the gender of the person doing the job, and certainly the contribution of women to society should be taught in social studies classes. What we take issue with here are the *radical* feminist ideas that have gained such a foothold in many segments of our society. This set of ideas extends far beyond equal pay and seeks to impose the entire Postmodern Marxist worldview on the rest of society—the baseless ideas that there are *no* differences between men and women, that women do not need men, and that the family, education, business, government, the military—our entire society—should be restructured to accommodate their radical vision for social relationships.

## COUNTERING POSTMODERN SOCIOLOGY

Francis Schaeffer describes a picturesque village in the Swiss mountains where Nietzsche spent several summers writing. A plaque honoring the famous philosopher is inscribed with a quote from one of Nietzsche's works. It reads, in part:

Oh man! Take heed
of what the dark midnight says…
The world is deep—more profound than day
would have thought…
Woe speaks; pass on.
But all pleasure seeks eternity—
a deep and profound eternity.[38]

Schaeffer comments on Nietzsche's words: "Surrounded by some of the most beautiful scenery in the world, Nietzsche knew… with no personal God, all is dead. Yet man… cries out for a meaning that can only be found in the existence of the infinite-personal God… and in the existence of a personal life continuing into eternity."[39]

> Like Nietzsche's view of life's meaning, multiculturalism is an idea at war with itself.

Nietzsche could not bear the reality his own worldview had constructed. He claimed to believe God was dead and that life had no meaning, yet his heart longed for a very different reality and for a different life-story—one of significance that goes beyond the grave, one of "a deep and profound eternity." Nietzsche's worldview met reality head-on, and was knocked to the ground, because in the real world, the Bible tells us God has set "eternity in the hearts of men…" (Ecclesiastes 3:11).

Like Nietzsche's view of life's meaning, multiculturalism is an idea at war with itself. To claim that all cultures are equally valid runs counter to what we intuitively know to be true. It is *not* defensible that sacrificing infants to a sun god, as practiced by the ancient Aztecs, is on equal footing with the biblical injunction that parents love and care for their children (see Ephesians 6:4 and Titus 2:3-4). Neither is the

Hindu custom of burning young widows with their deceased husbands—a practice that was outlawed through the tireless efforts of Christian missionary William Carey because of his concern for women (Luke 7:12-13; 1 Timothy 5:3-10). And it does not take much reflection to recognize that the mass slaughter of innocent men, women and children because of their race as carried out through Hitler's Holocaust against the Jews or Saddam Hussein's more recent ethnic cleansing of Kurds in northern Iraq runs counter to the idea that individuals have intrinsic worth—a concept stemming from the biblical notion that we are created in God's image (Genesis 1:27).

We should be careful to note, however, when talking about multiculturalism, that not every educator who teaches out of current history and social studies textbooks understands the worldview from which this perspective comes. As Alvin Schmidt, in *The Menace of Multiculturalism*, suggests:

> Some multiculturalist advocates, including many well-meaning teachers and school administrators, are not aware of the leftist (Marxist) concepts and assumptions operative in multiculturalism. Unwittingly, they often give aid and comfort to a radical leftist philosophy. If the unsuspecting advocates of multiculturalist practices were aware of the Marxist threads in the fabric of multiculturalism, they would be a lot less eager to advance its principles and policies.[40]

This makes it all the more critical that those involved in shaping educational policy *do* understand the background and danger of this postmodernist approach. Christians need to find a

| TITUS 1:3-4 |
| --- |
| *In the same way, older women are to be reverent in behavior, not slanderers, not addicted to much wine. [They are] to teach what is good, so that they may encourage the young women to love their husbands and children.* |

place on school boards, curriculum selection committees, as principals and teachers, and as officials on the state and federal levels of education to counter the destructive trends that have overrun public education in America.

| EPHESIANS 6:4 |
| --- |
| *And fathers, don't stir up anger in your children, but bring them up in the training and instruction of the Lord.* |

Instead of the multiculturalist approach, our children need to understand that the Western tradition is the source of the concepts of individual freedom and political democracy to which most of the world aspires today. And while the West in its darker moments has committed its own crimes against humanity, its higher ideals, rooted in biblical principles, have provided the necessary foundation for correcting such abuses of power. The Declaration of Independence records these words: "We hold these truths to be self-evident, that all men are created equal, that they are endowed by their Creator with certain unalienable Rights…" These twin ideas—of humankind's equality before God and God-given rights—motivated Christians in the 1800's to seek the eradication of slavery both in Great Britain and America. And it was these very same words Dr. Martin Luther King, Jr. drew upon in the 1960's when he called for revising the laws of our land to respect equality of the races in America. So even though Western Civilization has not always lived up to its own ideals, without them where would we be?

As multiculturalism fails to reflect cultural realities, radical feminism conflicts with what we know to be true about femininity, marriage, and the family. To get at the truth about the benefits of marriage, sociology professor Linda J. Waite developed original research and synthesized hundreds of

> ## Scripture Shows Respect for Women
>
> Just as He [Jesus] neared the gate of the town, a dead man was being carried out. He was his mother's only son, and she was a widow. A large crowd from the city was also with her. [13]When the Lord saw her, He had compassion on her and said, "Don't cry."
> —Luke 7:12-13
>
> Support widows who are genuinely widows. [4]But if any widow has children or grandchildren, they should learn to practice their religion toward their own family first and to repay their parents, for this pleases God. [5]The real widow, left all alone, has put her hope in God and continues night and day in her petitions and prayers; [6]however, she who is self-indulgent is dead even while she lives. [7]Command this, so that they won't be blamed. [8]Now if anyone does not provide for his own relatives, and especially for his household, he has denied the faith and is worse than an unbeliever. [9]No widow should be placed on the official support list unless she is at least 60 years old, has been the wife of one husband, [10]and is well known for good works—that is, if she has brought up children, shown hospitality, washed the saints' feet, helped the afflicted, and devoted herself to every good work.
> —1 Timothy 5:3-10

cross-disciplinary scientific studies in sociology, economics, medicine, psychology, sexology, and law. In her book, *The Case for Marriage,* she and co-author Maggie Gallagher document the ways in which marriage is good for husbands, wives, and children. Waite and Gallagher convincingly argue that:

> …by a broad range of indices, being married is actually better for you physically, materially, and spiritually than being single or divorced. Married people live longer, have better health, earn more money and accumulate more wealth, feel more fulfilled in their lives, enjoy more satisfying sexual relationships, and have happier and more successful children than those who remain single, cohabit, or get divorced. Statistics show, for example, that violence is less prevalent in married households and that divorce reduces male life expectancy on the order of a pack-a-day cigarette habit.[41]

*The Case for Marriage* confirms what the Bible affirmed centuries ago, "It is not good for the man to be alone. I will make a helper who is like him…. This is why a man leaves his father and mother and bonds with his wife, and they become one flesh" (Genesis 2:18, 24). In addition, Paul instructs husbands to "love your wives, just as also Christ loved the church and gave Himself for her… [and] love their wives as their own bodies" (Ephesians 5:25, 28). God has built into each of us a desire for this kind of loving relationship. As part of God's design, it is not only good for us as individuals, but it is good for society.

Another problem with multiculturalism and feminism is their focus on the group over the individual. They emphasize that individuals are products of their particular social settings, and this "group identity"

> Children need to understand that the Western tradition is the source of the concepts of individual freedom and political democracy to which most of the world aspires today.

keeps anyone from empathizing appropriately with those of another group, thus setting up barriers to communication and any sense of community. On the other hand, Christianity emphasizes the individual, not the group into which one is born. The Apostle Paul wrote that in Christ "there is no Jew or Greek, slave or free, male or female" (Galatians 3:28).

"Individualism, united with altruism," writes Karl Popper, "has become the

> **GENESIS 1:27**
>
> *So God created man in His own image; He created him in the image of God; He created them male and female.*

basis of our western civilization." This well-known philosopher of science and critic of Marxism continues, "It is the central doctrine of Christianity ('love your neighbor,' say the Scriptures, not 'love your tribe'); and it is the core of all ethical doctrines which have grown from our civilization and stimulated it."[42] Postmodernism's attack on the individual is tantamount to an attack on Christianity and the entire Western enterprise.

An article in *Newsweek* offers a summary of how multiculturalism, far from being the enlightened, progressive view claimed by its advocates, is a throwback to ancient, pre-Christian ways of looking at society:

Christianity "discovered" the individual. In the ancient world, individuals were recog-nized as members of tribes or nations or families, and conducted themselves accordingly...the Gospels are replete with scenes in which Jesus works one on one, healing this woman's sickness, forgiving that man's sins and calling each to personal conversion. He invites Jews and Gentiles alike to enter God's kingdom. "Christianity discovers individuality in the sense that it stresses personal conversion," says Bernard McGinn, professor of historical theology at the University of Chicago Divinity School. "This is a crucial contribution to Western Civilization because it releases the individual from the absolute constraints of family and society."[43]

In order for those who have been captured by our postmodern culture to hear and receive the Gospel, Christians must re-enter the discussion concerning multiculturalism and radical feminism and point out to any who have ears to hear how these ideas are destructive to individuals as well as society. This means teaching a biblical Christian worldview of sociology in our churches, initiating discussions on these issues with our neighbors and in our schools, and insuring that those in political leadership have a firm

> Postmodernism's attack on the individual is tantamount to an attack on Christianity and the entire Western enterprise.

understanding and commitment to the role of the family in society. To refrain from this battle of ideas in any of these arenas is to admit defeat and turn from Jesus' call to be the "salt and light" of society (Matthew 5:13-16). As Francis Schaeffer put it so succinctly, "The Christian must resist the spirit of the world in the form it takes in his own generation. If he does not do this, he is not resisting the spirit of the world at all."[44]

## RECOMMENDED READING

Carson, D. A., *The Gagging of God: Christianity Confronts Pluralism*. Grand Rapids, MI: Zondervan Publishing House, 1996.

Cottrell, Jack, *Feminism and the Bible: An Introduction to Feminism for Christians*. Joplin, MO: College Press Publishing, 1992.

Kassian, Mary A., *The Feminist Gospel: The Movement to Unite Feminism with the Church*. Wheaton, IL: Crossway Books, 1992.

Grant, George, *Grand Illusions: The Legacy of Planned Parenthood*, Franklin, TN: Adroit Press, 1992.

McCallum, Dennis, editor, *The Death of Truth*, Minneapolis, MN: Bethany House Publishers, 1996.

Schmidt, Alvin J., *The Menace of Multiculturalism*, Westport, CT: Praeger Publishers, 1997.

Waite, Linda J. and Maggie Gallagher, *The Case for Marriage: Why married People are Happier, Healthier, and Better off Financially*, New York: Doubleday, 2000.

## ENDNOTES

1. Alvin J. Schmidt, *The Menace of Multiculturalism*, (Westport, CT: Praeger Publishers, 1997) p. 29.

2. Irving Kristol, "Countercultures," *Commentary*. New York: Dec 1994, Vol. 98, Issue 6, p. 35.

3. George Barna, *The Frog in the Kettle: What Christians Need to Know About Life in the Year 2000* (Ventura, CA: Regal Books, 1990), p. 123.

4. Lawrence Cahoone, editor, *From Modernism to Postmodernism: An Anthology*, (Cambridge, MA: Blackwell Publishers, Inc., 1996), p. 102.

5. Quoted in Colin Brown, *Philosophy and the Christian Faith* (Downers Grove, IL: InterVarsity Press, 1968), p. 139.

6. Cahoone, *From Modernism to Postmodernism*, p. 102.

7. Michel Foucault, "Truth and Power," quoted in Cahoone, p. 380.

8. Karl Marx and Friedrich Engels, *The Communist Manifesto* (New York: Pocket Books, 1964), p. 91.

9. This statement is the title of a book, *That's Just Your Interpretation*, written by Paul Copan. It is an excellent examination of a number of common misconceptions about the Christian worldview.

10. Dennis McCallum, editor, *The Death of Truth* (Minneapolis, MN: Bethany House Publishers, 1996), p. 96.

11. Don Feder, *The Washington Times*, September 6, 1997.

12. B. K. Eakman, *Cloning of the American Mind*, (Lafayette, LA: Huntington House Publishers, 1998) p. 134.

13. Richard Bernstein, *Dictatorship of Virtue*, p. 227

14. Alvin J. Schmidt, *The Menace of Multiculturalism*, (Westport, CT: Praeger Publishers, 1997) p. 25.

15. Schmidt, *The Menace of Multiculturalism*, p. 164.

16. *World History: Perspectives on the Past* (D.C. Heath and Co, 1994), p. 333.

17. Howard La Fay, "The Maya: Children of Time," *National Geographic* (December 1975), p. 734, quoted in Schmidt, p. 46-7.

18. *World History*, p. 335.

19. Ibid.

20. See Thomas Sowell, *Conquests and Cultures* (New York: Basic Books, 1998), p. 276.

21. Thomas Sowell, *Conquests and Cultures*, p. 276-7.

22. *World History*, p. 188-9.

23. Ibid., p. 189.

24. Robert Payne, *The History of Islam* (N.Y.: Dorset Press, 1959), p. 46-7.

25. Ibid., p. 242.

26. David Horowitz, "The Queer Fellows," *American Spectator*, January 1993, p. 43.

27. B. K. Eakman, *Cloning of the American Mind*, p. 132-3.

28. George Grant, *Grand Illusions: The Legacy of Planned Parenthood* (Franklin, TN: Adroit Press, 1992), p. 53.

29. George Grant, *Grand Illusions*, p. 53.

30. Ibid., p. 65

31. David Horowitz, *Heterodoxy*, March 1999, p. 14.

32. Ibid.

33. Michael Levin, *Feminism and Freedom*, p. 26.

34. Phyllis Schlafly, *The Washington Times*, March 29, 2003, p. A 13.

35. Schlafly, *The Washington Times*, p. A 13.

36. The *Washington Times*, May 2, 1999, p. B6. Mrs. Stotsky is a research associate at the Harvard Graduate School of Education and her book is entitled: *Losing Our Language: How Multicultural Classroom Instruction Is Undermining Our Children's Ability to Read, Write and Reason.*

37. Irving Kristol, "Countercultures," *Commentary*. New York: Dec 1994. Vol. 98, Issue 6; pg. 35.

38. Francis Schaeffer, *How Should We Then Live?* (Old Tappan, NJ: Fleming H. Revell Co, 1976), p. 180.

39. Schaeffer, *How Should We Then Live?*, p. 180.

40. Schmidt, *The Menace of Multiculturalism*, p. 25.

41. Linda J. Waite and Maggie Gallagher, *The Case for Marriage: Why Married People Are Happier, Healthier, and Better Off Financially* (New York: Doubleday, 2000) Inside jacket cover.

42. Karl R. Popper, *The Open Society and Its Enemies* (Princeton University Press, 1971), p. 102.

43. *Newsweek*, March 29, 1999, p. 56.

44. Francis Schaeffer, *The God Who Is There*, vol. 1, bk. 1 of *The Complete Works of Francis A. Schaeffer* (Good News Publisher, 1982), p. 11.


(1) College campus: From Countering Culture video (2004 Summit Ministries: Manitou Springs, CO)

(2) Aztec sacrifice: From ClipArt.com

(3) Mohammed: From ClipArt.com

# CHAPTER 9

# Political Power Plays

"The [current campus culture] war is
fundamentally over what kinds of knowledge
universities should encourage their
students to acquire…"[1]
—PHILLIP JOHNSON

"Gay marriage is not some sideline issue;
it is the marriage debate. Losing it means
losing marriage as a social institution,
a shared public norm."[2]
— MAGGIE GALLAGHER

"The Texas sodomy case makes it clear that
conservatives are losing the culture war."[3]
—ARMSTRONG WILLIAMS

In the 1979 film version of *Les Miserables*, Police Inspector Javert says to Jean Valjean, "There is no God. There is only the law. Guilt and innocence do not exist outside the law."

Javert's comment agrees with postmodern beliefs: laws derive from the mind of man, not God. Similar to how the postmodernist understands the concept of "truth," law is perceived as a social construct used by those in power to force others to do their will. Yet, Nietzsche and Foucault, as we saw in the last chapter, pointed out that without God, there is no law. Given these two contemporary notions, if the screenplay of *Les Miserables* was rewritten for a postmodern audience, Inspector Javert would more likely say something such as: "There is no law. There is only power. Guilt and innocence do not exist except in the power structure of society."

It is interesting to note that today we find many postmodern "Javerts" in our midst. One example is Susan Estrich, Professor of Law and Political Science at the University of Southern California Law School and a syndicated columnist who has worked with many liberal politicians and appeared on numerous television talk shows. Estrich was asked once why she supported Anita Hill when Hill charged Clarence Thomas (during his confirmation hearings for the Supreme Court) with sexual harassment but opposed Paula Jones' sexual harassment allegations against President Clinton. Ms. Estrich replied simply, "You believe in principle; I believe in politics."

Ms. Estrich takes her cue from the playbook of Marx, Nietzsche and Foucault, implying that law is simply a tool of political power. Marx said, "Political power, properly so called, is merely the organized power of one class for oppressing another."[4] Estrich

> In a postmodern world, the survival of the fittest equals the survival of those in power.

intimates that she will use the law in any way necessary to get what she wants. Thus, the law is no longer a God-ordained, objective standard by which to judge men's actions and maintain an ordered society, but a weapon to beat political opponents into submission to your way of thinking.

The politics of power makes sense from the perspective of a Postmodern Marxist worldview. Starting with theological atheism and philosophical naturalism, the Postmodernist must rely on Darwinian evolution—"survival of the fittest." With blind evolutionary forces at work, man becomes simply a product of his environment, and ethics become a matter of social preferences that have benefited our survivability as a species. In light of this postmodern "creation" story, law is what men decide, and politics becomes the vehicle that the powerful use to get their way. In a postmodern world, the survival of the fittest equals the survival of those in power. As Marx put it, "The ruling ideas of each age have ever been the ideas of its ruling class."[5]

## UNBRIDLED POLITICAL POWER

Where does the politics of power take us? We only have to look back over the past century for the answer. R. J. Rummel studied extensively the archives of the former Soviet Union as well as documents from other pertinent sources to uncover the death and destruction brought about when governments institute a Marxist brand of power politics as the basis for law and no longer appeal to God as the Supreme Judge. In his landmark 20th century book, *Death By Government*, Rummel reveals the following:

In total, during the first eighty-eight years of this century, almost 170 million men, women, and children have been shot, beaten, tortured, knifed,burned, starved, frozen, crushed, or worked to death; buried alive, drowned, hung, bombed, or killed in any other of the myriad ways governments have inflicted death on unarmed, helpless citizens and foreigners. The dead could conceivably be nearly 360 million people. It is as though our species has been devastated by a modern Black Plague. And indeed it has, but a plague of Power, not germs.[6]

In Death by Government, R.J. Rummel shows that the number of people killed by totalitarian governments during the 20th century may be equivalent to the population of North America.

The "plague of Power" Rummel refers to is Marxism, specifically the communist stranglehold on the former Soviet Union, China, North Korea, Cambodia, and other Communist nations around the world. Here in America, we are moving in the direction of Marx's vision for society, except, unlike the sudden political upheaval that engulfed Russia and China and the wholesale slaughter it brought, socialism is coming to us on the installment plan, or as Lenin called it, according to the "salami tactic"—one slice at a time.[7]

The putdown of China's student protests at Tiananmen Square in June 1989 resulted in the deaths of more than 500 people and epitomizes the typical outworking of Marxist philosophy.

Conservative columnist and author Ann Coulter also describes the situation: "While undermining victory in the Cold War, [American] liberals dedicated themselves to mainstreaming communist ideals at home."[8]

Many Americans do not realize the shift in worldview that has taken place over the past half-century. Because this change has been gradual, the Marxist worldview is mostly hidden, and much of this is by design. "Practically no one is a 'communist' today," writes Balint Vazsonyi, "What happened?"[9] Vazsonyi is a Hungarian-born concert pianist and historian who lived under the iron hand of communism as a child, immigrated to America and was granted American citizenship in 1964. Vazsonyi answers his own question:

Fundamental attitudes don't disappear into thin air. People might die, but ideas rarely do, especially when the idea is one of only two major strains of political thought that excite the people, dominate the minds, and determine the affairs of man for centuries.... It must count among the most amazing spectacles of history to be inundated with the rhetoric, theory, and practice of communism, and see not one communist around. We read and hear daily about class warfare, redistribution of wealth, the 'dispossessed' masses, the disadvantaged, universal health care, speech codes, sensitivity training, restrictions on parents' rights, school-to-work—the list goes on and on. The agenda is with us; the Party is not.[10]

> Here in America, socialism is coming to us on the installment plan, or as Lenin called it, according to the "salami tactic"— one slice at a time.

Vazsonyi points out that, despite denials, the "salami tactic" has introduced the *practice* of communism in the form of multiculturalism and feminism (as brought out in chapter 8) as well as even more potent changes in our political landscape such as the adoption of political correctness and identity politics. We will examine these topics more closely in this chapter.

## POLITICAL CORRECTNESS: REVISING WHAT CHILDREN LEARN

Political correctness circumscribes the moral code for the politics of power. The PC crowd recognizes right and wrong, but instead of basing ethics on moral absolutes established by God, their standard for what is right revolves around their political objectives, hence the term *political* correctness. "The PC promoters may seem to have numerous goals," writes Alvin J. Schmidt in *The Menace of Multiculturalism*, "but in reality they amount to only two: (1) to impose multiculturalist values that relativize all knowledge and

standards of truth, except their own; and (2) to dismantle the Euro-American culture."[11] How does one go about dismantling a culture? In George Orwell's telling novel, *1984*, a totalitarian government reshapes society by exercising complete power over the lives of its citizens. In the 1984 society of Oceania, it is a "thoughtcrime" to think for oneself. One of the tactics used by "Big Brother" to manage people's thoughts is to rewrite history and control education, making sure all knowledge is filtered through government handlers.

> To suit politically correct sensibilities, textbook writers and publishers are rewriting what American students learn.

An ominously similar trend is happening here in America—textbook writers and publishers are rewriting what students learn to suit politically correct sensibilities. This is called "revisionism." We mentioned several examples in the last chapter related to history, but history is only one of a number of areas under revision. Diane Ravitch is a historian of education, a research professor at New York University, a senior fellow at the Brookings Institution, where she holds the Brown Chair in Education Policy, and author of *The Language Police: How Pressure Groups Restrict What Students Learn*. In an article titled "Education after the Culture Wars," she presents her evaluation of national language arts tests for fourth grade students. She comments, "what I learned in this setting suggests that the problems within American education run deep, and that these problems have grave implications, not just for America's primary schools, but also for its colleges and universities—and, indeed, for the future of our common culture."[12] She discovered how reading samples used in these tests had been revised, leaving out ideas and images that might be "offensive" to certain groups of people. Ravitch notes, "In an essay on a giant sequoia tree, for example, the editors deleted a phrase that compared the sequoia's shape to that of a Christmas tree because the analogy was considered religious and might be offensive to non-Christians. Another phrase in the same essay was dropped as sexist because it described a branch of the sequoia tree as so wide that a seven-foot man could stretch across it without being able to extend either his fingers or his toes over the edge."[13]

Ms. Ravitch then spoke with the publisher of these tests. "When I asked why so few reading pas-

To be politically correct, you just might not want to describe a Sequoiah tree as looking like a Christmas tree or having branches too large for a man to reach around.

Universities have installed "speech codes" to punish any student or faculty member who does not abide by the new ethics of equality for "disadvantaged" groups based on their sex, race, sexual orientation, or disability.

sages were drawn from classic children's literature, the publisher explained that it was a well-accepted principle in educational publishing that everything written before 1970 was rife with racism and sexism. Only stories written after that date, he said, were likely to have acceptable language and appropriate multicultural sensitivity."[14] She also discovered that every publisher of school textbooks has a list of guidelines to insure their texts and tests are screened for representational fairness, language usage, stereotyping, and controversial subject matter. "The language used in the tests was also carefully scrutinized for signs of bias," says Ravitch. "Almost any use of the word 'man,' whether by itself, in a suffix (as in 'salesman' or 'workman'), or in a colloquial phrase ('the man in the street' or 'mankind'), is treated as an unacceptable form of gender bias."[15] Here we see the feminist objective of equalizing the sexes rooted tangibly in educational practices. The classrooms of America have become politicized through the game of "power politics."

Writing on the same topic, columnist John Leo exposes other samples of how today's textbooks seek to eliminate any sense of bias:

Which of the following stories would be too biased for schools to allow on tests?
(1) Overcoming daunting obstacles, a blind man climbs Mount McKinley; (2) Dinosaurs roam the

Earth in prehistoric times; (3) An Asian-American girl, whose mother is a professor, plays checkers with her grandfather and brings him pizza.

As you probably guessed, all three stories are deeply biased. (1) Emphasis on a "daunying" climb implies that blindness is some sort of disability, when it should be viewed as just another personal attribute, like hair color. Besides, mountain-climbing stories are examples of "regional bias," unfair to readers who live in deserts, cities and rural areas. (2) Dinosaurs are a no-no—they imply acceptance of evolutionary theory. (3) Making the girl's mother a professor perpetuates the "model minority" myth that stereotypes Asian-Americans. Older people must not be shown playing checkers. They should be up on the roof fixing shingles or doing something vigorous. And pizza is a junk food. Kids may eat it—but not in a school story.

## SPEECH CODES

Revising textbooks is only part of the story. In order to establish a learning environment free from harassment and intimidation (as defined by PC supporters), universities have installed "speech codes" to punish any student or faculty member who does not abide by the new ethics of equality for "disadvantaged" groups based on their sex, race, sexual orientation, or disability. Speech codes prohibit anything that intentionally produces "psychological… discomfort, embarrassment, or ridicule,"[17] and includes such actions as telling jokes or even laughing at the wrong kinds of

> The goal of political correctness is not to educate students to become independent, morally upright, and involved citizens but rather to produce compliant comrades for the world community.

expressions. These campus policies are written in very broad, vague terms, relegating circumstances to a subjective exercise to determine whether or not the code has been violated.

While we agree students should be courteous in their remarks to one another, the significant point is that speech codes are not administered evenly. For example, it is *not* a breech of policy to call a white person a "honky" or "white fascist pig." On the other hand, for saying anything that might be offensive to women, people of color, or homosexuals, a student can be brought before the administrative tribunal, required to attend sensitivity classes and write public apologies, or face being suspended from college. In several cases, conservative campus newspapers that have published satirical editorials or cartoons directed at protected groups have been censored by college officials, copies of the offending newspapers confiscated, and the aberrant editor banished from the paper's staff.

The reason given for the differing standards is that certain groups, according to Marxist orthodoxy, historically have been oppressed. To level the playing field for these repressed people, the rights of those who have traditionally held the power (white males) must be subverted. Speech codes accomplish this goal of "liberating tolerance," to use the term coined by Herbert Marcuse, by taking a stand of "intolerance against movements from the Right, and toleration of movements from the Left."[18]

One stunning example of PC thought management occurred in October 2001 at the University of North Carolina at Wilmington in which the school ordered the opening and examination of private messages in a UNC-W professor's email account. The incident erupted when a student wrote an email with a scathing denouncement of President Bush's response and actions after the 9/11 terrorist attacks on the World Trade Center and the Pentagon. The student sent the email to a number of university faculty and concluded with an invitation to forward the email in the interest of "open, unbiased, democratic discussion."[19] One professor, Mike Adams, sent the student a brief reply and forwarded the student's message to others, several of whom responded directly to her. "Stung by sharp criticism, the student, in communications to the UNC-W general counsel, accused Professor Adams of intimidation, defamation, and false representation,"[20] and demanded that the university allow her to see the professor's emails in order to sue him. The administration capitulated.

Thankfully, some of these attempts by universities to censor student or faculty free speech have lost when taken to court. Nevertheless, college administrators have set the stage for accentuating differences among people which leads only to a further sense of cultural distance between them. But, again, this fits the Marxist view of social relations and class warfare, so the politics of power is brought to our centers of education.

## BUILDING A UTOPIAN WORLD

Sadly, the goal of political correctness is not to educate students to become independent, morally upright, and involved citizens but rather to produce compliant comrades for the world community—and to produce the *socialist* dream of a better society. This radical political agenda is a utopian vision, a longing for a time when all of society's ills and abuses will be eliminated. Religion, especially the Christian religion, is understood by Marxists to be the greatest hindrance to this utopian state. "[Leftist writer Walt] Whitman and

[humanist educator John] Dewey tried to substitute hope for knowledge," writes Richard Rorty, Stanford's Professor of Comparative Literature and well-known proponent of postmodern thought. "They wanted to put shared utopian

> To achieve their utopia, Marxists understand they must dismantle the current social system in America by undermining the moral law of God.

dreams—dreams of an ideally decent and civilized society—in the place of knowledge of God's Will, Moral Law, the Laws of History, or the Facts of Science... As long as we have a functioning political left, we still have a chance to achieve our country, to make it the country of Whitman's and Dewey's dreams."[21]

Notice Rorty's language of idealism. The goal of the radical left is nothing less than remaking society to match the dream world they have conjured. Thomas Sowell refers to this desire for the perfect society as "The Quest for Cosmic Justice." To achieve their utopia, Marxists understand they must dismantle the current social system in America by undermining the moral law of God. The fast track to achieving this goal is not only to control what students learn in school but also to subvert the home and the family by introducing young people to sexual licentiousness, including both heterosexual promiscuity and homosexuality.

## THE HOMOSEXUAL AGENDA

Homosexuality is not new. It has been practiced since ancient times, most notably in the nation-state of Sparta which mandated homosexual "education" as part of the military training of every male. Yet in every other nation throughout history, homosexual sex has been considered deviant behavior. In western civilization, which grew from a biblical foundation, homosexuality was condemned from the standpoint of God's divine moral law as well as the natural law written on the conscience of every person (see Leviticus 18:22 and Romans 1:26-27).

> **LEVITICUS 18:22**
>
> *You are not to sleep with a man as with a woman; it is detestable.*

Yet, in the early 1900's, prominent Marxists began to challenge traditional sexual mores. In the 1920's, George Lukacs headed the department of education for both the Soviet Union and, later, Hungary, where he launched an "aggressive sex education program which consisted, in part, of special lectures and literature in schools 'instructing' children in free love, presenting graphic portrayals of intercourse, undermining 'archaic' family structures, including the concept of monogamy, and emphasizing the irrelevance of religion, which, he said, deprived people of pleasure."[22]

Taking their cue from Lukacs, other Marxist radicals sought to establish a

> **ROMANS 1:26-27**
>
> *This is why God delivered them over to degrading passions. For even their females exchanged natural sexual intercourse for what is unnatural. The males in the same way also left natural sexual intercourse with females and were inflamed in their lust for one another. Males committed shameless acts with males and received in their own persons the appropriate penalty for their perversion.*

beachhead in American education by replacing a biblically based ethic, which confines sexual intimacy to marriage, with a no-holds-barred "pursuit of pleasure." Then, via the writings of Marx (who promoted sexual "liberation") and Freud (who equated sexual repression with a host of neuroses), many college students of the 1960's embraced the whole package, preferring to "make love, not war." "Free love" became their rallying cry, and the sexual revolution swept the nation, spreading from the campus to popular culture through rock musicians, film directors, and television producers. Yet this glorification of sexual license, like the legendary genie, does not stay in its bottle, and predictably has led to the legitimization of other kinds of sexual expression, namely homosexual practices.

As the latest "marginalized" minority group in the line-up of victims looking for liberation from their oppressors, homosexuals now assert their "rights" for acceptance into the American mainstream, and the educational establishment is once again the primary cheerleader for reorienting traditional attitudes toward homosexual practices. Their spokesmen are in every discipline, but seem to be especially attracted to humanities departments. According to an article in *Campus*:

> Looking for deviant sexual practices in classic literature is a favorite pastime for many Humanities professors. A professor at Duke University, Michael Moon, presented a paper to the Modern Language Association entitled "Desubliminating the Male Sublime: Autoerotics, Anal Erotics, and Corporal Violence in Melville and William Burroughs." At the same conference, English professor Eve Kosofsky Sedgwich presented the topics "Jane Austen and the Masturbating Girl" and "How to Bring Your Kids Up Gay."[23]

B. K. Eakman cites Lukacs' model as the inspiration to introduce sex education into American elementary and secondary schools, largely through organizations such as the Sexuality Information and Education Council of the United States.[24] SIECUS, along with the National Education Association, the largest teachers union in the nation, promotes a homosexual agenda that includes funding to alleviate discrimination against deviant sexual practices, support for gay and lesbian history month (celebrating the contributions of homosexuals—and supposed homosexuals—in history, much of it fabricated!), and the inclusion of "sexual orientation" in sex education programs.[25] In the process, rhetoric has changed subtly but profoundly, referring to sodomy, for example, as "sexual orientation"—a more morally neutral designation. This change in terminology rings of the politically motivated "newspeak" coined by George Orwell in *1984*. However, in the current situation, misleading language is not generated by government but by advocates of social change, and it is disseminated through the willing compliance of popular media. Unfortunately, as we reveal below, our lawmakers are not far behind in adopting the agenda.

In their book, *The Homosexual Agenda*, Sears and Osten chronicle a number of instances in which our publicly funded schools actively promote homosexuality. For instance, Ithaca, New York school officials require first and second graders to be evaluated on their tolerance levels, including how they respect others of varying "genders" (implying other than the two "traditional" genders, so as to include the "transgendered"). In Provincetown, Massachusetts, the school board voted to teach pre-schoolers about homosexual behavior. In Hayward, California, school policy allows

> As the latest "marginalized" minority group in the line-up of victims looking for liberation from their oppressors, homosexuals now assert their "rights" for acceptance into the American mainstream.

teachers and staff to talk openly with students during classroom instructional time about their homosexual behavior and to do so without parental permission. And as with university speech codes, diversity and tolerance goes only one direction. In Ann Arbor, Michigan, a local high school held a "Diversity Week" that allowed students to give speeches on race, religion, and homosexuality at an all-school assembly. School officials, however, turned down one student's request to present the biblical position regarding homosexual behavior, claiming that, according to Sears and Osten, "her religious view toward homosexual behavior was 'negative' and would 'water down' the 'positive' religious message they wanted to convey."[26] Not allowing dissenting views is another classic example of the totalitarian thought control portrayed in Orwell's fictional world but which is now becoming a part of our real world experience.

In yet another peculiar case, kindergartener Daniel Walz was not allowed to give to his classmates as a personal gift pencils imprinted with the message, "Jesus loves the little children." The 3rd U.S. Circuit Court of Appeals ruled that the school has a "legitimate area of control" regarding speech, and therefore could restrict Daniel's freedom in his choice of gifts to his friends at school.[27] For more examples of intolerance toward a biblical worldview, see David Limbaugh's *Persecution: How Liberals Are Waging War Against Christianity*.

Activist court judges also play a role in promoting homosexual inclusion. An extremely significant issue regarding homosexuality was decided by the U. S. Supreme Court during the summer of 2003. In what is almost certainly destined to become a landmark case, *Lawrence v. Texas*, the nation's highest court took the radical approach that "deviant sexual intercourse with another individual of the same sex" is a constitutionally protected act. According to family activist Tom Jipping, the court also "rejected the whole idea that legislatures can enforce community standards."[28] While the 6-justice majority wrote reassuringly that this

---

# SELECTED POSITION STATEMENTS OF THE SEXUALITY INFORMATION AND EDUCATION COUNCIL OF THE UNITED STATES (SIECUS)

(Source: www.siecus.org)

## SCHOOL-BASED SEXUALITY EDUCATION

Comprehensive school-based sexuality education that is appropriate to students' age, developmental level, and cultural background should be an important part of the education program at every grade. A comprehensive sexuality program will respect the diversity of values and beliefs represented in the community and will complement and augment the sexuality education children receive from their families, religious and community groups, and health care professionals. Because child development involves sexuality, all pre-kindergarten through twelfth-grade teachers should receive at least one course in human sexuality.

## SEXUALITY AND RELIGION

Religion can play a significant role in promoting an understanding of sexuality as an affirming expression of equality, mutual respect, caring, and love. Religious groups and spiritual leaders can helpfully involve themselves in sexuality education and in promoting the sexual health of their constituents, including those who are gay, lesbian, bisexual, young, elderly, and ill, or with physical, cognitive, or emotional disabilities. While recognizing that religious groups have diverging views on how sexuality is expressed, professional guidance can assist religious leaders in how best to minister to their constituents regarding their sexual needs. It is important for religious institutions to minister and allow full religious participation to individuals who are gay, lesbian, or bisexual.

## SEXUAL ORIENTATION

Sexual orientation is an essential human quality. Individuals have the right to accept, acknowledge, and live in accordance with their sexual orientation, be they bisexual, heterosexual, gay, or lesbian. The legal system should guarantee the civil rights and protection of all people, regardless of sexual orientation. Prejudice and discrimination based on sexual orientation is unconscionable.

## ABORTION

Every woman, regardless of age or income, should have the right to obtain an abortion under safe, legal, confidential, and dignified conditions, and at a reasonable cost. Every woman is entitled to have full knowledge of the alternatives available to her, and to obtain complete and unbiased information and counseling concerning the nature, consequences, and risks associated both with abortion and with pregnancy and childbirth. Abortion counseling and services should be provided by professionals specially trained in this field. Violence against abortion providers and harassment intended to impede women's access to these providers are unconscionable attempts to undermine women's reproductive health rights and should be decisively prosecuted by the justice system.

> Not allowing dissenting views is another classic example of the totalitarian thought control portrayed in Orwell's fictional world but which is now becoming a part of our real world experience.

ruling does not weaken marriage law, Justice Antonin Scalia said in his scathing dissent, "The court today pretends that… we need not fear judicial imposition of homosexual marriage, as has recently occurred in Canada…. Do not believe it."[29]

Justice Scalia understood the implications and logic of the ruling, as did those who are pushing the homosexual agenda. According to a CNS news article:

> Hours after the U.S. Supreme Court struck down a Texas sodomy statute, homosexual activists proclaimed their next target would be to overturn a host of laws they view as discriminatory, including those that limit marriage to opposite-sex couples. Now that the court has ruled that these sodomy laws are unconstitutional, homosexuals are pre p a r e d to eliminate other forms of discrimination, said Ruth Harlow, lead attorney for [litigates in the Texas case] Lawrence and Garner and legal director at the homosexual advocacy group Lambda Legal… Harlow said discrimination in marriage laws and by the U.S. military would be two of their targets. "By knocking out both sodomy laws and the justification of morality, this decision makes it much harder to defend those discriminatory schemes."[30]

Attorney Harlow also said "people with strong

Christian views are outnumbered by a majority of Americans who opposed these sodomy laws. They are more and more being pushed to the sidelines. We don't have any problems with individuals making their own choices and having their own religious views. But in our country, a minority of individuals cannot dictate those views for the whole country."[31]

While Harlow's statement may come as a surprise to many Americans, the goal of changing society's view of the family has been a part of the homosexual agenda for a number of years. Enrique Rueda explains:

> There is no question that one of the top priorities of the homosexual movement is to force a "redefinition" of the American family away from the traditional husband-wife-children model to a more "functional" definition based on the notion of economic unit or any other basis that does not require heterosexuality as its foundation. The notion that a family must involve persons of both sexes is profoundly inimical to the homosexual movement... As early as 1970, elements within the homosexual movement had identified the family as inimical to its interests. At a convention in Philadelphia, the "Male Homosexual" work shop included the following as one of its demands: "The abolition of the nuclear family because it perpetuates the false categories of homosexuality and heterosexuality."[32]

> "One of the top priorities of the homosexual movement is to force a 'redefinition' of the American family away from the traditional husband-wife-children model."
> —Enrique Rueda

It is interesting to note that this demand by homosexuals mimics Karl Marx's statement in his 1848 *Communist Manifesto* when he called for the "abolition of the family"![33] Marx gave a different reason for why the family must be eliminated, claiming that the "bourgeois family" is based on capital, private gain and the exploitation of women—a view championed by current day radical feminists in the battle of the sexes. Now, however, homosexuals have joined the fight, calling for destruction of the family because, for them, it promotes a false distinction between various "acceptable" sexual orientations.

## COUNTERING THE HOMOSEXUAL AGENDA

At this point, some may object that we are being homophobic. The objection is rooted in the notion that homosexuals are "born that way," and it is therefore unfair to consider their behavior deviant. While the "born that way" defense is often used, it has no foundation in scientific fact. Hyped by the media, research about discovering "gay genes" and studies linking heredity and homosexuality, on later inspection, are found to be based on an insignificantly small number of subjects, partial reporting of results, or unwarranted conclusions in light of actual findings. To find out more about the misinformation surrounding the "gay gene" theory or how to help those struggling

> The median age of death for homosexual men is 44 to 46—a full 30 years less than the life expectancy of heterosexual married men.

with homosexuality, we have listed a number of resources at the end of the chapter.

Most people are not aware of the flaws in the gay gene theory, nor are they informed about the often severe emotional and physical repercussions of a homosexual lifestyle. According to one study, the median age of death for homosexual men is 44 to 46—a full 30 years less than the life expectancy of heterosexual married men![34]

Today's young people are subjected to a skewed view from all cultural fronts: Hollywood, academia, and now the politicized courts—none of which offer the complete story on the homosexual lifestyle. How many college freshmen know, for instance, that over half of the AIDS cases in the U.S. are attributable to homosexual sodomy? Or that only two percent of people—men having sex with men—account for 60 percent of the AIDS cases in the state of Texas? Despite all the so-called reality television, no programs portray the struggle of the homosexual lifestyle for what it is. Where are the gay and lesbian couples suffering from HIV or gender identity confusion in *Will and Grace* or *It's All Relative*? In the name of equality, diversity, and inclusiveness, the country has shielded its youth from the truth about the devastating consequences of homosexuality. We do not say this to be harsh, but to be honest with all the facts, most of which are being withheld from the discussion regarding homosexuality.

Economist and author Jennifer Roback Morse explains that the assault on marriage "uses the rhetoric and language" of *choice* in the marketplace because it is "very seductive."[35] And a growing number of Americans are being taken in by the seduction. In 1988, 74.9 percent of Americans believed sex between two people of the same gender is always wrong. By 1998, that number had *fallen* to 54.6 percent.[36] And according to a 2003 Gallup poll, 39 percent of Americans believe homosexual marriage should be

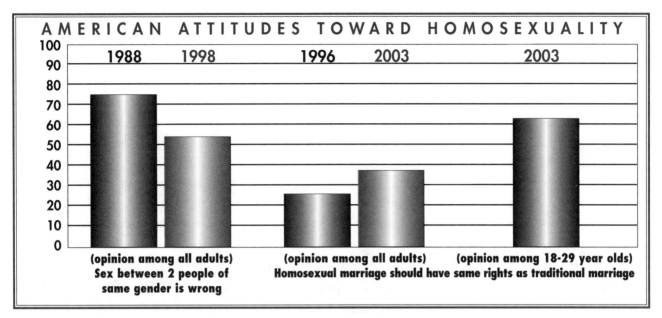

AMERICAN ATTITUDES TOWARD HOMOSEXUALITY

1988  1998     1996  2003           2003

(opinion among all adults)      (opinion among all adults)      (opinion among 18-29 year olds)
Sex between 2 people of      Homosexual marriage should have same rights as traditional marriage
same gender is wrong

recognized with the same rights and benefits as traditional marriage between a man and a woman. Yet just seven years ago, only 27 percent believed the same thing. Even more revealing of the success of the homosexual agenda is the level of approval for homosexual marriage among members of "Generation Y." On the heels of the *Lawrence v. Texas* sodomy case, 61 percent of Americans aged 18-29 believe homosexual marriages should be valid.[37]

## SALTY CHRISTIANS

Those of us who seek a truly stable foundation for individuals and society need to help our friends, neighbors, and public officials understand the seriousness of devaluing marriage. Maggie Gallagher warns of what will happen if we do not:

> If the law embraces this message [of undermining traditional marriage], government will become its carrier and promoter. School

textbooks, teen-pregnancy programs, and abstinence education (to mention just a few venues) will all be forced to carry this new unisex marriage vision. Religious people and social conservatives (not to mention marriage advocates in general) unwilling to champion this message, will retreat from the public square.[38]

Anyone who refuses to adhere to the government's mandated worldview will face the strong arm of the state. In some situations, this is already happening. For example, one college freshman asked the dorm housing authority if he could change roommates since his assigned roommate was an avowed homosexual who planned to have his lovers stay overnight in the dorm room. The university labeled the *straight* student bigoted and forced *him* to attend sensitivity training in order to correct his politically *in*correct views!

Ms. Gallagher gives the practical rationale for championing marriage. She writes:

> When men and women fail to form stable

marriages, the first result is a vast expansion of government attempts to cope with the terrible social needs that result. There is scarcely a dollar that state and federal government spends on social programs that is not driven in large part by family fragmentation: crime, poverty, drug abuse, teen pregnancy, school failure, mental and physical health problems.[39]

Of course, these problems would be anticipated from a biblical worldview, since God designed male/female

marriage to be the place where children learn to be moral, mature, contributors to society (see God's instructions to parents for raising godly children in Deuteronomy 6).

The cost of inaction on our part is measured in peoples' lives. We must argue for the truth of God's design for sex and marriage. C. S. Lewis admonishes the faithful in Christ to stand up and be heard. He writes, "As Christians we are tempted to make unnecessary concessions to those outside the Faith. We give in too much… we must show our Christian colors, if

## INSTRUCTIONS FOR RAISING GODLY CHILDREN

### (Deuteronomy 6)

This is the command—the statutes and ordinances—the Lord your God has instructed [me] to teach you, so that you may follow [them] in the land you are about to enter and possess. [2][Do this] so that you may fear the Lord your God all the days of your life by keeping all His statutes and commands I am giving you, your sons, and your grandsons, and so that you may have a long life. [3]Listen, Israel, and be careful to follow [them], so that you may prosper and multiply greatly, because the Lord, the God of your fathers, has promised you a land flowing with milk and honey.

[4]"Listen, Israel: The Lord our God, the Lord is One. [5]Love the Lord your God with all your heart, with all your soul, and with all your strength. [6]These words that I am giving you today are to be in your heart. [7]Repeat them to your children. Talk about them when you sit in your house and when you walk along the road, when you lie down and when you get up. [8]Bind them as a sign on your hand and let them be a symbol on your forehead. [9]Write them on the doorposts of your house and on your gates.

[10]"When the Lord your God brings you into the land He swore to your fathers Abraham, Isaac, and Jacob that He would give you—a [land with] large and beautiful cities that you did not build, [11]houses full of every good thing that you did not fill [them with], wells dug that you did not dig, and vineyards and olive groves that you did not plant—and when you eat and are satisfied, [12]be careful not to forget the Lord who brought you out of the land of Egypt, out of the place of slavery. [13]Fear the Lord your God, worship Him, and take [your] oaths in His name. [14]Do not follow other gods, the gods of the peoples around you, [15]for the Lord your God, who is among you, is a jealous God. Otherwise, the Lord your God will become angry with you and wipe you off the face of the earth. [16]Do not test the Lord your God as you tested [Him] at Massah. [17]Carefully observe the commands of the Lord your God, the decrees and statutes He has commanded you. [18]Do what is right and good in the Lord's sight, so that you may prosper and so that you may enter and possess the good land the Lord your God swore to [give] your fathers, [19]by driving out all your enemies before you, as the Lord has said.

[20]"When your son asks you in the future, 'What is the meaning of the decrees, statutes, and ordinances, which the Lord our God has commanded you?' [21]tell him, 'We were slaves of Pharaoh in Egypt, but the Lord brought us out of Egypt with a strong hand. [22]Before our eyes the Lord inflicted great and devastating signs and wonders on Egypt, on Pharaoh and all his household, [23]but He brought us from there in order to lead us in and give us the land that He swore to our fathers. [24]The Lord commanded us to follow all these statutes and to fear the Lord our God for our prosperity always and for our preservation, as it is today. [25]Righteousness will be ours if we are careful to follow every one of these commands before the Lord our God, as He has commanded us.'"

we are to be true to Jesus Christ. We cannot remain silent and concede everything away."[40] As former ambassador Alan Keyes remarked:

> More important than refutations of the particular sophistries that oppose us, however, is recognizing that the attack on marriage is an attack on the primal pattern of human life and is, accordingly, a breathtakingly cavalier and thoughtless project. It is the kind of irresponsible thing that we rightly associate with the worst attitudes of unreflective and inexperienced youth. The supporters of 'domestic partnership' know very well, in one sense, what they are doing. They know that they are attacking the privileged position of the marriage-based, two-parent family, and this apparently seems to them to be an eminently rational thing to do. So might the teen-ager who has taken the family car on a joy ride that ended in wreck and tragedy.... Sometimes refutation is not the best response. We need to recover our ability to look at such people and tell them, in charity, that they propose madness.[41]

When it comes to significant ethical issues such as the sanctity of life, we already have lost the battle and now must regain the high ground politically. In the case of marriage law, our backs are against the wall, and we must not give another inch, or it, too, will be lost.

We confront these issues, not to be unkind to homosexuals, but to show how a shift in worldview brings about a change in social mores and what is considered appropriate public policy. Christ died for sinners, which includes every one of us. And while, according to the Bible, any sex outside of marriage is wrong, Paul points out that homosexual sex is only *one* of the results of suppressing God's moral law. He

## THE OUTCOMES OF NOT ACKNOWLEDGING GOD
### (Romans 1:18-32)

For God's wrath is revealed from heaven against all godlessness and unrighteousness of people who by their unrighteousness suppress the truth, [19]since what can be known about God is evident among them, because God has shown it to them. [20]From the creation of the world His invisible attributes, that is, His eternal power and divine nature, have been clearly seen, being understood through what He has made. As a result, people are without excuse. [21]For though they knew God, they did not glorify Him as God or show gratitude. Instead, their thinking became nonsense, and their senseless minds were darkened. [22]Claiming to be wise, they became fools [23]and exchanged the glory of the immortal God for images resembling mortal man, birds, four-footed animals, and reptiles. [24]Therefore God delivered them over in the cravings of their hearts to sexual impurity, so that their bodies were degraded among themselves. [25]They exchanged the truth of God for a lie, and worshiped and served something created instead of the Creator, who is blessed forever. Amen.

[26]This is why God delivered them over to degrading passions. For even their females exchanged natural sexual intercourse for what is unnatural. [27]The males in the same way also left natural sexual intercourse with females and were inflamed in their lust for one another. Males committed shameless acts with males and received in their own persons the appropriate penalty for their perversion. [28]And because they did not think it worthwhile to have God in their knowledge, God delivered them over to a worthless mind to do what is morally wrong. [29]They are filled with all unrighteousness, evil, greed, and wickedness. They are full of envy, murder, disputes, deceit, and malice. They are gossips, [30]slanderers, God-haters, arrogant, proud, boastful, inventors of evil, disobedient to parents, [31]undiscerning, untrustworthy, unloving, and unmerciful. [32]Although they know full well God's just sentence—that those who practice such things deserve to die—they not only do them, but even applaud others who practice them.

describes homosexuality as "degrading" to those involved in it, an "unnatural" act in light of our male/female physical design, as "indecent," and a "perversion" of God's plan for expressing our sexuality. Yet, in his next statement, Paul delineates other outcomes of not acknowledging God: greed, gossip, and envy (Romans 1:18-32). We certainly do not suggest that homosexuals be treated with contempt or ridicule. We do suggest this: in the same way those who teach our children and preside over our courts of law should *not* be promoting greed or envy or adultery, they also should *not* be promoting homosexual sex.

As Christians seeking to be salt and light in our communities, we need to realize people will have a range of responses to our message. Some will steadfastly refuse to hear what we say. Others will hear but not understand. Yet, some will hear and be changed. We must insure that they hear God's truth shared with gentleness and compassion. The Apostle Peter instructs Christ's followers:

> Therefore, get your minds ready for action being self-disciplined, and set your hope completely on the grace to be brought to you at the revelation of Jesus Christ. As obedient children, do not be conformed to the desires of your former ignorance but, as the One who called you is holy, you also are to be holy in all your conduct... but set apart the Messiah as Lord in your hearts, and always be ready to give a defense to anyone who asks you a reason for the hope that is in you. However, do this with gentleness and respect... (1 Peter 1:13-15; 3:15-16)

This means taking a two-stage approach. First, we need a "pastoral" sensitivity to individuals who are caught up in a homosexual lifestyle. We do this not by

---

## THE GOVERNMENT'S MANDATE FROM GOD

*Genesis 9:6*
Whoever sheds man's blood, his blood will be shed by man, for God made man in His image.

*Romans 13:1-7*
Everyone must submit to the governing authorities, for there is no authority except from God, and those that exist are instituted by God. [2]So then, the one who resists the authority is opposing God's command, and those who oppose it will bring judgment on themselves. [3]For rulers are not a terror to good conduct, but to bad. Do you want to be unafraid of the authority? Do good and you will have its approval. [4]For government is God's servant to you for good. But if you do wrong, be afraid, because it does not carry the sword for no reason. For government is God's servant, an avenger that brings wrath on the one who does wrong. [5]Therefore, you must submit, not only because of wrath, but also because of your conscience. [6]And for this reason you pay taxes, since the [authorities] are God's public servants, continually attending to these tasks. [7]Pay your obligations to everyone: taxes to those you owe taxes, tolls to those you owe tolls, respect to those you owe respect, and honor to those you owe honor.

*1 Peter 2:13-14*
Submit to every human institution because of the Lord, whether to the Emperor as the supreme authority, [14]or to governors as those sent out by him to punish those who do evil and to praise those who do good.

singling them out as especially sinful but by explaining we all are sinful in God's sight and therefore are in need of a Savior. Further, because of the addictive nature of homosexuality, we need to help individuals process the emotional pain they have endured in past relationships—relationships that have contributed to their inappropriate attachment to people of the same sex. For suggestions in this regard, read the article at the end of this chapter, "When Someone in Your Congregation Says 'I'm Gay.'"

The second approach we need is to work in the political arena to halt the advancement of behavior detrimental to individuals and society. This means becoming involved with our time and money in the election campaigns of pro-moral candidates. Our first study, *Thinking Like A Christian*, made it clear that God has ordained the state to rule (Genesis 9:6; Romans 13:1-7; 1 Peter 2:13-14), and His followers need to be involved in government to insure that it functions as closely as possible to His moral will. This does not mean we should outlaw every vice imaginable, but on certain issues, such as homosexual marriage, we must draw the line for the sake of moral rectitude and social stability.

## WORLDVIEWS MATTER

In this chapter, we have analyzed the devastating results of a socialist approach to politics, from totalitarianism's devastation of individuals and the breakdown of the the family and education—stabilizing institutions of society—to the wholesale slaughter of innocent citizens. As seen from our review of how a worldview functions, these results are predictable. Because socialism begins with the wrong theology (atheism), it leads to a wrong philosophy (materialism), which in turn results in a wrong understanding

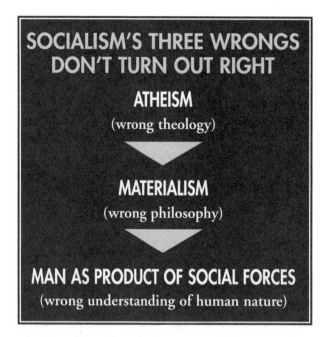

of the nature of man (man is a product of social forces). So, the push is on for social change through a wrong-headed approach to politics—trying to force an outward change upon society under the guise of doing "good."

Those who invest in learning history and observing the nature of man are aware of problems inherent in the quest for cosmic justice. J. R. R. Tolkien was one who did. In an early scene of *Lord of the Rings: The Fellowship of the Ring*, Tolkien presents a dialogue between Frodo, the Hobbit, and Gandalf, the wizard. Frodo, upon learning of the power of the "one ring" in his possession, frantically attempts to give it to

J. R. R. Tolkien understood what those on the left side of the political spectrum do not: because of our sinful nature, no man or group can be trusted, unchecked, with power over the lives and fortunes of others.

Gandalf. The wise wizard refuses to take it, saying, "Understand me, Frodo. I would use this ring from a desire to do good, but through me, it would wield a power too great and terrible to imagine." Tolkien understood what those on the left side of the political spectrum do not: because of our sinful nature, no man or group can be trusted, unchecked, with power over the lives and fortunes of others.

The founders of the United States rejected the socialist's utopian vision and sought to create a nation based on different, more realistic ideals—individual liberty and opportunity. And because they also understood man's sinful nature, they sought to put "chains" (their term) around government to keep at bay its tendency to abuse power. They knew the ultimate check on the politics of power is found in the opening phrase of the Constitution: "We, the people..." Their wisdom placed political power ultimately in the hands of citizens. If we do not take our responsibility seriously, we have only ourselves to blame when we lose our liberty to those who would seek to "do good."

In another scene from *The Two Towers*, the second *Lord of the Rings* book, Pippin and Merry have entreated the peace-loving Ents (ancient trees that walk and talk) to help battle the forces of the evil Sauron. When the trees refuse, Pippin tries to solace Merry by saying, "Maybe Treebeard is right. We don't belong here, Merry. This is too big for us. What can we do in the end? We've got the Shire. Maybe we should go home." To which Merry replies desperately, "The fires of Isengard will spread, and the woods of Tribru and Buckland will burn. And all that was once great and good in this world will be gone. There won't be a Shire, Pippin."

What Merry understood is a lesson for contemporary Christians. If we fail to act while we still have the freedom to speak our minds, there will come a day when the power-plays of political correctness will eliminate more and more of our liberties, and all that was once "great and good" about America will be gone. There will cease to be a land of the free.

A few years ago, the legendary, Oscar-winning screen actor Charlton Heston spoke at Harvard Law School, a modern bastion of political correctness. He forthrightly confronted the "newspeak" of that college. In his speech, he outlined the gravity of the problem with political correctness and took a bold stand for restoring sanity to our public conversation. We offer his words as a fitting conclusion to our discussion:

> It scares me to death, and should scare you, too, that the superstition of political correctness rules the halls of reason. You are the best and the brightest. You, here in the fertile cradle of American academia, here in the castle of learning on the Charles River; you are the cream. But I submit that you, and your counterparts across the land, are the most socially conformed and politically silenced generation since Concord Bridge. And as long as you validate that...and abide it... you are—by your grandfathers' standards—cowards.... If you talk about race, it does not make you a racist. If you see distinctions between genders, it does not make you a sexist. If you think critically about a denomination, it does not make you anti-religion. If you accept but don't celebrate homosexuality, it does not make you a homophobe.[42]

## WHEN SOMEONE IN YOUR CONGREGATION SAYS "I'M GAY"

Things to Remember

1. **No one is born gay**, and no one chooses to be gay. Because of relational brokenness in families and among peers, some people experience emotional needs that they try to meet in ungodly ways. Many of them are uncomfortable with their own gender; later, they discover they are attracted to others of the same sex, but this is not their choice. Acting on it, however, is.

2. **Change is possible**. Even going back to the first-century church, the apostle Paul wrote to former homosexuals in the Corinthian church, "...and such were some of you" (1 Cor. 6:11).

3. Because we live in a fallen world, **we are all broken**. Many people in our churches are sexually broken—victims of incest, pornography and masturbation addicts, and compulsive sex addiction. Homosexuality is only one form of brokenness.

4. **Homosexuality grows out of broken relationships and is healed in healthy relationships**, especially same-sex relationships. This is one of the reasons it is essential for recovering homosexuals and lesbians to be actively involved in the church, because this is where they can find healthy, God-honoring friendships. Their homosexuality is not contagious!

5. **Treat them with respect like you would anyone else**. They are people made in the image of God for whom Christ died-they are not their sexuality. Many people trying to come out of the gay lifestyle expect to find respect and acceptance only in the gay community. Finding it in church is immensely healing to their souls.

6. **Accept them where they are, just as Jesus did**. Choose to accept the person, but not sinful behavior. People don't change unless they experience the grace of acceptance first. But once they know they are loved and accepted, many of them are willing to do what it takes to live a life of holiness.

7. **Seek to see them with God's eyes** of love and acceptance, with His intention for their wholeness, healing and freedom. This means depending on the Holy Spirit for divine perspective and exercising humility to recognize that first impressions are often incomplete and inaccurate.

8. This is a great opportunity to lead people to an understanding of **what it means to have a personal relationship with Jesus Christ**. Some homosexual strugglers, especially men, feel that they have committed the unpardonable sin. They've heard they are going to hell no matter what they do, so they are permanently separated from God. They need to know this is a lie, because when we confess our sins, the blood of Jesus covers them ALL and cleanses us from all unrighteousness (1 John 1:9).

9. Because of abuse issues, most **strugglers seem to have an especially hard time relating to Father God** and to receiving His love. Yet it is the masculine voice (first in earthly fathers, and ultimately in our Heavenly Father) that calls gender out from both men and women, and it is the Father's personal and powerful love that is the most important healing agent in human hearts.

10. Because most pastors are men in authority, **most strugglers (men and women) are INCREDIBLY intimidated** by them. Pastors need to know this and really understand in order to minister to strugglers. This means respecting the fragility of strugglers' relationships with pastors and choosing to be deliberately tender and gentle. They really need "good shepherds." Verbalize to them that God can not only change them, but He is very proud of them (as you are) for sharing this with you and desiring to change.

11. **Most same-sex strugglers have very weak and broken boundaries**. Their deep neediness causes

them to lapse into emotionally dependent relationships with everyone who gets close. We encourage you to only counsel these folks at your office during regular business hours where others can be aware of your activities. This gives a sense of security to the struggler and a protection for you as the pastor.

12. The most success in overcoming same-gender attraction has occurred when strugglers experienced **God as Healer through heterosexual people who were willing to come alongside them** in their journeys-men helping men, and women helping women. It would be helpful for you to find someone willing to befriend and mentor the struggler. This takes a person willing to seriously invest in the life of a very needy person. They will need to be available and accessible. Their presence in the struggler's life can be powerful and healing.

13. **If someone comes in with an agenda** of arrogance, demanding acceptance of their sexual sin, don't let them bully you. There is a difference between welcoming the sinner and allowing him to continue in his rebellion. Homosexuality is sin. Lev. 18:22-23; Rom. 1:26-27, 1 Cor. 6:9-11. Note that these verses condemn homosexual behavior, not feelings.

*(The above information is taken from a brochure by Sue Bohlin, written for Living Hope Ministries. Sue serves on the Board of Directors of Living Hope and moderates one of the organization's online forums. The full text can be read at www.probe.org/docs/pastors-brochure.html.)*

## RECOMMENDED READING

Lapin, Rabbi Daniel. *America's Real War: An Orthodox Rabbi insists that Judeo-Christian Values are Vital for our Nation's Survival,* Sisters, OR: Multnomah Publishers, 1999.

Rummel, R. J. *Death By Government,* Transaction Publishers, 1997

Sowell, Thomas, *The Quest for Cosmic Justice,* New York: The Free Press, 1999.

Vazsonyi, Balint. *America's 30 Years War,* Washington, D.C.: Regnery Publishing, 1998.

HOMOSEXUALITY:

We recommend the following books and organizations for a better understanding of homosexual issues: For refutations of the research touting a genetic disposition toward homosexuality, www.cprmd.org/Myths/MYTHS_PAGE.htm is a helpful Web site, which documents 17 myths of homosexuality. Also read Jeffrey Satinover's *Homosexuality and the Politics of Truth* or go to the Web site of **The National Association for Research & Treatment of Homosexuality** at http://www.narth.com. For further information on the latest attempt to declare pedophilia normal check Dr. Laura Schlessinger's web site at www.drlaura.com.

To better understand and help those caught in the homosexual lifestyle read *A Parent's Guide to Preventing Homosexuality,* by Joseph Nicolosi & Linda Ames Nicolosi, *You Don't Have to be Gay,* by Jeff Konrad, and *Out of Egypt: One Woman's Journey Out of Lesbianism,* by Jeanette Howard. For more information on the political aspirations of the homosexual lobby, see *The Homosexual Agenda: Exposing the Principal Threat to Religious Freedom Today,* by Alan Sears and Craig Osten.

## ENDNOTES

1. Phillip E. Johnson, *Reason in the Balance* (Downers Grove, IL: InterVarsity Press, 1995) p. 112.

2. Maggie Gallagher, "The Stakes: Why we need marriage." *National Review,* online at http://nationalreview.com/comment/comment-gallagher071403.asp.

3. Armstrong Williams, "The Supreme Court and the Culture War," online commentary at http://www.townhall.com/columnists/Armstrongwilliams/aw20030722.shtml.

4. Karl Marx and Friedrick Engels, *The Communist Manifesto* (New York: Pocket Books, 1964), p. 95.

5. Marx and Engels, *The Communist Manifesto,* p. 91.

6. R. J. Rummel, *Death By Government* (Transaction Publishers, 1997), p. 9.

7. Balint Vazsonyi, *America's 30 Years War* (Washington, D.C.: Regnery Publishing, 1998), p. 176-7.

8. *Reason,* p. 289.

9. Vazsonyi, *America's 30 Years War,* p. 115.

10. Quoted in Vazsonyi, p. 115.

11. Alvin J. Schmidt, *The Menace of Multiculturalism* (Westport, CT: Praeger Publishers, 1997) p. 86.

12. Diane Ravitch, *Education After the Culture Wars*, an online article http://catholiceducation.org/articles/education/ed0188.html.

13. Ravitch, *Education After the Culture Wars*.

14. Ibid.

15. Idid.

16. John Leo, "Textbook Sensitivity Codes Function as Form of Censorship," June 29, 2003 column online at http://www.townhall.com/columnists/johnleo/jl20030629.s html.

17. Allan Charles Kors and Harvey A. Silverglate, *The Shadow University: The Betrayal of Liberty on America's Campuses* (New York: The Free Press, 1998), p. 179.

18. Kors and Silverglate, *The Shadow University*, p. 70

19. "UNC-Wilmington, Without Shame, Invades Professor's Privacy and Chills Everyone's Free Speech," December 19, 2001, www.thefire.org/issues/uncs_121801.php3.

20. Ibid.

21. Richard Rorty, *Achieving Our Country: Leftist Thought in Twentieth-Century America* (Harvard University Press, 1999), p. 106-7.

22. B. K. Eakman, *Cloning of the American Mind*, p. 146.

23. Tony Mecia, "Feminist College President Assumes Control of Duke," *Campus*, Spring, 1994, p. 6.

24. Ibid.

25. For a list the specific proposals regarding homosexual issues passed by the NEA, see their website at www.nea.org/reso-lutions.html.

26. Alan Sears and Craig Osten, *The Homosexual Agenda: Exposing the Principal Threat to Religious Freedom Today* (Nashville, TN: Broadman & Holman Publishers, 2003) p. 58-60.

27. Julie Duin, "Court Bans Religious Gifts to Classmates," *The Washington Times*, September 21, 2003, p. 1. www.washtimes.com/national/20030921-124437-4267r.htm.

28. Quoted in *World* magazine, "Robed Rulers," July 5, 2003, p. 20.

29. Quoted on the cover of *World* magazine, July 5, 2003.

30. *Homosexuals Push for Same-Sex Marriage After Sodomy Ruling*, (CNSNews.com, June 26, 2003), article linked from www.breakpoint.org/Breakpoint/ChannelRoot/CNSNewsArticle?ID=104830.

31. Ibid.

32. Enrique T. Rueda, *The Homosexual Network* (Devin-Adair Publishers, June 1986), p. 221.

33. Marx and Engels, *The Communist Manifesto*, p. 87.

34. Mr. Trey Kern, President of the Citizens for Parent Rights in Pasadena, Maryland has collected an impressive amount of data on studies documenting the diminished lifespan of active homosexuals. See www.cprmd.org, "Homosexual Myths: Homosexuals Live Long Lives, Fact Sheet." Studies include: G. Tardieu, 1858; M. Hirschfield, 1914, Kinsey, 1930's, 1940's; Mattachine Society, 1950's: Berger, 1960's, Kinsey Institute, 1969; Spada Report 1978; M. Mendola, 1979; Cameron, Playfair, Wellum, 1994; Hogg, R.S., et. al, *International Journal of Epidemiology*, 1997; Cameron, P, Cameron, K, Playfair, WL., *Psychological Reports*, 1998.

35. "Deceptive Rhetoric: Marriage and the Language of the Market," "BreakPoint" with Charles Colson, Commentary #030722 - 07/22/2003.

36. These statistics come from a National Opinion Research Center study from the University of Chicago, cited in Sears and Osten, *The Homosexual Agenda*, p. 30.

37. Statistics taken from 2003 Gallup Poll Social Series, *Moral Views and Values* (Princeton, NJ: The Gallup Organization, 2003), p. 19-23.

38. Maggie Gallagher, "The Stakes: Why we need marriage."

39. Ibid.

40. C.S. Lewis, *God in the Dock*, p. 262.

41. Alan Keyes, "Proposing madness," 2000 WorldNetDaily.com, www.worldnetdaily.com/news/article.asp?ARTICLE_ID=18 708 <http://www.worldnetdaily.com/news/article.asp?ARTI-CLE_ID=18708>

42. Charlton Heston, February 16, 1999, Harvard Law School Forum. (www.narila.org/ila/hestonhs.htm)

(1) Tiananmen Square: From Countering Culture video (2004 Summit Ministries: Manitou Springs, CO)

(2) North America graphic: From ClipArt.com

(3) Sequoiah tree: Photo by Gregory Webster (The Gregory Group: Lynnville, TN)

# SECTION IV
# COSMIC HUMANISM

The influence of Cosmic Humanist theology is evidenced by the number of people who believe all religions lead to the same God. According to George Barna's research, 44 per cent of American adults agree that the Bible, the Koran, and the Book of Mormon are all different expressions of the same spiritual truths, and 30 per cent of teens believe all religious adherents pray to the same God. Chapter ten explores New Age pantheism and specific ways Christians can confront these mistaken ideas.

A much larger percentage of Americans—including over 90% of those claiming to be "born again"—have adopted the New Age idea of relativism in truth and ethics. Chapter eleven shows Christians why relativism is logically untenable and provides the key questions they can use to guide New Age friends out of the relativistic fog which envelopes our nation.

Finally, chapter twelve concludes our study of the New Age worldview by focusing on the growing "self-esteem" movement in America and how it has taken over both our public schools and popular culture. This chapter explains how parents of school-aged children can engage the battle over their children's education by promoting a balanced approach to curricula driven by biblical approaches to family living, character, self-esteem, drug use, and sex education.

# CHAPTER 10

# The God of Our Choosing

"[Star Wars is] designed primarily to make
young people think about the mystery.
Not to say, 'Here's the answer.' It's to say,
'Think about this for a second. Is there a God?
What does God look like? What does God
sound like? What does God feel like?
How do we relate to God?'"[1]
—GEORGE LUCAS

"I've investigated a number of religions. I was
into Zen Buddhism for a while. But voodooism
is the one that stuck more. It's very interesting.
Not that I practice it or anything."[2]
—ACTRESS KRISTANNA LOKEN

"Elijah went before the people and said,
'How long will you waver between two worldviews? If the LORD is God, follow Him;
but if Baal is God, follow him.'"
—1 KINGS 18:21 (AUTHOR'S TRANSLATION)

"A leaderless but powerful network is working to bring about radical change in the United States.... Broader than reform, deeper than revolution, this benign conspiracy for a new human agenda has triggered the most rapid cultural realignment in history. The great shuddering, irrevocable shift overtaking us is not a new political, religious, or philosophical system. It is a new mind—the ascendance of a startling worldview that gathers into its framework breakthrough science and insights from earliest recorded thought."[3] Thus begins Marilyn Ferguson's watershed classic, *The Aquarian Conspiracy*. The "insights from earliest recorded thought" to which she refers are Eastern religions. Her "benign conspiracy" is the New Age movement.

In the twenty-four years since her book was released, the influence of New Age spirituality has expanded throughout our culture, especially with Gen Y'ers. In conceptualizing their own worldviews, students—even those raised in Christian homes—are prone to combine elements from divergent belief systems. Pollster George Barna notes the trend: "It is likely that from Christianity they will borrow Jesus' philosophy of love and acceptance. From Eastern religions they will borrow ideas related to each person being his or her own god, the center of the universe, capable of creating and resolving issues through his or her own power and intelligence."[4] Today's generation is no longer interested in organized religion such as Christianity but nevertheless exhibits a desire for spirituality. This proclivity results from the mainstreaming of what Ferguson calls "the new mind." We call it Cosmic Humanism.

The Cosmic Humanist worldview consists of two interrelated spiritual movements. One is known as the New Age movement (NAM), and the other is neopaganism, including occult practices, Native American spiritism, and Wicca (witchcraft, or The Craft). While the neopagan/witchcraft movement in America and other English-speaking nations shares certain commonalities with the New Age movement, it differs in several significant points. New Age theology, for example, makes no serious distinctions between religions, considering all to be ultimately the same. "In contrast," writes researcher John P. Newport, "neopagans generally believe that they are practicing an ancient folk religion, whether as a survival or a revival. Thus, being focused on the pagan religions of the past, they are not particularly interested in a New Age of the future."[5] Newport continues, "In the contemporary world, the neopagan movement is a leader in emphasizing God's manyness: He is both singular and plural; they are both male and female." In ancient societies, this polytheistic view is referred to as animism, nature worship, or spiritism, or the belief that "nature and all the objects

COSMIC HUMANISM CONSISTS OF TWO INTERRELATED MOVEMENTS

NEW AGE MOVEMENT (NAM)

NEOPAGANISM (OCCULT, SPIRITISM, WITCHCRAFT)

New Age theology makes no serious distinctions between religions, considering all to be ultimately the same.

of nature are peopled with, and possessed by, living spirits or gods."[6]

As neopagan ideas gain a larger following, some are even being presented in mainstream media, in television shows such as *Charmed* and *Buffy, the Vampire Slayer*. Yet, the total number of Americans who follow this particular variety of Cosmic Humanism is relatively small. For that reason, we will focus most of our discussion in this and the next two chapters on the New Age movement.

The New Age movement mixes ancient Eastern religions (especially Hinduism and Zen Buddhism) with a touch of other religious traditions, adds a smattering of scientific-sounding jargon, and imports the newly baked concoction into mainstream America. The contemporary movement has roots in the Romantic poets of the 1800's such as Ralph Waldo Emerson, Walt Whitman and Henry David Thoreau. These men rejected the Christian God who can be known by reading the Bible and wrote at length about a transcendent quality of spirituality experienced purely through personal introspection. These ideas did not attract a broad audience until the 1960's when popular recording artists, movie stars, and Eastern gurus traveling the lecture circuit began trumpeting their New Age views across the nation. More recently, well-known personali-

> The New Age movement mixes ancient Eastern religions with a touch of other religious traditions, adds a smattering of scientific-sounding jargon, and imports the newly baked concoction into mainstream America.

> The contemporary movement has roots in the Romantic poets of the 1800's such as Ralph Waldo Emerson, Walt Whitman and Henry David Thoreau.

ties such as Madonna and Alanis Morissette have identified themselves as having an interest in Hinduism, while Tiger Woods, Phil Jackson, and Richard Gere openly embrace Zen Buddhism.

Many other luminaries also express belief in scientology and an assortment of other Cosmic Humanist ideas. As a result, New Age ideas are disseminated not only through movies and television, but also through burgeoning book sales. Since its publication in 1993, *The Celestine Prophecy* has sold over 8 million copies in more than 32 countries, and it achieved distinction as the bestselling American hardcover book in the world for two consecutive years. Author James Redfield wrote in the Afterword to the 1997 printing, "we are manifesting nothing less than a new world view that will flourish in the next millennium." Another "modern day spiritual messenger" is Neale Donald Walsch, the author of fifteen books on spirituality and its application to everyday life. His first five books in the Conversations with God series all made the *New York Times* bestseller list (*Conversations with God–Book 1* placed on that list for well over two years). His books have been translated into 27 languages and have sold more than 7 million copies worldwide.

Because of this extensive New Age influence, it is important that Christians are equipped to counter New Age beliefs. This equipping begins with understanding Cosmic Humanism's answers to the questions of theology and philosophy.

# THE COSMIC HUMANIST VIEW OF GOD

Technically speaking, New Agers are neither atheists nor theists but are, rather, pantheists. Pantheism is the belief that everything is God, and God is everything. This idea is well illustrated in the New Age children's book, *What Is God?*:

> There are many ways to talk about God. Does that mean that everything that everybody ever says about God is right? Does that mean that God is everything? Yes! God is everything great and small! God is everything far away and near! God is everything bright and dark! And God is everything in between! If everything is God, God is the last leaf on a tree. If everything is God, God is an elephant crashing through the jungle. If everything is God, then God is the hot wind in the desert, and God is the freezing snow in the winter, and God is the big, yellow moon. If everything is God, then I am God, you are God, all of us are God![7]

Of course, if everything is God, then there is nothing that exists that is not God. This means God is not a personal Supreme Being, but instead is a general cosmic force. Cosmic Humanist theology posits no transcendent God "out there" apart from His creation. God *is* the creation. Says Marilyn Ferguson, "In the emergent spiritual tradition God is not the

> New Agers are neither atheists nor theists but are pantheists, believing everything is God, and God is everything.

*According to New Age thinking, nature itself is part of God.*

personage of our Sunday School mentality.... God is experienced as flow, wholeness... the ground of being.... God is the consciousness that manifests as Lila, the play of the universe. God is the organizing matrix we can experience but not tell, that which enlivens matter."[8]

The god-as-cosmic-energy concept has been popularized in George Lucas' now classic film series, *Star Wars*. In the 1977 original episode, Obi-wan Kenobi explains the nature of the god-force as he tells Luke Skywalker, "The Force is what gives the Jedi his power. It's an energy field created by all living things. It surrounds us and penetrates us and binds the galaxy together." During an extended scene in *The Empire Strikes Back*, Yoda, the Jedi master, instructs Luke in the ways of the Force. In true guru fashion, Yoda tells his young apprentice, "For my ally is the Force, and a powerful ally it is. Life breeds it, makes it grow. Its energy surrounds us and binds us. Luminous beings are we, not this crude matter. You must feel the force around you, here between you, me, the tree, the rock, everywhere, yes, even between land and ship."

Weaving pantheistic religion throughout *Star Wars* was not an accident. While most viewers enjoyed this film saga for its entertainment value, producer Lucas sees his role as an educator as well as entertainer. He notes, "I've always tried to be aware of what I say in my films because all of us who make motion pictures are teachers, teachers with very loud voices."[9]

Cosmic Humanist education with a more neopagan flair erupts in notable children's films such as *Pocahontas*—the main character sings "every rock and every tree has a spirit, has a name"—and *The Lion King*, notably in its theme song "The Circle of Life." A short list of other movies that exhibit generally Cosmic Humanist subtexts or major themes include *Poltergeist, Indiana Jones and the Temple of Doom,* The *Dark Crystal, Solarbabies, Mulan, The Exorcist, What Dreams May Come,* and *Sixth Sense.*

## EXPLORING COSMIC HUMANIST REALITY

As we noted in chapter 4, an early scene in *The Matrix* shows Neo asking, "This isn't real?" to which Morpheus responds with a classic definition of naturalism—a secular approach to philosophy. But the film goes still further. Later in the story, another answer to the question is given when a boy who looks the part of a Buddhist devotee is practicing bending a metal spoon through the power of his mind. He explains to Neo, "Don't try to bend the spoon. That's

> Zen Buddhist monks learn to dispense with reason and seek sudden illumination of truth by meditating on a paradoxical idea called a *koan*.

impossible. Only understand the truth." Neo then asks, "The truth?" to which the boy responds flatly, "There is no spoon." The boy's statement reflects a classic Hindu/Buddhist conception of reality—what we see is an illusionary world. There is no objective world, only the reality of our mental state.

The writers and directors of *The Matrix*, Larry and Andy Wachowski, are candid about their purpose in bringing up this subject, "We think the most important sort of fiction attempts to answer some of the big questions. One of the things that we had talked about when we first had the idea of *The Matrix* was an idea that I believe philosophy and religion and mathematics all try to answer. Which is, a reconciling between a natural world and another world that is perceived by our intellect."[10] In the same interview, the Wachowskis admit Buddhism plays a major role in their understanding of religion.

As pop culture commentator

> Like the Christian, the Cosmic Humanist rejects naturalistic philosophy because it ignores the supernatural dimension of the universe.

Roberto Rivera observes, "You can see Zen's fingerprints everywhere, including the way Morpheus talks to Neo. Instead of answering Neo's questions in a straightforward manner, he insists on koans such as, 'I can only show you the door, you must walk through,' and 'when the time comes, you won't need to dodge the bullet.' Or my favorite, '[the Oracle] didn't lie, she told you exactly what you needed to hear.'"[11]

Like the Christian, the Cosmic Humanist rejects naturalistic philosophy because it ignores the supernatural dimension of the universe. Yet contrary to biblical philosophy, the New Age belief that everything is divine leads to the idea that even what we call "nature" is divine. If everything is divine, then nothing is simply natural. Therefore, the philosophy of Cosmic Humanism is best termed *non-naturalism*, because nothing is merely natural (physical). Everything is supernatural (spiritual), or put another way, everything is God.

Ultimate reality for the Cosmic Humanist is a grand unity. Because everything is God, you are a part of God, I am part of God, your chair is part of God,

> For the Cosmic Humanist, everything is God—you are a part of God, I am part of God, your chair is part of God, garbage is part of God.

garbage is part of God, and so on. Everything is of one nature, of one essence. This is *monism*, the belief that there is only one reality. As New Age teacher David Spangler has written, "this worldview encourages us to treat all things not only as ourselves, as the holistic view would see it, but as honored and precious manifestations of God."[12] Or, as bestselling New Age author Neale Donald Walsch puts it, "All things are One Thing. There is only One Thing, and all things are part of the One Thing That Is."[13]

What substance makes up this god-force? The question is difficult to answer since every individual arrives at his own truth, and New Age thinkers often differ in their interpretations. Gary Zukav believes consciousness is ultimate reality and offers the following illustration to make his point:

All that is can form itself into individual droplets of consciousness. Because you are part of all that is, you have literally always been, yet there was the instant when that individual energy current that is you was formed. Consider that the ocean is God. It has always been. Now reach in and grab a cup full of water. In that instant, the cup becomes individual, but it has always been, has it not? This is the case with your soul. There was the instant when you became a cup of energy, but it was of an immortal original Being. You have always been because what it is that you are is God, or Divine Intelligence, but God takes on individual forms, droplets, reducing its power to small particles of individual consciousness.[14]

Other Cosmic Humanists have additional answers, based on their personal "experience" of the truth. Cosmic Humanists acknowledge their godhood but prefer to avoid dogmatic views regarding its final nature. Marilyn Ferguson states, "We need not postulate a purpose for this Ultimate Cause nor wonder who or what caused whatever Big Bang launched the visible universe. There is only the experience."[15]

Some Cosmic Humanists, deriving their worldview more from Hinduism, believe our perception of the physical universe is *maya*, an illusion. But this is not the majority view among New Agers. Having been strongly influenced by Western values and worldviews, New Agers readily affirm the reality of the physical world and seek to transform it according to their worldview. "The Western… tradition," write Corinne McLaughlin and Gordon Davidson, "does not view physical life as simply 'maya' or illusion to be transcended, as in some teachings of the East, but rather as a field for service and active reform." In other words, there are two dimensions to reality. McLaughlin and Davidson further explain:

*The Cosmic Humanist God caught on film in its many forms.*

The Ageless Wisdom [New Age movement] takes the view that we are both spiritual and material beings and we must honor all dimensions of ourselves. To do this we need to maintain awareness of the third principle—the Soul—which is the bridging consciousness between Spirit and matter… As the Souls, we would not become so detached from the world as to ignore humanity's need for help, nor would we become so over identified with material reality as to forget our true spiritual identity.[16]

The umbrella of Cosmic Humanist philosophy, then, covers a range of beliefs regarding the nature of ultimate reality, from a cosmic consciousness on one end to a combined spirit/material being on the other. The common belief among all New Age adherents is their understanding of how we know whatever reality there is to know.

## HOW DO THEY KNOW?

The theory of knowledge, or *epistemology*, of the Cosmic Humanist worldview emphasizes emotions. If you *feel* something is true, then, according to this worldview, it *is* true. As New Age spokeswoman Shirley MacLaine writes, "You must learn to trust your feelings more and refrain from approaching so many issues in life from strictly an intellectual perspective. Intellect is too limited. Feelings are limitless. Trust your heart…"[17] The extremely popular New Age author Neale Donald Walsh agrees, claiming to write the words of God:

Stop it! Get out of your mind. Get back to your senses! That is what is meant by getting back to your senses. It is a returning to how you feel, not how you think. Your thoughts are just that—thoughts. Mental constructions. 'Made up' creations of your mind. But your *feelings*—now *they* are *real*.[18]

This Cosmic Humanist theme—gaining knowledge through feelings instead of conscious thoughts—also is portrayed in *Star Wars: A New Hope*. Obi-wan trains Luke in the tactics and art of using a light saber: "This time, let go your conscious self and act on instinct… Your eyes can deceive you, don't trust them… Stretch out with your feel-ings… You see, you can do it… You've taken your first step into a larger world." Luke eventually learns his lesson, and in the film's climactic battle scene, he guides his X-wing fighter to its target and destroys the Death Star after hearing Obi-wan's voice urging him to "Use the Force, Luke. Let go, Luke. Luke, trust me… Remember, the Force will be with you, always." Obi-wan's last sentence is notewor-thy in that his direction echoes Jesus' final words to His disciples as found in Matthew 28:20. George Lucas apparently draws from Christianity as well as Buddhist traditions in order to create his cosmic myth.

> According to the Cosmic Humanist worldview, if you feel something is true, then it is true.

## RESPONDING TO COSMIC HUMANISM

When defending a biblical worldview in the market-place of ideas—whether it takes the form of a letter to the editor of your local paper or a face-to-face dialogue with a neighbor—the Christian must keep two things in mind. According to 2 Timothy 2:24-26, we must present the truth in order set free those who have been captured by deceptive philosophies, and secondly, we are to be kind and gentle as we do so. Both our con-tent and our charac-ter are important. And since New Age adherents place a premium on peace and harmony, this approach is espe-cially needed when trying to lead them to God's truth.

> **MATTHEW 28:20**
> *And remember, I [Jesus] am with you always, to the end of the age.*

One particularly attractive component of New Age theology to its devotees is its non-judgmental approach to religion. According to Neale Donald Walsch, God communicated to him: "No path to God is more direct than any other path. No religion is the "one true religion…."[19] In an interview with Bill Moyers, filmmaker George Lucas said, "The conclu-sion I've come to is that all the religions are true."[20] This conviction is shared in the wider population, even among many Christians. According to George Barna, 48 per cent of those surveyed who claim to be "born again" agree that "Christians, Jews, Muslims, Buddhists, and others all pray to the same God, even though they use different names for that God."[21]

Although in our rush to be non-judgmental many Americans may choose to believe "all the religions are true," that notion is a logical impossibility. The first law of logic, the law of non-contradiction, states specifically what we know intuitively: two things can-not be the same and different at the same time and in the same way. In other words, something cannot be

> "No path to God is more direct than any other path. No religion is the 'one true religion'…."
> —Neale Donald Walsch

both true and false at the same time. When we apply the law of non-contradiction to the religions of the world, we find that Hindus, Buddhists, Jews, and Muslims deny what Christians affirm: that Jesus is God incarnate, the third person of the Trinity. Either Jesus is, in fact, a member of the Trinity, or He is not. If He is not, then Christians are wrong about their belief and those of other religions are right. On the other hand, if Christians are right, then the other religions are wrong. It cannot be both ways. While it is a *possibility* all religions of the world are false, it is a *certainty* they cannot all be true.

So the first step in setting free those who have been captured by New Age theology is to point out the illogic of their beliefs. They will likely counter that logic and rational thought cannot be trusted, that one must instead trust his or her feelings. If they raise such an objection, then ask this simple question: Did you just make a rational statement concerning what can be trusted? Since they have to answer "yes" to your question, you can point out their statement is self-refuting since they made a rational statement that says rational statements cannot be trusted.

Logic cannot be forever denied. God has designed

> ## Although many Americans may choose to believe "all the religions are true," the idea is a logical impossibility.

our minds to operate rationally, so even when someone rejects rationality, we can use it to our benefit to shed light on the reality of clear thinking. And once again, this affirms the reality of the biblical view of God.

When claiming that all religions lead to God, some New Agers use the "all roads lead to Rome" illustration to make their point. One way to counter this idea is to gently point out that this conclusion does not follow from the "all roads" example. First of all, if you look on at the globe you discover that all roads do *not* lead to Rome. Some are dead ends while others are separated from Rome by an ocean. Furthermore, if a road actually does connect to Rome, a traveler must be heading the *right direction* on that road in order to get to Rome. Since it is possible to be going away from the destination as well as toward it, it is likewise possible someone could be heading the wrong way and end up moving further *away* from God.

This brings up the issue of how New Agers know *their* view is correct. Since New Age believers insist all religions contain some truth, they are prone to cherry-pick various religious traditions for the parts they like and assimilate those ideas into their worldview. So, a legitimate question arises: "How do you know you are selecting the correct beliefs from each religion?" The principle problem of picking and choosing is that there is no way to be sure when you have selected the right ideas. And although a common New Age response is that each knows the right answers within him or herself

> ### 2 TIMOTHY 2:24-26
> *The Lord's slave must not quarrel, but must be gentle to everyone, able to teach, and patient, instructing his opponents with gentleness. Perhaps God will grant them repentance to know the truth. Then they may come to their senses and escape the Devil's trap, having been captured by him to do his will.*

> ## While it is a possibility all religions of the world are false, it is a certainty they cannot all be true.

(again, the "feelings" argument), that answer fails under the weight of logic—even New Agers hold conflicting views as to the nature of God. Everyone's views cannot all be right!

## THE BLIND MEN AND THE ELEPHANT

Cosmic Humanists often cite a Hindu parable to defend the belief that all religions are the same. In thieir illustration, six blind men touch an elephant. One handles the tail and exclaims that an elephant is like a rope. Another grasps a leg and describes the elephant

*Does an elephant have an objectively verifiable form?*

as a tree trunk. A third feels the tusk and says the animal is similar to a spear. The remaining three touch other parts and give correspondingly different descriptions since each feels only a small portion of the whole elephant. The New Age conclusion is that various religions describe God in different terms simply because each tradition touches only a very small part of the whole, and yet all are describing the same God.

How would you respond to this parable? One way is to ask your New Age friends how they knows the men are all touching the same elephant. This brings out the crucial—but not necessarily valid—assumptions built into the parable. First, the parable assumes each man can discern only part of the truth about the

nature of the elephant and second, that somehow we know something that the blind men don't—there is a real elephant they are all touching. Yet the first assumption rests on a questionable New Age belief regarding the nature of truth, and the second assumes knowledge about what God is really like. In other words, the elephant parable does not *demonstrate* the point it is making, it simply *illustrates* what New Agers already *believe* to be the case. But the question is, "What is the source of this knowledge?" As we've discovered from their own admissions, they simply *feel* this is the right way to understand God. But is it possible their feelings could be wrong? And if their feelings about God differ from someone else's feelings about God, how does one determine who has the right feelings?

After pointing to the faulty thinking of such New Age beliefs, a Christian then can explain that Christianity—rather than assuming a blind search for God—begins with the idea that God has revealed Himself in the objective revelation found in the Bible. In our previous study of a biblical Christian worldview, *Thinking Like A Christian*, we offered several reasons for the Bible's reliability (archeology and prophecy) and the historicity of Christ's resurrection (eyewitness accounts and the implausibility of other explanations). Although the Bible describes God as a Being who cannot be fully known (we cannot completely understand all that God is), we *can* know certain things, such as His transcendence, imminence, and other attributes such as holiness, love, mercy, forgiveness, and judgment of sin.

When it comes to the nature of God and

> **HEBREWS 11:1**
> *Now faith is the reality of what is hoped for, the proof of what is not seen.*

reality, the Christian worldview offers confidence not found in Cosmic Humanism. Hebrews 11:1 explains that biblical faith is not based on intuition or subjective feelings, but upon "reality" and "proof." In contrast to the idea that "all roads lead to God," the historical evidence maps out only *one* road leading to God, and it passes through the life, teachings, death and resurrection of Jesus Christ. *This* we can know with certainty (John 8:31-32; Colossians 2:2; 2 Peter 1:16-18; 1 John 5:20).

## RECOMMENDED READING

Campbell, Joseph. *The Power of Myth*. New York: Doubleday, 1988.

Ferguson, Marilyn. *The Aquarian Conspiracy: Personal and Social Transformation in Our Time*, New York: Tarcher/Perigee Books, 1980.

Gawain, Shakti. *Living in the Light*, San Rafael, California: New World Library, 1986.

Newport, John P. *The New Age Movement and the Biblical Worldview: Conflict and Dialogue*, Grand Rapids, MI: Eerdmans Publishing Co, 1998.

Spangler, David. *Emergence: The Rebirth of the Sacred*, New York: Delta/Merloyd Lawrence, 1984

## ENDNOTES

1.  "Of Myth and Men: A Conversation between Bill Moyers and George Lucas on the meaning of the Force and the true theology of *Star Wars*," *Time*, April 26, 1999, p. 93.

2.  Kristanna Loken, *Rolling Stone*, July 24, 2003, p. 46.

3.  Marilyn Ferguson. *The Aquarian Conspiracy: Personal and Social Transformation in Our Time* (New York: Tarcher/Perigee Books, 1980) p. 24.

4.  George Barna, *The Frog in the Kettle* (Ventura, CA: Regal Books, 1990) p. 71.

5.  John P. Newport, *The New Age Movement and the Biblical Worldview: Conflict and Dialogue* (Grand Rapids, MI: Eerdmans Publishing Co, 1998) p. 214.

---

## SCRIPTURAL ASSURANCES ABOUT THE REALITY OF JESUS CHRIST

*John 8:31-32*
So Jesus said to the Jews who had believed Him, "If you continue in My word, you really are My disciples. You will know the truth, and the truth will set you free."

*Colossians 2:2*
[I want] their hearts to be encouraged and joined together in love, so that they may have all the riches of assured understanding, and have the knowledge of God's mystery—Christ.

*2 Peter 1:16-18*
For we did not follow cleverly contrived myths when we made known to you the power and coming of our Lord Jesus Christ; instead, we were eyewitnesses of His majesty. For when He received honor and glory from God the Father, a voice came to Him from the Majestic Glory: This is My beloved Son. I take delight in Him! And we heard this voice when it came from heaven while we were with Him on the holy mountain.

*1 John 5:20*
And we know that the Son of God has come and has given us understanding so that we may know the true One. We are in the true One—that is, in His Son Jesus Christ. He is the true God and eternal life.

---

6.  Newport, *The New Age Movement and the Biblical Worldview*, p. 216.

7.  Etin Boritzer, *What Is God?* (Westport, CT: Firefly, 1990), n.p.

8.  Marilyn Ferguson, *The Aquarian Conspiracy* (Los Angeles: J.P. Tarcher, Inc., 1980), p. 383.

9.  Quote attributed to George Lucas in

www.pbs.org/wnet/americanmasters/database/lucas_g.html.

10. Interview with Larry and Andy Wachowski, November 6, 1999. Online article at www.dvdwb.com/matrixevents/wachowski.html.

11. Roberto Rivera, "So, What Is The Matrix? Rethinking Reality." Online article at www.boundless.org/1999/departments/atplay/a0000115.html.

12. David Spangler, *Emergence: The Rebirth of the Sacred* (New York: Delta/Merloyd Lawrence, 1984), p. 83.

13. Neale Donald Walsch, *The New Revelations: A Conversation with God* (New York: Atria Books, 2002), p. 360.

14. Gary Zukav, *The Seat of the Soul* (New York: Simon and Schuster, 1990), pp. 85-6.

15. Marilyn Ferguson, *The Aquarian Conspiracy* (Los Angeles: J.P. Tarcher, Inc., 1980), p. 383.

16. Corrine McLaughlin and Gordon Davidson, *Spiritual Politics: Changing the World from the Inside Out* (New York: Ballantine Books, 1994), p. 14-15, 46.

17. Shirley MacLaine, *Out on a Limb* (New York: Bantam Books, 1983), p. 203.

18. Neale Donald Walsch, *Conversations with God: An Uncommon Dialog* (Charlottesville, VA: Hampton Roads, 1997), p. 215.

19. Neale Donald Walsch, *The New Revelations: A Conversation with God* (New York: Atria Books, 2002), p. 97.

20. "Of Myth and Men: A Conversation between Bill Moyers and George Lucas on the meaning of the Force and the true theology of *Star Wars*," *Time* Magazine, April 26, 1999, p. 92.

21. George Barna, *What Americans Believe*, 1991, p. 212.

1) Natural arch: Photo by Gregory Webster (The Gregory Group: Lynnville, TN)

(2) Photo montage—horse, salamander, tractor, wind surfers, walrus: From ClipArt.com

(3) Elephant: From ClipArt.com

# CHAPTER 11

# Boundless Relativism

"It's taking everything you've learned from your
parents and school and finding out what works
for you and what you have to offer.
The important question is,
'What feels right for you?'"[1]
—ACTOR BRAD PITT

"…growing up with my sister
(older sister Tanya is gay), I learned that
whether it be her being with women or men
being with other men, there's never a wrong or a
right thing about it. Society has never
played a part in my beliefs."[2]
—ACTRESS KRISTANNA LOKEN

"The complete moral gridlock over moral issues
such as abortion, euthanasia, and homosexuality,
a gridlock that seems to make peaceful
coexistence impossible in our culture,
is ultimately caused by two rival moral
universes colliding."[3]
—BENJAMIN WIKER

"In a world of postmodern fad," sings popular recording artist, Jewel, "What was good now is bad. It's not hard to understand. Just follow this simple plan: Follow your heart, your intuition. It will lead you in the right direction. Let go of your mind. Your intuition is easy to find. Just follow your heart, baby."[4] Jewel's song, "Intuition," is a lucid expression of popular culture's view that truth is what you believe and morality is what *feels* right to you.

> ### JOHN 18:38
> *"What is truth?" said Pilate.*

According to researcher George Barna, this "follow your heart" mentality has left its mark on today's teenagers. As Barna discloses in his book, *Real Teens*, "Seven out of 10 teens say there is no absolute moral truth, and 8 out of 10 claim that all truth is relative to the individual and his or her circumstances."[5] But Barna's investigation into the teenage mind also turns up a puzzling twist. While "three-quarters of teens agree that you can tell if something is morally right by whether it works in your life," the same majority asserts the opposing idea that "the Bible provides practical, defined standards by which we should live our lives."[6] This state of confusion reveals the inner struggle the current generation faces when confronted with the question of what is morally right—Is it my way or God's way?

Jewel's song begs the question, "Is that view true?" Which leads to a more fundamental question, "What is truth?" This issue has been around a long time. It was Pontius Pilate's question as he interrogated Jesus (see John 18:38), and as we mentioned earlier, in a more contemporary setting it was Truman's question to Christof when he asked, "Was nothing real?" To respond to this fundamental philosophical query, we must make a distinction between two different kinds of truth. The first relates to the existence of absolute truth, and the second involves the reality of whether or not there are universally true moral absolutes. As a foundational element of their worldview, Cosmic Humanists have an answer.

## TRUTH IS RELATIVE

Thirty-year veteran professor of classic literature, Allan Bloom, in his book, *The Closing of the American Mind*, writes "There is one thing a professor can be absolutely certain of: almost every student entering the university believes, or says he believes, that truth is relative."[7] The idea that truth is relative is the fruit of both a secular worldview and a Cosmic Humanist mentality. If there is no God, there is no basis for absolute knowledge. All that remains are man's ideas, and "who's to say which of man's conflicting ideas are right?" Even what we think of as scientific "truths" are often revealed to be false when new discoveries are made. The conclusion atheists reach is that truth is simply what individuals or society happens to believe at the moment. Truth is relative to the times.

> "There is one thing a professor can be absolutely certain of: almost every student entering the university believes, or says he believes, that truth is relative."
> —Allan Bloom

The other side of the relativistic coin is New Age pantheism. With pantheism, the starting point is cosmic evolution—the view that the universe-that-is-God is changing and growing—so that our concept of truth also changes and grows over time. To the Cosmic

Humanist, truth is not an objective article "out there" that we must discover, but instead truth is understood as something very personal, discerned through one's feelings—*intuition*, as Jewel says. That's why *Star Wars* Jedi Master and spiritual advisor Yoda instructs Luke not to use his rational mind, but instead to "*feeeel* the Force." This internal focus means something may be true for one person and yet not be true for all people. The common slogan reflecting this view is, "That may be true for you, but not for me."

New Age promoter Neale Donald Walsch agrees. In his book, *Conversations with God*, Walsch writes:

> (God is speaking) "I do not communicate by words alone. In fact, rarely do I do so. My most common form of communication is through *feeling. Feeling is the language of the soul.* If you want to know what's true for you about some thing, look to how you're *feeling* about it…. Hidden in your deepest feelings is your highest truth."[8] (Italics in the original)

How does Walsch know God was communicating these feelings to him? He recounts that in 1992 he was depressed and wrote a letter to God to vent his anger and confusion, when, "To my surprise, as I scribbled out the last of my bitter, unanswerable questions and prepared to toss my pen aside, my hand remained poised over the paper, as if held there by some invisible force. Abruptly the pen began *moving on its own*. I had no idea what I was about to write, but an idea seemed to be coming, so I decided to flow with it."

> Walsch's pragmatism may seem to confirm God's voice, but upon closer inspection it becomes a mumbo jumbo of sweet sounding platitudes that make no contribution to solving the nitty-gritty issues of real life.

Out came a response from God, in first person singular![9] "Before I knew it," Walsch continues, "I had begun a conversation…and I was not writing so much as *taking dictation*. That dictation went on for three years…"[10] Walsch believes this unique experience is evidence of God communicating with him. This method of communication with the spirit world—called automatic writing—is not new. It is a traditional means used by psychics over the years to receive information from spirit guides and those who have passed on to "the other side."

What is the content of God's communication? According to Walsch, God said, "…not all feelings, not all thoughts, not all experience, and not all words are from Me…. The challenge is one of discernment…. *Mine is always your Highest Thought, your Clearest Word, your Grandest Feeling. Anything less is from another source.*"[11] He goes on to define these highest thoughts, clearest words, and grandest feelings as joy, truth, and love.

How do we know these thoughts or feelings are God's ideas? Walsch explains, "You should apply it and see what works. Incidentally, put every other writing that claims to be a communication from God to the same test."[12] The reason Walsch gives for believing what he writes is pragmatism—because it works. The pragmatic approach to truth is summarized in the popular slogan, "It works for me." As Christians who are concerned about matters of truth, how should we interact with people who have embraced this New Age concept of truth?

# RESPONDING TO RELATIVISM

While the "it works for me" mentality may sound compelling—meditating on joy and love and all good things—a thinking person must face a central question: "Does pragmatism offer a reliable way to determine what is true?" We suggest that it does not.

As a way of determining truth, pragmatism has many pitfalls. It fails, first, because it provides no clear guidelines to measure "what works." For example, having an abortion may "work" for the woman who is pregnant because the procedure elimi-

> Cosmic Humanists muddle the distinction between taste and truth.

nates a "problem" pregnancy, yet it does not answer the question of whether it was right for the unborn child. And after having an abortion—sometimes days, sometimes years later—many women feel extreme remorse and depression over the choice they made. In those cases, it may be the abortion that "worked" for them in the first circumstance now no longer "works." Or, what if someone is seeking to love others, and the love is not reciprocated, but instead hatred and violence is returned? Does love "work" in that case? What is the loving thing to do when one is being physically assaulted? Or when the assault is on one's sibling, spouse, parent, neighbor, or child?

While at first glance Walsch's pragmatism may seem to confirm God's voice, upon closer inspection it becomes unworkable, a mumbo jumbo of sweet sounding platitudes that make no contribution to solving the nitty-gritty issues of real life. With no objective criteria to judge between what works and what does not, we are left with only personal feelings. Can it be that personal feelings are not a solid foundation for determining

what is actually true? If not, what is?

At this point we need to help our relativistic friends understand the distinction between what philosopher Mortimer Adler calls "matters of truth" and "matters of taste."[13] Matters of taste are expressions of personal preference, and include statements like the following:

- Papa John's has the best pizza.
- I like vanilla ice cream.
- *The Lord of the Rings* was a great movie.

Matters of truth, on the other hand, are statements of fact that correspond to reality. For example:

- Abraham Lincoln was the 16th president of the United States.
- That Lexus SC sport convertible is red.
- 2 plus 2 equals 4.

Cosmic Humanists muddle the distinction between taste and truth. For instance, if a Christian says, "Jesus is the Son of God," the response by many in our society is, "Well, that may be true for you, but not for me." This places the Christian's claim on par with the comment, "I like vanilla ice cream." But the Christian is not making a remark about his or her personal preference. Regarding Christ, a statement of preference would be, "I like Jesus." The truth claim about Jesus' deity is in the same category as "2 plus 2 equals 4." Either the claim is true, or it is false. It would be silly to say that "two plus 2 equals 4 may be true for you but not for me."

> If truth is nothing more than our subjective experience, then how does one feel 2 plus 2 equals 4?

The confusion about which sort of statement is being made is what logicians call a category fallacy—placing the statement in the wrong grouping of ideas.

But unlike personal preferences, there are ways to validate a truth claim. Despite their sometimes creative mental machinations, people cannot sidestep absolute truth. Simply by making a statement such as, "That is true for you but not for me," they are admitting to one universal truth: That all truth is relative to the person. But here we find a crucial logical fallacy. Their truth statement self-destructs. The relative truth claim has the same Achilles' heel as the statement, "Everything I say is false." If everything I say is false, then if the statement itself is true, it can't be because it says my statements are false.

To the one who says "That may be true for you but not for me" we can ask simply, "Is that statement true only for you?" We then can elaborate with the following: "If it is not, and you intend for it to apply to everyone, including me, then you are making an absolute statement that contradicts what you just said. If it is true only for you, then why should I pay attention to your personal preference?"

In the Walsch passage cited above, he asserts that a person's "highest thoughts" and "grandest feelings" are from God and are linked to joy, truth, and love. Walsch's unspoken premise is that joy and love are morally good standards by which to distinguish from sorrow and hate. So even while claiming subjective feelings are the ultimate guide to what is true, Walsch unwittingly admits to an absolute standard of truth—that we all can agree on what comprises joy, truth, and love—a standard not based on his personal feelings but a shared, objective reality!

There is another problem with the idea that truth is only what we experience. If truth is nothing more than our personal, subjective experience, then we are limited in what we can know. How, for example, does one *feel* 2 plus 2 equals 4? Or if I have never experienced the electrical charge of an electron or the taste of a boysenberry, does that mean electrons and boysenberries do not exist? These examples reveal the absurdity of the idea that truth is only what can be experienced. Truth *must* be something other than what we feel.

This leads us to consider what the Bible affirms regarding truth. The Christian view holds that truth is that which corresponds to the facts, or the real world. This "correspondence theory" of truth is discussed by philosopher J. P. Moreland when he writes, "If a thought really describes the world accurately, it is true. It stands to the world in a relation of correspondence."[14] "In fact," Moreland continues, "something can be true even if no one has ever thought about it at all. For example, if protons really do exist and have positive charge, then this fact was true during the Middle Ages. But no one knew it was true…"[15] Later, Moreland adds, "Truth does not change. Something either is or is not true."[16] This is what we mean when we claim that truth is absolute—it is true at all times, in all places, for all people.

The reason that Christians hold to a correspondence concept of truth is because our biblical theology

> **PSALM 95:3-5**
> *For the Lord is a great God, a great King above all gods.*
> *The depths of the earth are in His hand, and the mountain peaks are His. The sea is His; He made it. His hands formed the dry land.*

> When the relativist says truth is relative, he is making an absolute truth claim that is itself narrow-minded, since he is excluding every other claim about truth.

informs us that God created a real universe that exhibits certain laws of cause and effect (see Genesis chapters 1-2; Job chapters 38-42; Psalm 95:3-5; and Psalm 104).

Also, the Bible affirms that Jesus Christ is the Logos of God, or the Word (John 1:1,14). Logos, or logic (rational thought) is an attribute of the Godhead from all eternity. God chose to communicate to mankind primarily through language (the written Word) and Jesus Christ (the incarnate Word). Look through the Gospel of Matthew at the number of times Jesus used the phrase, "I tell you the truth"or "I assure you"—it averages one every chapter!

Jesus placed a priority on his teaching ministry when he told his followers "I assure you: Anyone who hears My word and believes Him who sent Me has eternal life and will not come under judgment but has passed from death to life. I assure you: An hour is coming, and is now here, when the dead will hear the voice of the Son of God, and those who hear will live." (John 5:24-25). Jesus is not referring to a subjective experience here, but an affirmation of his verbal teaching that leads to an objective reality in the after life. In another place, Jesus said, "If you continue in My word, you really are My disciples. You will know the truth, and the truth will set you free." (John 8:31-32). Again, the focus is on his teaching that sets us free, not an inner light or experience. While there is a subjective aspect to what He is saying, i.e., a person feels a sense of emotional peace and freedom when they accept Jesus' offer of forgiveness, this feeling comes as a *result* of accepting that His words are true. And Jesus discloses the source of truth—God's word—when he prayed to the Father, "Sanctify them by the truth;

> "The alarmingly fast decline of moral foundations among our young people has culminated in a one-word worldview: 'whatever.'"
> —George Barna

Your word is truth" (John 17:17).

In addition, in the book of Acts, the Bereans are held up as a model for Christians to follow as Luke commends their attitude concerning their search for the truth. We read, "The people here [Beroea] were more open-minded than those in Thessalonica, since they welcomed the message with eagerness and examined the Scriptures daily to see if these things were so." (Acts 17:11). The Beroeans were studying the Scriptures to find out if Paul's words corresponded with God's words, a demonstration of the correspondence theory of truth. These factors strongly support the case that God communicates truth primarily with words, not feelings.

Some people object to the idea of absolute truth, saying Christians are narrow-minded to claim Christianity is true and all non-Christian systems are false. Yet, Norman Geisler rebuts that idea by noting, "the same is true of non-Christians who claim that what they view as truth is true, and all opposing beliefs are false."[17] Narrow-mindedness is not the sole territory of Christians. When the relativist says truth is relative, he is making an absolute truth claim that is itself narrow-minded, since he is excluding every other claim about truth. Truth by definition is narrow. Yes, to say "2 plus 2 equals 4" is a narrow truth. There are countless ways to make that statement false (2 plus 2 equals 5, for starters), but there is absolutely one and only one way it can be true. What we find then, is that every claim by relativists to discredit logic or absolutes fails because they must use logic and their own absolute standard when trying to refute the biblical view.

## MORALS ARE RELATIVE

When on September 11, 2001 terrorists flew commercial jetliners into the twin towers of New York City and a section of the Pentagon in Washington and crashed another in rural Pennsylvania, killing more than 3,000 unsuspecting men, women, and children, Americans unanimously decried the acts as a textbook example of evil. This suggests people do understand intuitively the reality of right and wrong. Yet, when asked the question directly, only a small minority of Americans claim to believe in the existence of absolute moral truth.

The same year of the grim 9/11 terrorist attacks, the Barna Research Group documented that only 22 per cent of adults and 6 per cent of teens affirm moral absolutes. Among Christian young people, the numbers were only slightly higher, with one out of ten "born-again" teenagers holding to a belief in unchanging moral truth.[18] According to these statistics, even those raised in the church are heeding the call of our popular culture that cries out "Morals are relative." George

Barna also noted "the alarmingly fast decline of moral foundations among our young people has culminated in a one-word worldview: 'whatever.' The result is a mentality that esteems pluralism, relativism, tolerance, and diversity without critical reflection of the implications of particular views and actions."[19]

Barna's research also found that by far the most common basis for moral decision-making is to do whatever feels right or comfortable in a situation. Nearly four out of ten teens (38%) and three out of ten adults (31%) agreed that is their primary consideration. Among adults, other popular means of moral decision-making were: the principles taught in the Bible (13%) and whatever outcome would produce the most personally beneficial results (10%). Teenagers were slightly different. One out of six (16%) said they make choices on the basis of whatever would produce the most beneficial results for themselves, and just 7 per cent said their moral choices were based on biblical principles.

This view of moral relativism, according to Christian authors Frank Beckwith and Greg Koukl, asserts "there are no universally objective right or

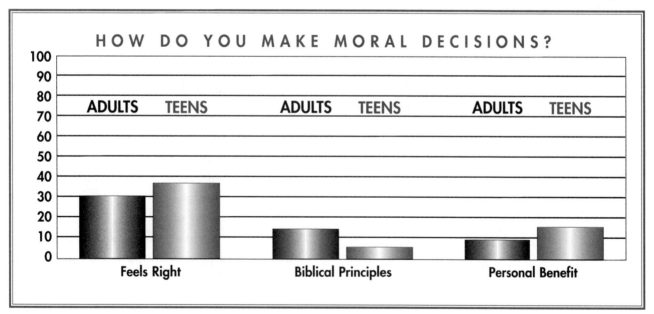

wrong answers, no inappropriate or appropriate judgments, and no reasonable or rational ways by which to make moral distinctions that apply in every time, in every place, and to every person… only subjective opinions exist, which are no different from one's feelings about a favorite football team, movie star, or ice cream flavor."[20] This attitude is reflected in fashionable buzzwords, slogans, and pat answers, such as: "Don't push *your* morality on me!" or "Who are *you* to judge?"

As with relativistic thinking about the nature of truth, moral relativism grows from either an atheistic or pantheistic worldview. If there is no God or if the individual is the ultimate authority, there is no transcendent moral law. One simply creates his or her own moral paradigm and this, of course, can and will change from individual to individual, making morality a subjective experience, dependent solely on the person.

To build their case for moral relativism, many secularists argue that the human moral impulse can be explained through atheistic, Darwinian evolution. An ethical standard has evolved over time that gives Homo sapiens a selective advantage, leading to increased survivability. Groups of hominids that did not develop the "moral" gene have

> The conclusion of both atheists and pantheists is that morals are relative.

been largely eliminated from the gene pool. As zoologist Richard Dawkins puts it, "We are survival machines, robot vehicles blindly programmed to preserve the selfish molecules known as genes."[21]

A similar line of reasoning comes from a pantheistic position, except here cosmic evolution posits a changing, growing universe-which-is-God and in which man participates as a drop in the cosmic consciousness. In this scenario Walsch reminds us, "true morality as an unchanging, objective criteria does not

*Lacking the ultimate authority of God's law, earthly legislators are left with only the whims of relativism to guide them.*

exist. It *cannot* in any evolving society, for the nature of evolution itself is change."[22] Therefore, the conclusion of both atheists and pantheists is that morals are relative.

The issue of what is moral can be boiled down to two basic choices. To quote Beckwith and Koukl, "Morality is either objective, and therefore absolute in some sense, and universal, or not objective, and therefore personal and subjective, mere opinion. These are the only choices."[23] How then, do we defend a biblical view of moral absolutes against the growing tide of relativism?

## RESPONDING TO MORAL RELATIVISM

The first step in defending a Christian view of ethics is to show how other views are not valid. When someone says all morals are relative, the simplest way to deflate that idea is to ask, "Relative to what?" As soon as anyone attempts to answer that question by giving a fixed reference point, he or she has just provided an "absolute" standard and thus ceases to be a relativist!

Another way to help people realize they actually

do believe in moral absolutes is to take from them something they value, like a wallet or CD player. When they object to this action, turn the tables and ask, "Why are you upset? You're not trying to force *your* morality on *me*, are you?" When it comes to things people hold dear, all become moral absolutists! Isn't it interesting, while some claim not to know what is always just, right, or fair, they seem to know innately what isn't just, right and fair when it affects them personally.

To critique the "ethics have evolved" argument, the biblical thinker can point out three major flaws. First, the argument itself assumes at least one moral absolute—it is good to do that which will aid in the survival of one's species. But if there is one absolute, it is possible there could be others, which, in either case, means moral relativism is false.

Second, the "ethics have evolved" story can give only *descriptive* accounts of what is right and wrong, but cannot be *prescriptive*. In other words, it can loosely explain why people have behaved a certain way in the past—description—but it cannot explain why we should behave in a particular way in the future—prescription. It begs the question, "Why should I not steal or murder tomorrow if it aids my survival?" Yet, what our *intuition* (to borrow Jewel's term) actually tells us is there are some things people *ought* to do or not do. We ought not steal, murder, rape, or pillage.

And third, "ethics as evolution" cannot account for moral laws that seem to stand contrary to the notion of "survival of the fittest." For example, rape could be considered a productive way to ensure the

> While some claim not to know what is always just, right, or fair, they seem to know innately what isn't just, right and fair when it affects them personally.

> The foremost problem with moral relativism is that it is incongruent with how we actually live and think.

survival of the human race, yet civil societies universally restrain its citizens from this act and severely punish rapists, citing ethical concerns as a justification for passing judgment.

Even an atheist such as Princeton's Peter Singer (who believes we have evolved into rational beings[24]), acknowledges the fact that "we cannot do without all our ethical principles." and if we base ethics on the free use of biological and cultural explanations this "would leave us in a state of deep moral subjectivism."[25] Therefore, Professor Singer tries to find a basis for morality in the principle of utilitarianism (a moral action is one that brings about the greatest happiness for the greatest number of people).

One of Singer's books, *Practical Ethics*, is widely used as a college text for ethics courses. In it, he teaches that all "persons" should be treated equally, but he defines a "person" as a being that is rational and self-aware. Of course, by this definition, cows and chickens are persons, and unborn humans and infants less then 3 or 4 months old are not. Given his ethical absolute of utilitarianism, Singer argues it is morally right to kill a severely disabled new-born since that action will bring about more happiness for the parents by relieving them of the emotional stress and financial strain of caring for a handicapped child.

Yet, Dr. Singer cannot practice what he teaches. During an interview with *The New Yorker*, Singer admits to spending considerable amounts of money on nursing care for his elderly mother who is suffering from Alzheimer's disease. Peter Berkowitz explains:

> After all, Singer's mother has lost her ability to reason, and to remember, and to recognize others. She has ceased to be a person in her son's technical sense of the term. In these circumstances, Singer's principles surely require him to take the substantial sums of money that he uses to maintain her in comfort and in dignity and spend them instead to feed the poor and save the lives of innocent children.[26]

This brings us to the foremost problem with moral relativism: it is incongruent with how we actually live and think. People everywhere (even ethical relativists) cannot get away from the idea that *they* ought to be treated with compassion, justice, and truthfulness—values that presuppose a transcendent and objective moral law. Yet according to their worldview, there is no source from which this moral code originates. Starting from the atheist's position, where nature is all there is, we find no "moral law" written into the universe of molecules in motion. As for the pantheist's view of reality, if God is everything, evil is as much a part of God as is good. Thus, there is no standard of goodness by which to evaluate what is considered evil. Moral judgments become impossible in the Cosmic Humanist universe.

Whether they recognize it or not, it is impossible for ethical relativists to live consistently with their own moral position. This chink in the relativist's armor can be used open their minds and let in a glimmer of the reality of a

> **LUKE 10:27**
>
> *Love the Lord your God with all your heart, with all your soul, with all your strength, and with all your mind; and your neighbor as yourself.*

transcendent moral law given by a moral Lawgiver. A biblical worldview informs us about this knowledge of right and wrong that is built into the structure of our minds. Paul says as much in Romans 2:15, "[Non-believers] show that the work of the law is written on their hearts. Their consciences testify in support of this, and their competing thoughts either accuse or excuse them." Or, as Professor J. Budziszewski puts it, there are things "we can't not know."[27]

> As image-bearers of God, all people have an innate sense of right and wrong, an "oughtness" associated with behavior.

As image-bearers of God, all people have an innate sense of right and wrong, an "oughtness" associated with behavior. This accounts for the goodness we observe in others, the acts of kindness and generosity. But on the other hand, we find people ignoring these absolute standards of goodness, resulting in acts of hatred and violence. Only the biblical worldview explains what we actually see lived out in the world around us, the moral lapses as well as the moral heroism. We know instinctively it is always wrong to murder your fellow human being, to steal his wife, to covet his home and car. Isn't it always wrong to steal from a blind man's cup and torture children? On the other hand, we know it is always morally right to love your neighbor as yourself, to be the Good Samaritan instead of the thief or Pharisee. And it is always right to love your Creator who endowed you with a rational mind and moral conscious.

Everyone's view of truth and morality ultimately rests on a theological foundation. Secular Humanists and postmodernists begin with atheism, and Cosmic Humanists begin with pantheism, but they both lead to various forms of moral relativism. Christianity, on the other hand, begins with theism, a moral order based on the nature of God and moral imperatives—love God and your neighbor as yourself (Luke 10:27).

# CONCLUSION

In a May 2003 Gallup survey, Americans are nearly three times as likely to say moral values in the United States are getting worse (67%) than better (24%). In another survey, Gallup asked respondents if they felt that various institutions in society are currently doing a good job in raising the moral and ethical standards of the nation. Although "the church or religious leaders" topped the list, this response received only a 29 per cent "good job" rating. The even sadder news is that this number is *down* from 36 per cent in 1994. At the same time, 60 per cent of Americans believe that the church and religious leaders *could* have a significant influence on raising the moral standards in America.[28] This means that the majority of Americans are looking to the church to set the pace in bringing about a moral revival in our nation.

*Most Americans believe church and religious leaders are in a position to significantly influence our moral standards for the better.*

George Barna comments on the importance of teaching morals within a biblical worldview when he writes, "Christian families, educators and churches must prioritize this matter if the Christian community hopes to have any distinctiveness in our culture. The virtual disappearance of this cornerstone of the Christian faith… is probably the best indicator of the waning strength of the Christian Church in America today."[29]

The waning strength of the church's moral influence on society should be a wake-up call to all Christians who take God's cultural commission seriously. Are you prepared to defend a biblical Christian view of absolute truth and morality in your schools, your place of employment, and the political arena? To do so

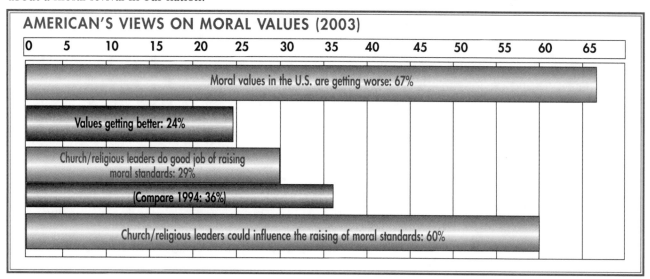

**AMERICAN'S VIEWS ON MORAL VALUES (2003)**

| 0 | 5 | 10 | 15 | 20 | 25 | 30 | 35 | 40 | 45 | 50 | 55 | 60 | 65 |
|---|---|----|----|----|----|----|----|----|----|----|----|----|----|

Moral values in the U.S. are getting worse: 67%

Values getting better: 24%

Church/religious leaders do good job of raising moral standards: 29%

(Compare 1994: 36%)

Church/religious leaders could influence the raising of moral standards: 60%

is part of your Christian call to be salt and light in our increasingly immoral and dark culture. As Paul reminds us, "So we must not get tired of doing good, for we will reap at the proper time if we don't give up." (Galatians 6:9).

As our founders understood so well, when it comes to the connection between morality and a free and civil society, the future of our nation is at stake. In George Washington's farewell address to the nation, he invoked principles that ring as true today as when he first spoke them 200 years ago. Washington emphasized the importance of morality based on religion, and he was clearly referring to Christianity, not a vague New Age spirituality. We quote him at length for you to appreciate the implications of his words for educating today's young people as well as generations yet to come:

> Of all the dispositions and habits which lead to political prosperity, religion and morality are indispensable supports. In vain would that man claim the tribute of patriotism who should labor to subvert these great pillars of human happiness—these firmest props of the duties of men and citizens. The mere politician, equally with the pious man, ought to respect and to cherish them. A volume could not trace all their connections with private and public felicity. Let it simply be asked, "where is the security for property, for reputation, for life, if the sense of religious obligation desert the oaths which are the instruments of investigation in courts of justice?" And let us with caution indulge the supposition that morality can be maintained without religion. Whatever may be conceded to the influence of refined education on minds of peculiar structure, reason and experience both forbid

us to expect that national morality can prevail in exclusion of religious principle. It is substantially true that virtue or morality is a necessary spring of popular government. The rule indeed extends with more or less force to every species of free government. Who that is a sincere friend to it can look with indifference upon attempts to shake the foundation of the fabric?[30]

## RECOMMENDED READING

Beckwith, Frank and Greg Koukl. *Relativism: Feet Firmly Planted in Mid-Air*, Grand Rapids, MI: Baker Books, 1998.

Copan, Paul. *True for You, But Not for Me: Deflating the Slogans that Leave Christians Speechless*, Minneapolis, MN: Bethany House, 1998.

Copan, Paul. *That's Just Your Interpretation*, Grand Rapids, MI: Baker Books, 2001.

Wiker, Benjamin. *Moral Darwinism: How We Became Hedonists*, Downers Grove, IL: InterVarsity Press, 2002.

TO TEACH YOUR GROUP HOW TO RESPOND TO MORAL RELATIVISM, Chuck Edwards has compiled a 6-lesson study guide for Frank Beckwith's and Greg Koukl's book, *Relativism: Feet Firmly Planted in Mid-Air*. Included with the teaching package is a video interview with the authors. This resource, is available at Summit Ministries' Web site at http://store.summit.org/index.jsp. Click on "Ethics/Morality" and look for the "Relativism Package," or call 719-685-9103 to order over the phone.

## ENDNOTES

1. Brad Pitt answering a question about what defines the teenage years, *Teen People*, August 2003, p. 112.

2. Kristanna Loken ("T3" movie) answering whether she liked girls, *Rolling Stone*, July 24, 2003, p. 46.

3. Benjamin Wiker. *Moral Darwinism: How We Became Hedonists* (Downers Grove, IL: InterVarsity Press, 2002) p. 24.

4. "Intuition," by Jewel. From her *0304* CD released June, 2003.

5. George Barna, *Real Teens: A Contemporary Snapshot of*

*Youth Culture* (Ventura, CA: Regal Books, 2001), p. 92.

6.  Barna, *Real Teens*, p. 92.

7.  Allan Bloom, *The Closing of the American Mind* (New York: Simon and Schuster, 1987), p. 25.

8.  Neale Donald Walsch, *Conversations with God: Book 1* (New York: G. P. Putnam's Sons, 1995), p. 3.

9.  Walsch, *Conversations with God: Book 1*, p. 1.

10. Ibid., p. 2.

11. Ibid., p. 4.

12. Neale Donald Walsch, *The New Revelations* (New York: Atria Books, 2002), p. 118.

13. Mortimer J. Adler, *Truth in Religion: The Plurality of Religions and the Unity of Truth* (New York: MacMillan, 1990), 2-5.

14. J. P. Moreland, *Scaling the Secular City* (Grand Rapids, MI: Baker Books, 1987), p. 82.

15. Moreland, *Scaling the Secular City*, p. 190.

16. Ibid.

17. Norman L. Geisler, *Baker Encyclopedia of Christian Apologetics* (Grand Rapids, MI: Baker Books, 1999), p. 745.

18. George Barna, "Americans Are Most Likely to Base Truth on Feelings," February 12, 2002, on the Web at www.barna.org/cgi-bin/PagePressRelease.asp?PressReleaseID=106&Reference=C. This report was based on a random telephone survey conducted in Oct/Nov 2001 across the continental U.S. (1010 adults and 604 teens, 13-18, were surveyed).

19. Barna, "Americans Are Most Likely to Base Truth on Feelings."

20. Frank Beckwith and Gregory Koukl, *Relativism: Feet Firmly Planted in Mid-Air* (Grand Rapids, MI: Baker Books, 1998), p. 12-13.

21. Richard Dawkins, *The Selfish Gene* (Oxford: Oxford University Press, 1989), preface to the 1976 edition.

22. Walsch, *The New Revelations,* p. 173.

23. Beckwith and Koukl, *Relativism*, p. 12-13.

24. See Peter J. Colosi, "The Intrinsic Worth of Persons: Revisiting Peter Singer and His Critics" in *Journal of Inter-Disciplinary Studies*, Vol. XV, Nos. 1-2, 2003, p. 3ff.

25. Peter Singer, *The Expanding Circle* (Oxford, UK: Clarendon Press, 1981) p. 84-5.

26. Peter Berkowitz, "The Utilitarian Horrors Of Peter Singer: Other People's Mothers," *The New Republic Online*, January 10, 2000. http://www.tnr.com/011000/coverstory011000.html.

27. J. Budziszewski, *The Revenge of Conscience: Politics and the Fall of Man* (Dallas, TX: Spence Publishing, 1999) p. xv.

28. George H. Gallup Jr., "Which National Principles Keep America Strong?," *Religion & Values Survey*, November 4, 2003. http://www.gallup.com/poll/tb/religvalue/20031104.asp.

29. Barna, "Americans Are Most Likely to Base Truth on Feelings."

30. "Washington's Farewell Address, 1796." Online at www.yale.edu/lawweb/avalon/washing.htm.


(1) U.S. Capitol building: From Countering Culture video (2004 Summit Ministries: Manitou Springs, CO)

(2) Church steeple: From Countering Culture video (2004 Summit Ministries: Manitou Springs, CO)

(3) Holocaust victims: From Countering Culture video (2004 Summit Ministries: Manitou Springs, CO)

# CHAPTER 12

# Self Esteem for a New Age

"For my ally is the Force, and a powerful ally
it is. . . . Its energy surrounds us and
binds us. Luminous beings are we,
not this crude matter."

—YODA, JEDI MASTER

"…you are only a step away from
understanding a larger truth. Which is?
That you and God are One."[1]

—NEALE DONALD WALSCH

"In a growing number of classrooms throughout
the world, education is beginning to move into
a new dimension. More and more teachers are
exposing children to ways of contacting their
inner wisdom and their higher selves...
New Age education has arrived...."[2]

—JACK CANFIELD

In *The Truman Show*, when Truman asks Christof, "Who am I?" the director responds, "You're the star!" Like Truman, everyone on planet earth is vitally interested in the question of who he or she is—really. And in one sense, Christof's answer parallels the Cosmic Humanist reply. Truman was the star of his own show without realizing it. Similarly, New Age psychology teaches that humanity's fundamental problem is that we do not realize we are god, the unwitting stars of our own "show." As we will discover in this chapter, this view is gaining influence in various segments of society—especially in psychology and education—and from these strongholds has foisted a remarkable mindset on the wider culture.

More than thirty years ago, Charles Reich recognized a novel understanding of the self rapidly spreading across the country. In his New Age manifesto, *The Greening of America*, Reich heralded the dawning of a new consciousness that "declares that the individual self is the only true reality. Thus it returns to the earlier America: 'Myself I sing.' The first commandment is: thou shalt not do violence to thyself."[3] This expansive individualism leads to Reich's second commandment: "No one judges anyone else."[4] Reich describes an unbounded relativism of self and tolerance that, as outlined in the last chapter, is the fruit of New Age pantheism.

Everywhere today we hear the message of "self"— it's even the name of a magazine dedicated to, what else, the self (www.self.com). In her hit single, "The Greatest Love Of All," actress and recording artist Whitney Houston sings, "I found the greatest love of all inside of me. The greatest love of all is easy to achieve. Learning to love yourself; it is the greatest love of all." Some may respond: "What's wrong with that? Haven't studies indicated that a strong self-image is important for a psychologically healthy person? And

didn't Jesus say to love others as you love *yourself*?" These are legitimate questions. But the response depends on the place of self within the larger worldview. This chapter examines the meaning of "self" in New Age psychology.

## EVERY PERSON IS GOD

Echoing Truman's question to Christof, Meher Baba declares, "There is only one question. And once you know the answer to that question there are no more to ask.... Who am I? And to that question there is only one answer—I am God!"[5] In fact, actress and New Age promoter Shirley MacLain recommends everyone begin each day by affirming his or her own godhood. "You can use I

> "Who am I? And to that question there is only one answer— I am God!" —Meher Baba

am God or I am that I am as Christ often did, or you can extend the affirmation to fit your own needs."[6]

John Bradshaw expresses the focal point of New Age psychology when he writes, "Each of us has access to a supraconscious, creative, integrative, self-organizing, intuitive mind whose capabilities are apparently unlimited. This is the part of our consciousness that constitutes our God-likeness."[7] Bradshaw professes that our conscious mind links each of us to God. Many Cosmic Humanists state the case even more forcefully. Ruth Montgomery supposedly channeled a spirit that spoke through her, claiming, "We are as much God as God is a part of us . . . each of us is God ... together we are God... this all-for-one-and-one-for-all... makes us the whole of God."[8] New Ager John White optimistically asserts, "sooner or later every human being will feel a call from the cosmos to ascend to godhood."[9]

## MONISM: ALL IS ONE

The idea that every individual is God and God is every individual is tied to the concept of monism, the belief that all of reality is essentially one essence and that this ultimate essence is God. Because Cosmic Humanists retain this "all is one" mentality, they believe humanity can become attuned to all the powers of its godhood by achieving a unity of consciousness.

> Monism is the belief that all of reality is essentially one essence and that this ultimate essence is God.

"Once we begin to see that we are all God," says Beverly Galyean, "that we all have the attributes of God, then I think the whole purpose of human life is to reown the Godlikeness within us; the perfect love, the perfect wisdom, the perfect understanding, the perfect intelligence, and when we do that, we create back to that old, that essential oneness which is consciousness."[10]

Monism has sweeping implications for psychology. If all is one, then the One that we are as humans is not only God but also is good. As Neale Donald Walsch puts it:

> The promise of God is that you are His son. Her offspring. Its likeness. His equal…. It is your first nature to be unconditionally loving…. What the soul is after is—the highest feeling of love you can imagine. This is the soul's desire. This is its purpose. The soul is after the feeling…. The highest feeling is the

experience of unity with All That Is. This is the great return to Truth for which the soul yearns. This is the feeling of perfect love.[11]

Or, as Robert Muller says, "Only the unity of all can bring the well-being of all.[12]

## REINCARNATION AND KARMA

Any answer to the question, "Who am I?" necessarily confronts the issue of what happens when a person dies. The concept of mankind's unity, our essential "oneness," supports the concept of reincarnation. Virtually every "orthodox" adherent of the New Age movement believes that each individual's soul was present in other material forms earlier in history and that the soul will manifest itself in still other forms after its present body dies. The body may pass away, but the soul will continue its quest for godhood in other bodies. This belief in reincarnation caused Shirley MacLaine, when recalling her daughter's birth, to muse, "When the doctor brought her to me in the hospital bed on that afternoon in 1956, had she already lived many, many times before, with other mothers? Had she, in fact, been one herself? Had she, in fact, ever been my mother? Was her one-hour-old face housing a soul perhaps millions of years old?"[13]

This line of thinking suggests that in order to understand oneself (and one's path to godhood), a person must be cognizant of at least some of his or her past lives. Gary Zukav explains:

> If your soul was a Roman centurion, an Indian beggar, a Mexican mother, a nomad boy, and a medieval nun, among other incarnations, for example, . . . you will not be able to understand your proclivities, or interests,

or ways of responding to different situations without an awareness of the experiences of those lifetimes.[14]

Reincarnation serves little purpose unless people know about and learn from their past lives. For this reason, Cosmic Humanists advocate the laws of karma. Most New Agers believe that, between incarnations, individual souls have an opportunity to decide how to address their bad karma in their next life. Thus, they believe what befalls us in our lifetimes—whether good or evil—happens because we chose for it to happen.

This belief has led several New Age promoters to claim there are no such things as victims. "We are not victims of the world we see," writes Shirley MacLaine. "We are victims of the way we see the world. In truth, there are no victims. There is only self-perception and self-realization."[15] Neale Donald Walsh writes, "There are no victims, and there are no villains."[16] New Age speaker Shakti Gawain provides an example of how this works. When a woman in her workshop told Gawain she had been raped, Gawain responded that she had chosen for this to happen and that she needed to discover the power in the pain she chose for herself. Gawain explains:

> A woman in one of my workshops shared that she'd been awoken from her sleep and raped. At first it was impossible for her to see her power in this situation or see how she could have chosen such a painful, frightening way to heal herself. Her rape left her feeling powerless, afraid that this could happen to her again. To remove her fear, I felt it was important for her to see why she might have created

this situation. She began to look more deeply into the cause of her rape. For years she had feared being abused by a man and deeply believed that this could happen to her. In general, she saw others as having power over her, while she herself had little choice but to submit to the powers that be. I believe she created an external situation that mirrored and intensified what she felt inside.[17]

Neale Donald Walsch likewise believes the circumstances of our lives happen only because we choose for them to occur. "We create our own reality," says Walsch. Thus, when he comments on the horrors of Hitler and the Jewish Holocaust—where millions upon millions of Jews were tortured, starved, gassed, shot and experimented upon—he actually claims that "Hitler did nothing wrong," and that "Hitler did no harm to those whose deaths he caused." He even says what Hitler did was to release these "butterflies from their cocoons."[18] Walsch believes this because his worldview melds good and evil. He comments, "The first thing to understand about the universe is that no condition is 'good' or 'bad.' It just *is*. So stop making value judgments. The second thing to know is that *all conditions are temporary. Nothing stays the same, nothing remains static. Which way a thing changes depends on you.*"[19] (Italics his)

## HIGHER CONSCIOUSNESS

The belief that an individual can hasten the work of evolution by achieving a higher consciousness is tied closely to Cosmic Humanist psychology. Achieving

> Most New Agers believe that what befalls us in our lifetimes—whether good or evil—happens because we chose for it to happen.

higher consciousness is the central goal for any member of the New Age movement, and only psychology provides the means to unlock the secrets of this superior mindset.

Cosmic Humanists sometimes refer to their approach to psychology, with its emphasis on higher consciousness, as "fourth force" psychology.

*Cosmic Humanists assert that no one should make value judgments—even Hitler "did nothing wrong" to victims of the Holocaust.*

John White explains: "Fourth force psychology covers a wide range of human affairs. All of them, however, are aimed at man's ultimate development—not simply a return from unhealthiness to normality—as individuals and as a species."[20] Carl Jung is credited with developing the main outlines of fourth force psychology, which includes the idea that "an individual can gain wholeness if he can set up some communication with the Self through opening himself to the world of the unconscious."[21] To identify the unconscious self as being the *true* self fits neatly within the New Age framework of cosmic consciousness and as a result has been embraced by many Cosmic Humanists.

The realization of cosmic unity, according to the New Age movement, represents the only truly healthy mental state. Marilyn Ferguson writes, "Well-being cannot be infused intravenously or ladled in by prescription. It comes from a matrix: the bodymind. It reflects psychological and somatic harmony."[22] One's consciousness affects both body and soul, and only a constant state of higher consciousness can ensure mental and physical well-being. Thus, psychology plays a crucial role in Cosmic Humanism's worldview, not only because it can hasten the evolution of all mankind to a collective God-consciousness, but also because it works to ensure perfect health for every individual.

# MIND OVER MATTER

The message from Cosmic Humanist psychologists to people suffering health problems is simple: mindset is responsible for health. People who suffer painful sickness are doing so because they have not yet achieved a higher consciousness. "Every time you don't trust yourself and don't follow your inner truth," says Shakti Gawain, "you decrease your aliveness and your body will reflect this with a loss of vitality, numbness, pain, and eventually, physical disease."[23]

This same failure to contact the "God within" also creates criminal tendencies. Vera Alder explains that in the New Age:

> A criminal or an idler will be recognized as a sick individual offering a splendid chance for wise help. Instead of being incarcerated with fellow unfortunates in the awful atmosphere of a prison, the future 'criminal' will be in much demand.[24]

Criminals can be put in touch with their higher consciousness, thereby becoming capable of leading healthy lives—spiritually, physically, and ethically.

By attaining higher consciousness, we guarantee ourselves excellent all-around health. "Health and disease don't just happen to us," says Ferguson. "They are active processes issuing from inner harmony or disharmony, profoundly affected by our states of consciousness, our ability or inability to flow with experience."[25] Further, those enlightened individuals who maintain higher consciousness can solve more than their own personal problems. Shirley MacLaine found: "Somewhere way underneath me were the answers to everything that caused anxiety and confusion in the world."[26] If this is true, of course, then the most important thing any individual can do is attain higher consciousness. Personal "salvation," and indeed, the salvation of the world, depends upon it.

## METHODS OF THE FOURTH FORCE

What means does "fourth force" psychology employ to induce states of higher consciousness in willing individuals? Most often, it relies on meditation, frequently aided by crystals or mantras. A writer in *Life Times Magazine* states emphatically, "My message to everyone now is to learn to meditate. It was through meditation that many other blessings came about."[27] According to the Cosmic Humanist, higher consciousness flows naturally from meditation—one of its many "blessings." But other "blessings" may manifest themselves as well. For example, meditation can create in an individual the ability to channel spirits. According to Kathleen Vande Kieft: "Almost without exception, those who channel effectively meditate regularly. The process of channeling itself is an extension of the state of meditation... the best way to prepare, then, for channeling is by meditation."[28]

Channeling is the Cosmic Humanist belief that

> Channeling is the Cosmic Humanist belief that spirits sometimes speak to and through a particularly gifted individual engaged in meditation.

spirits sometimes speak to and through a particularly gifted individual engaged in meditation. Elena, a spirit allegedly channeled by John Randolph Price, describes beings like herself as "angels of light—whether from earth or other worlds. They search, select and guide those men and women who may be suitable subjects."[29]

Not every member of the New Age movement acknowledges much significance in channeling, but most New Agers embrace meditation as an important psychological tool for attaining higher consciousness. Channeling and other practices (including astrology, firewalking, ouija boards, and aura readings) often are suggested by New Age psychologists as means to enhance the higher consciousness achieved through meditation.

Regardless of the specific psychological package prescribed by individual Cosmic Humanists, New Age psychology is based on a simple rule: commune with the God within. This is the fundamental difference between New Age and Christian meditation. New Age meditation focuses on the "God within" while Christian meditation focuses on the God outside ourselves—our Maker, Judge and Savior—and on His objective, external revelation of truth found in the Bible. This distinction is spelled out dramatically in the New Age children's book *What Is God?*—a book that teaches Cosmic Humanist meditation couched in more "traditional" terms:

> And if you really want to pray to God, you can just close your eyes anywhere, and think about that feeling of God, that makes you

> New Age meditation focuses on the "God within" while Christian meditation focuses on the God outside ourselves—our Maker, Judge and Savior.

part of everything and everybody. If you can feel that feeling of God, and everybody else can feel that feeling of God, then we can all become friends together, and we can really understand, 'What is God?' So, if you really want to feel God, you can close your eyes now, and listen to your breath go slowly in and out, and think how you are connected to everything, even if you are not touching everything.[30]

This New Age practice of meditation parallels some programs that have become popular in schools across America. This is where cosmic psychology meets public education.

## NEW AGE EDUCATION

While driving her children to school one morning, Nancy noticed her daughter Kim was unusually quiet as her brother picked on her. Kim's eyes were closed, and Nancy was alarmed that Kim didn't respond when she called her name. Nancy stopped the car and gently shook her daughter to arouse her from a trance-like state. Kim responded, "Don't worry, Mommy, I was relaxing, painting my mind picture and was with my friend Pumsy." Nancy asked where she learned this, and the second grader answered, "From school."[31] Part of the school's guidance counseling curricula, *Pumsy: In Pursuit of Excellence* is used in an estimated 40 percent of the schools across America.

In another instance involving a student at the other end of the educational spectrum from second-grade Kim, Mark attended a prestigious private university to pursue a pre-med degree. While taking abnormal psychology during his sophomore year, Mark read three required books which focused on

New Age psychology. Although reared as a Christian, Mark jettisoned Christianity and followed the path to cosmic spirituality as a result of studying these texts. For the next 16 years he practiced transcendental meditation and amassed a large library of New Age books.[32]

These real life examples demonstrate the degree to which New Age psychology has permeated every level of education across America and around the world. As with Secular Humanism and postmodernism, New Age ideology has been intentionally introduced into public school curricula. This is affirmed by Jack Canfield, chairman of the California Task Force on Self-Esteem and a frequent keynote speaker in education seminars and workshops, when he writes in *New Age* magazine: "In a growing number of classrooms throughout the world, education is beginning to move into a new dimension. More and more teachers are exposing children to ways of contacting their inner wisdom and their higher selves... New Age education has arrived.... An influx of spiritual teachings from the East, combined with a new psychological perspective in the West has resulted in a fresh look at the learning process."[33]

> The New Age practice of meditation parallels some programs that have become popular in schools across America.

In *The Aquarian Conspiracy*, too, Marilyn Ferguson reveals the infiltration of New Age adherents in education. "Of the Aquarian conspirators surveyed," Ferguson writes, "more were involved in education than in any other category of work... teachers, administrators, policymakers, educational psychologists."[34] Much of the work of these individuals is behind the scenes, moving quietly to implement the worldview they believe is best for children.

These New Age ideas have been at work for more than thirty years. In a lead article of the *Journal of Transpersonal Psychology* written in 1973, Frances Clark wrote:

> Increasing interest in transpersonal psychology has led to innovative programs in higher education which are called transpersonal. Transpersonal education is concerned primarily with the study and development of consciousness, particularly with those states commonly called higher states of consciousness and with the spiritual quest as an essential aspect of human life.... It focuses on the process of discovery and transcendence of self which results from spiritual practice, affirming subjective experience as valid and even essential for determining the nature of reality and the relative validity of revealed truth.[35]

> As with Secular Humanism and postmodernism, New Age ideology has been intentionally introduced into public school curricula.

In other words, subjective experience—especially encounters with altered states of consciousness—is a better source of understanding the "nature of reality" (i.e., truth) than are sources of "revealed truth," such as sacred texts like the Bible. The result is a proliferation of courses on the elementary, high school, and college level that encompass Eastern religion and New Age beliefs. Some college courses, with titles such as "Kundalini Yoga and Meditation" or "Metaphysical Training," overtly promote pantheistic ideas. In other cases, a Cosmic Humanist worldview is smuggled into the subject matter, such as the two examples cited above involving the elementary school class on self-esteem and the college course in abnormal psychology.

Dr. Barbara Clark sheds additional light on the underlying ideas that shape New Age education. Clark is professor of education at California State University and author of the popular and widely used textbook for teachers, *Growing Up Gifted.* Professor Clark promotes "integrative education" or "transpersonal learning." She suggests that educators use such New Age religious techniques as "guided fantasies and dreams, recognition and use of altered states of consciousness and centering activities" to develop a student's "intuitive abilities." These activities are important because "Reality is seen as an outward projection of internal thoughts, feelings and expectations. Energy is the connector.... You create your own reality."[36] Here we find blatant religious indoctrination masquerading as a program for gifted students.

> "You create your own reality."
> —Barbara Clark

This Cosmic Humanist psychology of self animates the *Pumsy* "self-esteem" curriculum for young children. In one exercise, for example, after a teacher guides children into a meditative state in which they paint "mind-pictures" and dialogue with imaginary friends, the children conclude the session by chanting in unison, "I am me, and I am enough...I am me, and I am enough...I am me, and I am enough." After another exercise, the teacher leads the children to chant, "I can choose how I feel...I can choose how I feel...I can choose how I feel."

The above admissions by respected educators derive from an all-encompassing worldview, revealing that their approach to education is the fruit of prior beliefs. From a worldview perspective, before the question of education can be addressed (i.e., what and how should a child be taught?) a more fundamental question must be answered: what is the nature of the child (the question of psychology)? But the answer to that question flows from a belief in what is real (the question of philosophy). But that question cannot be addressed until an answer is given to the question of the existence and nature of God (theology). Thus, "worldview" analysis demonstrates, once again, that every social issue is rooted in religious beliefs about the nature of God. The field of education is no exception to this rule.

Can learning take place in a religiously neutral environment? Worldview thinking reveals the answer: "Absolutely not!" Religiously neutral education is an impossibility. The educational enterprise cannot even get off the ground until the educator understands the nature of the person being taught. Only after affirm-

> Religiously neutral education is an impossibility.

ing a psychology, can a philosophy of education be developed to best suit the learning needs of the child. What we find in transpersonal education is a commitment to a pantheistic worldview that sees every child as a god and whose main problem is not appreciating his or her godhood. Hence, meditative techniques are introduced into the classroom to encourage children to get in touch with their inner selves, the supposed repository of all that is true. The approach has permeated

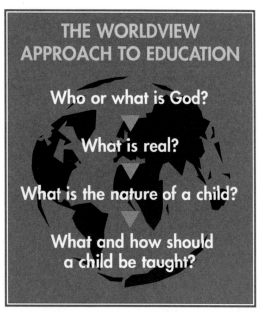

THE WORLDVIEW APPROACH TO EDUCATION

Who or what is God?

What is real?

What is the nature of a child?

What and how should a child be taught?

the overall direction of public education, leading to a decreased emphasis on learning facts, such as history, math, and reading skills, and to an increase in exposure to psychological experiences, emphasizing self-esteem and personal decision-making.

The transpersonal model of effective, nondirective decision-making is the basis of most drug and sex education courses, as well as for many courses for gifted students and guidance counseling programs. These programs are based on the belief that if children can be guided to feel good about themselves (self-esteem), then they can be empowered to make healthy choices about sex and drugs.

The influence of transpersonal psychology on educational philosophy is significant. Marilyn Ferguson surveyed and presented an anthology of goals, accomplishments, and strategies of New Age thinkers and activists across the social and technical spectrum. She asked respondents to name individuals whose ideas influenced them. Psychologists Carl Jung, Carl Rogers, and Abraham Maslow ranked two, three, and four among writers from every kind of background and discipline.[37]

While Rogers and Maslow are known primarily for their secular worldview, a New Age connection is apparent in some of their writings. For example, Rogers wrote: "The basis of values will need to be recognized as discoverable within.... The rich resources of the inner world need to be explored and utilized...in our expansion into alternate states of consciousness, to our growing use of psychic forces and psychic energy."[38] And Maslow considered that psychology was headed in a "New Age" direction when he wrote: "I consider Humanistic, Third Force Psychology to be transitional, a preparation for a still 'higher' Fourth Force Psychology, transpersonal, transhuman, centered in the cosmos rather than in human needs and interest, going beyond humanness, identity, self-actualization and the like."[39] And as mentioned earlier, the guru of the transpersonal psychology to which Maslow refers is Carl Jung.

## RESPONDING TO NEW AGE EDUCATION

In response to New Age content in public schools, concerned parents are asking school personnel that their children not be subjected to New Age indoctrination in the classroom. Many educators resist this concern, however. Rather than honestly addressing the facts, they often caricature the complaining parents as "censors" or part of the "Radical Right."

Unfortunately, many government school educators do not perceive the New Age assumptions in some curricula. This is, at least in part, because most people in the West do not have a working understanding of

> Many educators do not perceive New Age assumptions in curricula because most people in the West do not understand the New Age or Eastern mystery religions.

the New Age or Eastern mystery religions. Therefore, parents must approach teachers and school administrators with care, seeking to educate them in worldview thinking so they can understand how content is based on a *religious* foundation. The principles you have learned in this text have given you the tools needed to examine the worldview assumptions and implications inherent in any curriculum presented in

public schools.

For instance, we mentioned the "self-esteem" curriculum that teaches children to chant, "I am me, and I am enough." From a worldview perspective, that statement represents the fruit of psychology. As we've said many times, when the fruit is traced to its roots—to its theological source—there are only a few options open to us: either there is no God, God is personal (distinct from ourselves), or God is all. The declaration, "I am enough," is nourished from either a pantheistic or atheistic root. Either theology lends itself to the view that man is autonomous. Yet this is starkly different from a biblical view of God as Creator and Sustainer of life (Colossians 1:17). This view logically leads to a different kind of fruit, where man is understood to be a dependent creature, one relying on the power of Christ's sufficiency. As Paul confessed, "For me to live is Christ..." (Philippians 1:21).

It is important here to clarify a common misconception. Supreme Court and lower court decisions regarding religion in schools dealt only with religious *practice*, such as devotional Bible reading and prayer. In fact, the courts made it clear that teaching *about* the Bible is appropriate in a classroom setting. In the 1963 *Abington v. Schempp* decision regarding reading the Bible in school, Justice Clark, writing for the majority, stated, "Nothing we have said here indicates that such study of the Bible or religion, when presented objectively as part of a secular program of education, may not be effected consistently with the First Amendment." Justice Arthur Goldberg concurred: "Neither government nor this Court can or should ignore the significance of the fact that...many of our legal, political, and personal values derive historically from religious teachings." It should be noted that historically, the religious teachings Goldberg alludes to were from a biblical worldview, not atheism or pantheism.

To assist educators in how to appropriately teach the Bible, the National Bible Association published "The Bible and Public Schools:

> **COLOSSIANS 1:17**
> *He is before all things, and by Him all things hold together.*

A First Amendment Guide" (A copy can be found online at www.teachaboutthebible.org). This guide serves as a blueprint for teaching the Bible in literature, history, and social studies—something that surveys show three out of four Americans want. The guide is endorsed by 18 different Jewish, Christian, and Muslim groups, including: the National Council of Churches, the National Association of Evangelicals, the Christian Legal Society, the Anti-Defamation League, the American Jewish Committee, the American Jewish Congress, and People for the American Way. Even the two largest teacher unions, the American Federation of Teachers and the National Education Association, as well as the National School Boards Foundation, have signed on to this guideline.

So while our courts have ruled it is illegal to lead children in specific religious practices, such as Christian prayer or New Age meditation, the courts are clear that teaching *about* various religions, including Christianity, is not only consistent with the First Amendment, but necessary in order for a student to be considered well educated. Public school teachers, for example, *can* teach that Thanksgiving is a national

> "Neither government nor this Court can or should ignore the significance of the fact that…many of our legal, political, and personal values derive historically from religious teachings."—U.S. Supreme Court Justice Arthur Goldberg

holiday to thank God for His blessings. Consider this statement endorsed by 17 organizations including the National Education Association, The American Federation of Teachers, the American Jewish Congress, and the American Association of School Administrators:

> The study of religious holidays may be included in elementary and secondary curricula as opportunities for teaching about religions. Such study serves the academic goals of educating students about history and cultures as well as about the traditions of particular religions in a pluralistic society.

Additional resources for the proper use of religious content in the classroom can be obtained from *Gateways to Better Education*, a national organization dedicated to helping public school students and educators gain a better understanding of the value and contributions of Christianity to society and the world. Their website (www.gtbe.org) contains many practical ideas for how to create an environment for presenting the positive contributions of Christianity in ways that are legal and appropriate in a public school setting. You also will find tips on interacting with teachers and administrators who may resist these efforts.

On the university level, students can speak up in class and alert classmates to viewpoint discrimination (for instance, not allowing a Christian perspective on the subject) or, on the other hand, religious indoctrination, as when professors present their personal religious views as facts, as in

## Excerpts from "The Bible and Public Schools: A First Amendment Guide"

*(Source: www.teachaboutthebible.org/bps/bpsfaguide01.htm)*

### THE BIBLE AND THE RELIGIOUS-LIBERTY RIGHTS OF STUDENTS

Many Americans continue to hold the mistaken view that the Supreme Court decisions in the 1960s concerning prayer and devotional Bible-reading prohibited students from expressing their faith in a public school. Actually, the Court did not eliminate prayer or the Bible from public schools; it barred state-sponsored religious practices, including devotional use of the Bible by public school officials.

### STUDENT RELIGIOUS EXPRESSION

In "Religion in the Public Schools: A Joint Statement of Current Law," 35 religious and civil liberties organizations give the following summary of the rights of students to express their faith in a public school:

> Students have the right to pray individually or in groups or to discuss their religious views with their peers so long as they are not disruptive. Because the Establishment Clause does not apply to purely private speech, students enjoy the right to read their Bibles or other scriptures, say grace before meals, pray before tests, and discuss religion with other willing student listeners. In the classroom students have the right to pray quietly except when required to be actively engaged in school activities (e.g., students may not decide to pray just as a teacher calls on them). In informal settings, such as the cafeteria or in the halls, students may pray either audibly or silently, subject to the same rules of order as apply to other speech in these locations. However, the right to engage in voluntary prayer does not include, for example, the right to have a captive audience listen or to compel other students to participate.

Mark's case mentioned earlier.

Also, students can write a letter-to-the-editor for the campus newspaper or actively participate in a Christian or conservative political student organization. Those who have graduated can stay informed of attempts to squelch religious freedom on campus or join with other alumni to monitor the status of the "culture wars" at their alma mater. One organization that keeps tabs on repressive campus policies is the Foundation for Individual Rights in Education (F.I.R.E.). Their Web site (www.thefire.org) provides stories of the latest developments in political correctness and what informed students are doing to reverse these disturbing trends.

# COUNTERING NEW AGE PSYCHOLOGY

Concerning the grip of New Age ideas on Americans, a 2002 survey by Barna Research Group found that 35 per cent of adults believe it is possible to communicate with the deceased. This is up from 18 per cent just twelve years earlier. Similarly, a Gallup poll found belief in reincarnation grew from 21 to 24 percent among a cross-section of all age groups. These numbers indicate New Age ideas are gaining influence across our society. So how does a Christian present the truth in love in the face of these trends?

As stated earlier, our first approach in countering non-Christian ideas is to start with the assumptions of a biblical worldview. We follow the logic that, beginning with a personal God, all men are created in God's image and have stamped upon their consciousness the knowledge of Him, even though this knowledge has been suppressed (Romans 1:18-20). Because of this refusal to embrace the truth, many fall prey to deceptive philosophies (Colossians 2:8). To rescue those who

> **COLOSSIANS 2:8**
>
> *Be careful that no one takes you captive through philosophy and empty deceit based on human tradition, based on the elemental forces of the world, and not based on Christ.*

have been captured by these philosophies, we remind non-Christians of the truth they know but have suppressed, pointing out areas where they have been deceived in their thinking, then moving to the good news of God's forgiveness through Jesus Christ. You may recall we outlined in Chapter 1 how the Apostle Paul proceeded through these steps as he spoke to the atheistic and pagan philosophers in Athens.

When approaching someone who has been captured by the New Age worldview, we can affirm his or her desire for greater spirituality in the midst of our materialistic culture. Their longing for inspiration and wonder in life is legitimate, as well as their craving for a sense of personal worth. Yet we also need to explain that they are selling themselves short by seeking personal fulfillment in a non-personal source—the New Age cosmic-energy-force-God. Only a personal God can meet their deepest need for love and unconditional acceptance.

In addition, we can agree with the New Age concern for karma as it reflects our innate sense of justice—the idea of reaping what you sow, as the Bible mentions in Galatians 6:7. Yet, the idea of karma does not measure up to the Bible's assertion that our past faults can be forgiven and cleansed and that we can be united with the God who created us to have a relationship with Him.

Here are some additional questions

> **GALATIANS 6:7**
>
> *Don't be deceived: God is not mocked. For whatever a man sows he will also reap.*

related to psychology that may help stimulate discussion with a New Age devotee:

• **"Help me understand how you, a person, can come from an It, an impersonal force?"** (A person has a mind, will, emotions, etc., while an impersonal force, by definition, does not. Of course, there is no answer to this important question from a New Age perspective. This shows the New Age view of man to be a contradiction in terms, thus undermining the foundation of the New Age worldview.)

• **"How can love come from an impersonal force?"** (Recall Walsch's claim that God is impersonal energy, but man's first nature is "unconditionally loving." The law of cause and effect tells us that an effect cannot be greater than its cause. So how can we arrive at love by starting with non-love, for how can an impersonal force love?)

• **"If reincarnation is the system whereby we pay off our past karmic failings, how did this process get started?"** (New Age reincarnation assumes evil and suffering in life is ultimately the result of one's free choices in previous lives, and that individuality itself is a result of ignorance—a form of suffering and evil. But if you were originally a part of "the one," why did you become individualized into this illusion of life in the first place? This question raises a major contradiction for reincarnation. If one goes back in past lives far enough, he must come to a *first* incarnation. But in this first life, there is no karmic debt to pay because there were no prior lives, hence, no reason to exist as an individual in the first place.)

• **"Do you believe in animal rights?** (If yes,

then ask…) What is the source of 'rights'?" ("Rights," as in animal rights, implies there is a difference between a right way to act toward animals and a wrong way to act. In a pantheistic system, where all is ultimately "one," there is no difference between right and wrong, good or evil, cruelty or non-cruelty. Pantheism cannot account for these concepts. Therefore, there is no such thing as legal "rights," animal or human.)

• **"Should you help a person in need?** (If yes, then ask…) Wouldn't that interfere with a person's karma?" (The traditional Hindu idea is that one should never interfere with someone else's karma, which is why Hindus and Buddhists did not found hospitals. Hospitals were begun by Christians who were following Jesus' teaching about loving one's neighbor, as in the Good Samaritan, and His instruction that sickness is not the result of sin (see John 9:1-5). Some may point to Mahatma Gandhi, a Hindu and humanitarian who was concerned with the needs of the poor. Yet Gandhi acknowledges that Christian missionaries, not his own religion, "awakened in him a revulsion for the caste system and for the maltreatment of outcastes."[40] Gandhi acted *inconsistently* with his Hindu presuppositions and instead, incorporated a biblical system of ethics. The same is true for most New Agers—they cannot live consistently with the implications of their worldview when it comes to helping others.)

• **"How do you know if you are following your inner truth?** What if you feel like murdering someone? Should you follow that inner truth?" (There must be an *external* standard of truth and morality, as discussed in the last chapter, in order to answer these questions. Otherwise, we are left only with our subjective feelings. But an objective, external standard undermines the notion of getting in touch with the god within.)

After focusing on the weaknesses of New Age psychology, we can present a biblical understanding of how, beginning with a personal Creator, there is a solid foundation for building a psychology of man, as created in God's image. Only in the Bible do we find an adequate understanding of our personhood, with a soul comprised of will, intellect, and emotions. Biblical psychology answers the question of why we sense an awareness of a spiritual dimension to life as well as a distinctiveness from the rest of the created world. As the psalmist writes:

> **1 Peter 1:23**
>
> *…you have been born again—not of perishable seed but of imperishable—through the living and enduring word of God.*

> What is man that You remember him,
> the son of man that You look after him?
> You made him little less than God and
> crowned him with glory and honor.
> You made him lord over the works of
> Your hands; You put everything under his
> feet: all the sheep and oxen, as well as
> animals in the wild, birds of the sky,
> and fish of the sea passing through
> the currents of the seas. O LORD,
> our Lord, how magnificent is Your
> name throughout the earth![41]

The Bible also explains why there is evil in the world. The fall of man provides a rational explanation for why there is hate in our hearts (Jeremiah 17:9), and indeed, why the entire universe "groans" (Romans 8:20-22). On a personal as well as a cosmic level, the biblical account resonates with what we actually observe about our world and ourselves.

In the Bible, we also find hope and healing in the midst of our fallenness. Unlike other worldviews where there is not purpose to life, love actually makes sense from a Christian worldview, for the Bible presents a God who acts with unconditional love to bring us out of our sinful state of rebellion and brokenness. His love is supremely displayed through the willing sacrifice of His son, Jesus Christ (Romans 5:6-8).

By acknowledging God's love through Jesus Christ, people seeking spiritual unity with God can turn their belief in the continuing cycle of reincarnation to the one-time rebirth as a child of God (1 Peter 1:23). Once that rebirth happens, growth in understanding God takes place. Paul tells believers in Rome "to be transformed by the renewing of your mind"—not by your feelings (Romans 12:1-2). And to Timothy, Paul instructs, "Be diligent to present yourself approved to God, a worker who doesn't need to be ashamed, correctly teaching the word of truth." (2 Timothy 2:15). As Christians, we can do no better than to heed Paul's admonitions.

---

### ROMANS 12:1-2

*Therefore, brothers, by the mercies of God, I urge you to present your bodies as a living sacrifice, holy and pleasing to God; this is your spiritual worship. Do not be conformed to this age, but be transformed by the renewing of your mind, so that you may discern what is the good, pleasing, and perfect will of God.*

## RECOMMENDED READING

Ankerberg, John and John Weldon. *Encyclopedia of New Age Beliefs*, Eugene, OR: Harvest House Publishers, 1996.

Beckwith, Francis J. and Stephen E. Parrish. *See the Gods Fall*, Joplin, MO: College Press Publishing, 1997.

Newport, John P. *The New Age Movement and the Biblical Worldview*, Grand Rapids, MI: Eerdmans Publishing, 1998.

## ENDNOTES

1. Neale Donald Walsch, *The New Revelation* (New York: Atria Books, 2002) p. 139.

2. Jack Canfield and Paula Klimek, "Education for a New Age," *New Age*, February 1978, p. 27.

3. Charles A. Reich, *The Greening of America* (New York: Random House, 1970), p. 225.

4. Reich, *The Greening of America*, p. 226.

5. Meher Baba, cited in Allan Y. Cohen, "Meher Baba and the Quest of Consciousness," in *What Is Enlightenment?*, John White, ed. p. 87.

6. Cited in F. LaGard Smith, *Out on a Broken Limb* (Eugene, OR: Harvest House, 1986), p. 181.

7. John Bradshaw, *Bradshaw on the Family* (Pompono Beach, Florida: Health Communications, 1988), p. 230.

8. Ruth Montgomery, *A World Beyond* (New York: Ballantine/Fawcett Crest Books, 1972), p. 12.

9. John White, ed., *What Is Enlightenment?* (Los Angeles: J.P. Tarcher, 1984), p. 126.

10. Cited in Francis Adeney, "Educators Look East," *Spiritual Counterfeits Journal*, Winter 1981, p. 29. SCP Journal is published by Spiritual Counterfeits Project, P.O. Box 4308, Berkeley, CA 94704.

11. Neale Donald Walsch, *Conversations with God, Book 1* (NY: G. P. Puttnam's Sons, 1997), p. 75, 78, 83.

12. Cited in Benjamin B. Ferencz and Ken Keyes, Jr., *Planethood* (Coos Bay, OR: Vision Books, 1988), p. 92.

13. Cited in Smith, *Out on a Broken Limb*, p. 12.

14. Gary Zukav, *The Seat of the Soul* (New York: Simon and Schuster, 1999), p. 29.

15. Shirley MacLaine, *Dancing in the Light* (Bantam, 1986), p. 115.

16. Neale Donald Walsh, *Questions and Answers on*

*Conversations with God* (Hampton Roads Publishing, 1999), p. 183.

17. Shakti Gawain, *Living in the Light* (San Rafael, California: New World Library, 1986), p. 95-6.

18. Neale Donald Walsch, *Conversations with God, Book 2* (Charlottesville, VA: Hampton Roads, 1997), p. 26, 42, 55.

19. Walsch, *Conversations with God, Book 1*, p. 79.

20. John White, *Frontiers of Consciousness* (New York: Julian Press, 1985), p. 7. NOTE: The science of psychology has been viewed as progressing through four phases. The First Force represents the behaviorism of B. F. Skinner. Sigmund Freud is considered the originator of Second Force, or psychoanalytic psychology. Humanistic psychology and the Human Potential Movement (Abraham Maslow, Carl Rogers, etc.) developed after World War II and became know as Third Force. And more recently, Forth Force refers to the Transpersonal psychology of Carl Jung and others.

21. John P. Newport, *The New Age Movement and the Biblical Worldview* (Grand Rapids, MI: Eerdmans, 1998), p. 109.

22. Marilyn Ferguson, *The Aquarian Conspiracy* (Los Angeles: J.P. Tarcher, 1980), p. 248.

23. Gawain, *Living in the Light*, p. 156.

24. Vera Alder, *When Humanity Comes of Age* (New York: Samuel Weiser, Inc., 1974), p. 82.

25. Ferguson, *The Aquarian Conspiracy*, p. 257.

26. Shirley MacLaine, *Out on a Limb* (Toronto: Bantam, 1984), p. 96.

27. "The Joys and Frustrations of Being a Healer," *Life Times Magazine*, vol. 1, no. 3, p. 61.

28. Kathleen Vande Kieft, *Innersource: Channeling Your Unlimited Self,* (New York: Ballantine Books, 1988), p. 114.

29. John Randolph Price, *The Superbeings,* (Austin, Texas: Quartus Books, 1981), p. 51-2.

30. Etan Boritzer, *What Is God?* (Ontario: Firefly Books Ltd., 1990), p. 30.

31. Quoted in "Public Education Or Pagan Indoctrination?: A Report on New Age Influence in the Schools" by Craig Branch, Christian Research Institute, www.equip.org.

32. Personal communication with Chuck Edwards by Mark (not his real name—changed to protect his privacy).

33. Jack Canfield and Paula Klimek, "Education for a New Age," *New Age*, February 1978, p. 27.

34. Ferguson, *The Aquarian Conspiracy*, p. 280.

35. Frances Clark, "Rediscovering Transpersonal Education," *Journal of Transpersonal Psychology,*" vol. 1, 1974, p. 1.

36. Barbara Clark, *Growing Up Gifted* (Columbus, OH: Merrill Publishing Co., 1990), p. 582-3.

37. Ferguson, *The Aquarian Conspiracy*, p. 420.

38. Quoted in John Carlson, "Health, Wellness, and Transpersonal Approaches to Helping," *Elementary School and Guidance Counseling*, vol. 14, no. 2, December 1979, p. 91.

39. Abraham Maslow, *Toward a Psychology of Being*, 2nd ed. (New York: Van Nostrand Reinhold, 1968), p. iii-iv.

40. John Warwick Montgomery, *Human Rights and Human Dignity* (Grand Rapids: Zondervan, 1986), p. 113.

41. Psalm 8:4-9.


(1) Holocaust victims: From Countering Culture video (2004 Summit Ministries: Manitou Springs, CO)

# EPILOGUE

In ancient Israel, Elijah squared off with the prophets of Baal on Mt. Carmel. He proposed a dramatic contest by challenging them to enlist their gods in a dual of strength with his God. Elijah understood that this was a battle between gods, not men. So he confronted the people: "How long will you hesitate between two opinions? If Yahweh is God, follow Him. But if Baal, follow him."[1]

When David and Goliath faced each other in the valley of Elah, both knew this was more than a skirmish between two mortals. David asked those around him, "Just who is this uncircumcised Philistine that he should defy the armies of the living God?"[2] As the two combatants positioned for the fight, the giant cursed David "by his gods," and David shouted back, "Today, the LORD will hand you over to me.... Then all the world will know that Israel has a God."[3] Everyone at the scene understood this was a test of whose God was supreme—another battle of the gods.

In New Testament times, Paul engaged the religious philosophers of Athens. He knew his role in the battle of the gods as he declared the Athenians' objects of worship to be simply metal and mortar, mere man-made images compared with the Creator of heaven and earth and of all living things.[4]

In our own day, little has changed. God's followers still face the self-styled prophets, champions, and philosophers of foreign gods. Whether they worship an impersonal god within, or mortal man as the ultimate power, they stand arrayed to do battle against the God of the Bible.

*Countering Culture* has attempted to make clear that the real issues of our day are not women's rights, gay rights, or animal rights. Our problems do not stem from economics, society, or politics. And the solutions are not found in education, introspection, or meditation. The answer to all of life's questions is ultimately determined by whose God is real. The main problem people face today is theology. Who will they acknowledge as God? This always has been mankind's greatest challenge. And it will continue to be.

If Christians are genuinely concerned about the world they will leave for their children, grandchildren, and great grandchildren, they must engage in the battle now. There are no "cities of refuge." Those who seek to destroy us have already mounted the walls and broken the gates.

It is time for us to go on the offensive. We must confront the false ideas that bring misery, sickness, and sorrow to each generation. Armed with the truth, we go forth in love, and we seek those who will turn their hearts and minds to the Savior. Jesus met the physical needs of those around Him, but he also confronted the false ideas that had shaped his culture.

God's truth ultimately will prevail. Meanwhile, we are not called simply to hold the fort but to charge the gates of false ideas, seeking those who will repent and return to God's truth.

---

[1] 1Kings 18:21
[2] 1Samuel 17:26
[3] 1 Samuel 17:46
[4] Acts 17:22-34
[5] In Matthew 28:19-20, Jesus commissioned His followers to "Go..."

## TIPS FOR USING THE LEADER'S GUIDE CD

The CD included in the back of this textbook features support materials you will need to turn *Countering Culture* into a valuable and memorable learning experience for any group. There are four tracks of study available, depending on the context and maturity level of those you will be leading:

*1. Home School. Support materials include lesson plans, teaching outlines, pupil handouts, recommended assignments, quizzes, and exams that allow you to present to your home school student a comprehensive course on worldview studies. This study provides extremely valuable perspective on other home school subjects such as civics, science, philosophy, Bible, and economics.*

*2. High School Youth Group or Sunday School. Support materials include lesson plans, teaching outlines and pupil handouts that provide a high-energy experience to build a high schooler's confidence in his or her biblical worldview.*

*3. College Study Group or Sunday School. Support materials include lesson plans, teaching outlines, and pupil handouts that offer a compelling apologetic for the Christian worldview and enough background information to refute the opposing perspectives which every student will encounter during his or her college experience.*

*4. Adult Small Group Study or Sunday School. Support materials include lesson plans, teaching outlines, and pupil handouts to help adults handle the real-life issues that challenge the worldview thinking of even a person of strong faith commitment.*

The *Countering Culture* video (sold separately) is an integral part of each lesson. This documentary-style learning tool introduces learners to experts who discuss various aspects of each worldview. While the lessons can be taught without showing the video segments, it is a useful tool for enhancing the teaching process. Each lesson incorporates short segments of approximately five minutes.

## ADDITIONAL RESOURCES AND WORLDVIEW TRAINING

Summit Ministries equips tomorrow's servant leaders to analyze competing worldviews and champion the Christian faith, inspiring them to love God with their heart, soul, mind, and strength.

For more information on training in worldview analysis and in how to take a principled stand for truth, visit the Summit Ministries Web site. There you will find details about Summit's seminars and summer conferences for youth, college students, and adults. Summit also offers curriculum designed for Christian schools, churches and Bible studies as well as resource articles covering a wide range of topics and an online bookstore featuring the top authors for helping you counter the culture.

You also can receive by mail the *Summit Journal*, a monthly review of news and cultural events edited by Dr. David Noebel, or "Truth & Consequences," a brief analysis of how worldview ideas intersect current issues (sent to your in-box once a month).

Summit Ministries
P. O. Box 207
Manitou Springs, CO  80829
(719) 685-9103
info@summit.org
www.summit.org